JACK LONDON AND THE KLONDIKE

JACK LONDON AND
THE KLONDIKE

The Genesis of an American Writer

———————————

Franklin Walker

with a foreword by Earle Labor

THE HUNTINGTON LIBRARY
SAN MARINO, CALIFORNIA

Publisher's note:
The E. A. Hegg photographs described
on page 267 have been replaced by historic
photographs of the Klondike acquired by the
Huntington Library since 1966.

Cover design by Avelina Moeller

Contents

Illustrations

Foreword

This new edition of *Jack London and the Klondike: The Genesis of an American Writer* is a welcome reminder of how much the world of Jack London owes to Franklin Walker and to the Huntington Library, who were far-sighted and courageous enough to publish this book in 1966, at a time when London was still regarded by many critics as little more than a writer of popular dog stories for children. Excepting the appearances of Hendricks and Shepard's *Letters from Jack London* and Hensley Woodbridge's monumental *Bibliography* the year before—and a handful of thoughtful essays by such brave scholars as Sam Baskett, Gordon Mills, Clell Peterson, Alfred Shivers, and Walker himself (e.g., "Jack London's Use of Sinclair Lewis Plots, published in the November 1953 issue of the *Huntington Library Quarterly*)—except for these, virtually no significant London work had been published by members of the academic establishment for more than a generation. In fact, no book-length critical study of London's extraordinary contributions to American literature had ever been published. *Jack London and the Klondike* was the first.

During the three decades since then, London scholarship has flourished. Scores of substantial articles have appeared in the leading scholarly journals as well as in the four periodicals devoted exclusively to Jack London. And more than a dozen significant London books have appeared, including publications from several university presses. The authenticity of this London renascence (*nascence* might be the more accurate term) is confirmed by the Huntington's hosting of the 1994 International Jack London Symposium. London has clearly "arrived" at last, and his arrival is due in considerable measure to the pioneering work of Franklin Walker—and to the faithful support of the Huntington staff.

Jack London and the Klondike was not only the first book-length critical study of London's work; it prevails as the definitive study of a crucial phase of London's career. Walker explains that his aim is threefold: to provide "a vivid and valid picture" of the great Klondike Gold Rush, to present a "most important segment" of Jack London's life, and—by giving an account of London's methods—"to throw light on his creative talent." Undertaken by anyone but a dedicated veteran scholar, this project might have become another of those biographical botches that long ago prompted Harry Hartwick to remark that "More bad literature has been written about Jack London . . . than he wrote himself." But *Jack London and the Klondike* is distinguished by the author's remarkable scholarly integrity, as witnessed by his conscientious research (Walker not only sifted through the trove of London holdings at the Huntington but also traveled through the Yukon country, consulting sourdoughs and official records alike); by his tactful synthesis of document, hearsay, and fiction (one of the book's most pleasing features is Walker's skillful interweaving of factual research with illustrative quotations from London's own works); and—above all—by his essential honesty and good sense.

There is no doubt that London's year in the Northland was the most crucially important experience in his literary career. What the sea had been for Herman Melville, and what the Congo had been for Joseph Conrad, the Klondike was for Jack London. This experience—a genuine rite of passage—did not merely change the youth into the man: it transformed the man into the author, the amateur into the professional. "It was in the Klondike I found myself," London later testified. "There nobody talks. Everybody thinks. You get your true perspective. I got mine." As Walker points out, Jack was telling only half the truth, since it was from the talk of his fellow argonauts that he drew much of the substance for his Northland fiction: "Talk he did, but most important of all, he listened and observed during those months in the draughty cabins near the mouth of the Stewart; he stored memories, thought ideas through, felt the stirrings of the creative artist." The "stirrings" had manifested themselves earlier, during a couple of frenzied bursts of creativity, but the results had been mediocre at best. Yet within two years of his return from the Klondike, his stories had started to appear in such prestigious magazines as the *Overland* and *Atlantic* monthlies, and his first book had been published by Houghton, Mifflin Company of Boston. And within five years *The Call of the Wild* had won him international recognition. Walker reports that London brought home less than five dollars in gold dust, but his Klondike diggings ultimately yielded a dozen books and a half-hundred shorter works—one of the great literary bonanzas of all time.

The first seven chapters of Walker's book vividly recount the details of London's Northland adventure. Walker's own narrative style is as refreshing as London's: invariably clear and unpretentious, at times even poetic, as in his description of London's six-week stay in Dawson City:

> The weather of late October was fitful and changeable; finally, when the freeze, which would make sledding possible both to the mines

and upriver to the Stewart and on to the Chilkoot and Dyea, seemed about at hand, a warm Chinook came along to prolong the suspense. The birches and aspens along the Yukon and on the slopes of Moosehide Mountain back of Dawson had long since turned fiery yellow-red and dropped their leaves; their ashen trunks had stood naked in the autumn winds for nearly two months. The Arctic hare and ptarmigan had turned from brown to white, the bears had gone into caves for their winter sleep, and the grey days had grown very short indeed before the longed-for-freeze-up finally arrived. At last, one morning at the end of the first week in November men woke to find the river frozen. (p. 108)

The last three chapters of *Jack London and the Klondike* are an eloquent testament to Walker's critical acumen. Gracefully missing are the pretension and jargon which characterize so much of what has come to pass as academic criticism. The opening of chapter 7 is exemplary: "The story of how Jack London became a successful writer is one which features talent, perseverance, and good luck. It is as difficult to weigh all the ingredients today as it was for London to do so." Such difficulties notwithstanding, Walker does a masterful job of weighing and balancing. Without sidestepping the awkward implications of London's Anglo-Saxon sympathies, he justly emphasizes those qualities in Jack's fiction that account for this great author's universal appeal: vitality, sincerity, romance, courage, and humanism. Nowhere have London's virtues been more cogently summed up than in Walker's conclusion:

He was passionately of the conviction that man could be a reasonable creature, that he had the elements of greatness in the face of adversity, that he could survive in the wilderness and build a better society in the cities. Because he based his hope on the natural rather than the supernatural, but also because he had his transitory doubts of man's capabilities as well as a recurring confidence in his future, he seems today most human and most timely. (p. 265)

Because Franklin Walker based his own work on the fundamental principles of professional integrity and critical honesty, *Jack London and the Klondike* likewise still "seems today most human and most timely."

EARLE LABOR
Centenary College of Louisiana
Shreveport
1994

Preface

My debt to the trustees and staff of the Henry E. Huntington Library for making this work possible is a very great one. I wish to thank them for giving me permission to consult their Jack London collection, for providing me with a Huntington Library grant during 1952–1953 to further my research, and for publishing the completed work in its present form. I am also grateful to the John Simon Guggenheim Foundation for a fellowship to make it possible for me to complete the writing during 1960–1961. Particularly I am indebted to Mr Irving Shepard, holder of the Jack London copyrights, for permission to quote from London's holograph and typed letters and manuscripts, as well as from London's printed works and from Charmian London's *The Book of Jack London*. All manuscript material so quoted has been identified in the text or in the 'Note on Sources'. No such manuscript material used in this book may be quoted in print without the consent of Mr Shepard except for purposes of review. All Jack London's printed works have been quoted from the first editions.

Further permissions to quote copyrighted material include the following:

From *Jack London and His Times*, by Joan London, copyright 1939 by Joan London. Reprinted by permission of Doubleday and Co., Inc., New York.

From *Sailor on Horseback: The Biography of Jack London*, by Irving Stone, copyright 1938 by Irving Stone. Reprinted by permission of Doubleday and Co., Inc.

From *Jack London's Tales of Adventure*, edited by Irving Shepard, copyright 1956 by Doubleday and Co., Inc. Reprinted by permission of Doubleday and Co., Inc.

From *The Klondike Fever*, by Pierre Berton, copyright 1958 by Pierre Berton. Reprinted by permission of Alfred A. Knopf, Inc., New York, and of W. H. Allen & Company, London.

I also wish to thank Mr James Mitchell Clarke and Mr James D. Hart for reading the book in manuscript and advising me on various points concerning it.

FRANKLIN WALKER
Mills College
Oakland, California
May 2, 1966

I · BACKGROUND TO ADVENTURE

WHEN asked by his first publishers for biographical information, Jack London opened his account with the following data:

My father was Pennsylvania-born, a soldier, scout, backwoods-man, trapper, and wanderer. My mother was born in Ohio. Both came west independently, meeting and marrying in San Francisco, where I was born January 12, 1876. What little city life I then passed was in my babyhood. My life, from my fourth to my ninth years, was spent upon California ranches. I learned to read and write about my fifth year, though I do not remember anything about it. I always could read and write, and have no recollection antedating such a condition. Folks say that I simply insisted upon being taught. Was an omniverous [*sic*] reader, principally because reading matter was scarce and I had to be grateful for whatever fell into my hands.[1]

It is noteworthy that Jack London, who was twenty-four years old when he sent this information to Houghton Mifflin Company, revealed many of his dreams and his fears in the first paragraph of his letter. He was, he tells us, a child of wandering parents. Even in his boyhood he had alternated between city and ranch life, as he was to do later on. His earliest passion was for reading and writing. The reading emerged as a result of his own initiative: 'Folks say that I simply insisted upon being taught.' Here one glimpses the Jack London who always felt that he had to fight for what he got, who wrestled for learning as if he were fighting for recognition. It also reflects the creed of the self-made man operating at the age of five! In saying that little reading matter was available, he refers to what he always asserted was the bareness of his childhood—the poverty and niggardliness of a substandard environment. He also speaks of writing, writing which he did because he loved to do it, long before he discovered that he might make a living by such an occupation. And in referring to John London he emphasized experiences which were traditionally related to the frontier. He was a 'scout, backwoodsman, trapper, and wanderer'. Jack London thus proclaimed himself a son of the frontier, a claim he was to make again and again in the future. In many ways the search for this frontier was one of the key elements in his life, and the reflection of it one of the pervasive elements in his writing.

Not only was Jack London born in San Francisco, the heart of America's most spectacular frontier, but he found the first successful theme for his writing in a last frontier splurge—the rush to the Klondike, which was to have its first bizarre and violent stirrings in that mercurial city. Moreover, he was to learn to write in the tradition of Bret Harte, who had turned the sweat and tears of Sierra mining society into matter for wonder and sentiment; and he was to express himself with something of the savagery and morbidity of Ambrose Bierce, who had earned his spurs as a short-story writer and satirist in California. He developed little of the humour of a Mark Twain, but he displayed both a restlessness and an impatience with the established institutions which had been characteristic of the 'Washoe Giant' when he had begun his career in the Far West thirty years before London wrote his first Klondike tale. Ina Coolbrith, sweetheart of the San Francisco frontier school, helped to guide his reading as a boy, and Joaquin Miller, still capitalizing on his frontier experiences, was his neighbour in Oakland and a fellow adventurer in the Yukon. Frank Norris, who insisted that adventure was still the substance of the West even as he chronicled men's misfortunes there with a Zolaesque formula, was London's principal competitor for fame among California writers. Restlessness, independence, resourcefulness, exaggeration, crudity were all traits strong in London and strong in his writing. He did not by any means owe them entirely to his frontier background, but this background played a prominent part in making him one of the most widely-read writers of his period. And the reflection of the frontier has continued to be one of the strong elements of appeal to countless readers, not only in America, but in Europe and Asia.

When he was twenty-one and on the threshold of a short but highly productive writing career which ended with his death at forty, Jack London went from San Francisco to the Klondike as a component part of an extraordinary mass movement which drew men from all over the world to take part in one of the most preposterous adventures of modern times. The difficulties they faced were truly formidable. The task merely of getting to the Klondike, as London described it, was bad enough: 'With heavy packs upon their backs men plunged waist-deep into hideous quagmires, bridged mountain torrents by felling trees across them, toiled against the precipitous slopes of the ice-worn mountains, and crossed the dizzy faces of innumerable glaciers. When after incalculable toil they reached the lakes, they went into the woods, sawed pine trees into lumber by hand, and built it into boats. In these, overloaded, unseaworthy, they battled down the long chain of lakes. . . . At the rapids they ran their boats through, hit or miss, and after infinite toil and hardship, on the breast of a jarring ice flood, arrived at the Klondike.'[2] He should have added that they had to pack in everything they were going to wear, eat, or use; that they knew they would suffer through a severe Arctic winter as they huddled in inadequate shelters; that they planned to mine in perpetually frozen ground; and that they sensed even before they arrived that all the rich claims had already been staked by sourdoughs who had been in the area at the time of the strike. Yet they went, anyway, by the tens of thousands. It is as if they fought their way there and back just in order to get something out of their system.

The Klondike rush was, in fact, as insane a gamble for fortune, as perverse a movement toward the wilderness to escape a crowded world, as that world has known to date. Hamlin Garland, who also became a Klondiker (by the almost impassable overland Ashcroft route) summed up one aspect of the madness very well. 'I believed that I was about to see and take part in a most picturesque and impressive movement across the wilderness. I believed it to be the last march of the kind which could ever come in America, so rapidly were the wild places being settled up. . . . I wished to return to the wilderness also, to forget books and theories of art and social problems, and come again face to face with the great free spaces of woods and skies and streams.'

Jack London's more succinct comment was: 'I had let career go hang, and was on the adventure-path again in quest of fortune.' He was also aware of another factor which played a prominent part in the rush, a rush that took place during a depression decade. 'In one of its cyclopean moments the race had arisen and shoved back its frontier several thousand miles. Thus, with unconscious foresight, did mature society make room for its adolescent members. True, the new territory was mostly barren; but its several hundred thousand square miles of frigidity at least gave breathing space to those who else would have suffocated at home.'[3]

Though he had tried energetically during the spring before he went to the Klondike to break into the writing game, Jack London kept few notes and wrote no articles or stories during his winter in the Yukon. Nor did he ever record a detailed account of his experiences, in spite of the tremendous vogue for Klondike reminiscences. He achieved fame, however, by writing fiction based on those experiences, fiction much of which continues to figure among his most popular writings. The substance of the present study is based largely on this fiction, with the thought always in mind that London wrote best when he developed his stories from what he had seen or done.

The purpose of this synthesis from London's fiction is threefold. In the first place, it is my belief that a vivid and valid picture of the famous rush can be constructed in this manner, and, although there have been many books about the Klondike, there is ample room for another good one. In addition, it is my intent to give as accurately as possible a segment, and most important segment, of London's biography. Finally, through an examination of London's use of his experiences and source materials on the Klondike, I plan to present an account of his writing methods and to throw light on his creative talent. Knowing much of the 'reality' from which he made his stories, we can judge what he added to experience to create forceful writing. No vital experience is wholly to be comprehended without its background. Accordingly, a quick glance at London's first twenty years will make his big adventure more meaningful.

*   *   *

Though Jack London often declared himself a son of the frontier, he did not raise his first squall in San Francisco until seven years after the completion of the transcontinental railroad, which had effectively ended California's isolation. At the time of his birth, on January 12, 1876, the city of a quarter million, barely a generation old, was more concerned with housing and labour problems than with gold nuggets and free land. It was struggling through the depression which had hit the nation in 1873; ironically economic disorder was to condition London's early boyhood, just as it was to impel him to seek adventure during the depression of the nineties by joining the gold rush to

Yukon Territory. Hard times supplemented the ineptitude and improvidence of John London and Flora Wellman London in making a living. Instability was the keynote of Jack London's earliest years.

When one of Jack London's characters in *The Star Rover* made the statement that as a boy he moved 'on an average of six times a year', we suspect he was reflecting young Jack's experience. Though the London average ran a little below that, a constant change could be said to be the rule rather than the exception for the restless family. During the three years which London spent in San Francisco, there were several houses which might be called home. A couple of months after he was born at 615 Third Street, south of Market but in a district by no means a slum and in a house by no means a hovel, his mother, weak after giving birth to a child a tenth her weight and unable to provide him with milk, turned Jack over to the capable care of a Negro woman who had lost her child and was glad to serve as wet nurse. For several months, perhaps for a year, Jack stayed with his beloved foster mother, Mammy Jennie (Virginia Prentiss), while Flora worked at picking up a little money by sewing and giving music lessons. In the meantime, John London was finding it increasingly difficult to get odd jobs at carpentry and gardening in a city deep in depression. For a while he canvassed for a leading department store (The Emporium), and then turned from this frustrating activity to attempting to sell Victor sewing machines on commission. City directories and family records list a half-dozen different addresses for this period. The San Francisco wandering ended when, at the age of three, Jack became seriously ill in one of San Francisco's frequent diphtheria epidemics. John London's eagerness to leave the city and try once more his luck as a farmer was given impetus by this crisis; for the next six years he did his best to re-establish himself on the land, searching ever for the lucky spot in the Bay Region.

The first Oakland directory listing came in 1879, naming John London partner with G. H. Stowell in a fruit and produce store in West Oakland. The store was an ambitious adjunct of London's truck farming on land now part of Emeryville; the 1880 directory lists a new address for the London family but mentions no store. Family tradition has it that the joint grocery venture was a failure because Stowell skipped with the cash. By the time Jack was five, John London was farming a tract for Matthew Davenport across the estuary in Alameda, and it was here that the youngster first went to school. (Apparently already behind him was the episode he refers to in a note he made for a short story: 'My fear—alone in room of house in Oakland, 3 years old, while they are beating carpets in yard—twilight coming on—& then they disappear from yard & I am wholly alone—the primitive fear in me—.')[4]

By the time Jack was seven, the family was down the peninsula below San Francisco, on the 'bleak fog-girt coast' somewhere between Pedro Point and Moss Beach in San Mateo County. It was from this ranch, according to *John Barleycorn*, that Jack rode into the city with his father to deliver potatoes, finding the saloons at Colma and San Francisco warm havens after a cold ride—havens where a lonesome boy could get soda crackers or a glass of sweet grenadine while his father drank his mug of beer. And it was in the Moss Beach area, according to the same source, that he was frightened by the Italian neighbours, whom his mother scorned as not truly American stock, into drinking so much red wine that he nearly died of the burning surfeit. The last move on the land was back across the bay and a few miles inland to Livermore, with its tawny hills and bee-loud glades. But to the eight-year-old boy who was later to hymn the return to the land so vigorously, the country was not then nourishing to the imagination: '. . . the hills and valleys around were eyesores and aching pits, and I never loved them till I left them'.[5]

By the end of Jack London's ninth year, presumably in 1885 or early 1886, John London had given up hopes of making an adequate living from the soil—neither truck gardening in Alameda nor potato growing at Moss Beach nor chicken ranching at Livermore had been sufficiently lucrative to make for settling down. Though times had improved, John London's health was beginning to fail him. Flora, still ambitious but never too practical about investments—her spiritualist beliefs often encouraged her to try a fling on the lotteries or in wild-cat mining stock—was better able to help support the family in the town than in the country. Her most ambitious venture after returning to Oakland, rooming and boarding girls from Scotland who worked at the California Cotton Mills, failed through over-extension. Thereafter John London, past sixty and nearly an invalid, ceased farming and carpentering and worked as deputy constable, night watchman, and canvasser.

The other London residences during the period when Jack was going to grammar school, delivering papers, and absorbing the contents of the public library in huge gulps, were nearly all in the western and most shabby section of Oakland. The home which was to play the most vivid part in his fiction was the little house on Pine Street where Saxon and Billy lived in *The Valley of the Moon*. This was a neat little cottage near the railroad shops on the Point. But there were other houses—perhaps a half dozen—which briefly sheltered the family before Jack graduated from the Cole Grammar School in 1890. Thus, to the time his regular schooling ended at fourteen, his roots had hardly pierced the surface and a great restlessness was upon him.

Pinched though the family had been at times, Jack London's boyhood was far from being that of a hopeless dweller in the slums. If not as filled with adventure as Mark Twain's, it certainly was an improvement on that of Charles Dickens. Later London was to look back on this early period and comment: 'I had lived my childhood on California ranches, my boyhood hustling newspapers on the streets of a healthy Western city, and my youth on the ozone-laden waters of San Francisco Bay and the Pacific Ocean.'[6] At another time, much nearer to this boyhood, he was in a different mood and wrote a friend a complaining letter about how much he had had to work as a boy. 'Up at three o'clock in the morning to carry papers. When that was finished I did not go home but continued on to school. School out, my evening papers. Saturday I worked on an ice wagon; Sunday I went to a bowling alley and set up pins for drunken Dutchmen. . . . I turned over every cent and went dressed like a scarecrow.'[7] Doubtless part of his grammar school days were lived in the way described in this letter; often his family called on him for help; early he learned to share the cost of his board and room; and, always given to excess, he took on two newspaper routes rather than one. There was little cheer at home and not much opportunity to read—a recreation which he pursued when he could to the point of getting 'the jerks', which he naïvely called 'St Vitus dance'. Many of the books he read told about how poor boys such as President Garfield became famous, or gave detail on what lay beyond the horizon, as did Paul du Chaillu's African journeys; or they carried Jack into a dream world of romance, as did Washington Irving's *Alhambra* and Ouida's *Signa*. The latter novel, with its theme of how an Italian foundling made good as a musician, was a favourite with London for years. But the golden thread that ran throughout his boyhood years was his life on the water, first with John London on fishing trips in the bay and later in his own boats.

First there was the row-boat just big enough for himself and Rollo, his dog; it cost only two dollars, it had no centreboard, it never stopped leaking, but it provided lots of fun. Then came the decked-over, fourteen-foot centreboard skiff in which the twelve-year-old boy could sail out of the estuary which separates Oakland and Alameda, into the wider bay—not yet as far as the Golden Gate or Carquinez Straits but at least as far as Yerba Buena and Asparagus Island. Here was true adventure, with the shores lined with sailing vessels from the seven seas, the channel tricky, and the breeze fresh on one's cheeks. Possibly the twelve-year-old sailor even saw the *Casco*, which lay for a while in 1888 just off the Webster Street pier in the estuary, waiting for Robert Louis Stevenson, another adventurer, to take it to the South Seas. The waters of San Francisco Bay, which are now muddy and polluted, were then clear and inviting. And they provided more than sailing! Close at hand were crabs, soft-shell clams, and succulent oysters. And plentiful in deep water were smelt, red-tailed and silver perch, rock cod, striped bass, shad, porgies, sturgeon and salmon, not to mention seals, sea lions, and marauding sharks.

Jack London left a most attractive picture of himself at this age in a scene in *The Valley of the Moon*, in which the despondent heroine, Saxon Roberts, is cheered up by a boy in a boat, who is clearly young London.

A grinning small boy, in a small, bright-painted and half-decked skiff, sailed close in to the wall and let go his sheet to spill the wind.
'Want to get aboard?' he called.
'Yes,' she answered. 'There are thousands of big rats here. I'm afraid of them.'
He nodded, ran close in, spilled the wind from his sail, the boat's way carrying it gently to her.
'Shove out its bow,' he commanded. 'That's right. I don't want to break my centerboard. . . . An' then jump aboard in the stern—quick!—alongside of me.'
She obeyed, stepping in lightly beside him. He held the tiller up with his elbow, pulled in on the sheet, and as the sail filled the boat sprang away over the rippling water.
'You know boats,' the boy said approvingly.
He was a slender, almost frail lad, of twelve or thirteen years, though healthy enough, with sunburned freckled face and large

gray eyes that were clear and wistful. Despite his possession of the pretty boat, Saxon was quick to sense that he was one of them, a child of the people.

As Saxon sailed with the boy out to Goat Island to fish for rock cod, she was fascinated by his skill in handling his boat and excited with his story of his life and adventures. He had saved up six dollars to buy the boat and had put an additional five dollars and fifteen cents into paint, oars, and sail. Another boy had agreed to take over one of his afternoon paper routes for the day—'I give'm ten cents, an' all the extras he sells is his'—while he put his books under the stern sheets and sailed out a little way toward Japan and Alaska and the Solomons. As he manoeuvred his skiff out to Goat Island, a point more easily attained, though it was reached through choppy waters, he boasted about his Anglo-Saxon ancestors, and about his father, who was a Civil War scout and spy, and before that a buffalo-hunter and trapper. He confided that, though he would like to be called Erling, or Swen, or Jarl, to indicate his Viking ancestry, he had been named 'only John'. But he added quickly: 'I don't let 'em call me John. Everybody's got to call me Jack. I've scrapped with a dozen fellows that tried to call me John, or Johnnie—wouldn't that make you sick?—Johnnie!'

The moment they had set the fishing line, the boy pulled out a copy of a library book, *Afloat in the Forest*, which was about the marvellous Amazon, and explained that he used two library cards at the Free Library to get all the books he wanted—books by Mayne Reid, and Captain Marryatt, and Ballantyne and many another who had adventured in distant parts. Later he explained that he planned to sell his catch, together with some driftwood he hoped to snag, on the way back, to make up for the day off from his paper route. He had already confided that at his mother's insistence he was using his earnings to take shorthand lessons in order to learn to be a court reporter so that he might earn as much as twenty dollars a day! But he didn't really want to be a reporter at all. When Saxon asked him what he did want, he replied:

'What do I want?...' Turning his head slowly, he followed the skyline, pausing especially when his eyes rested landward on the brown Contra Costa hills, and seaward, past Alcatraz, on the Golden Gate. The wistfulness in his eyes was overwhelming and went to her heart.

'That,' he said, sweeping the circle of the world with a wave of his arm.

He was already half-way to the Klondike.

*   *   *

Grammar school behind him, the fourteen-year-old Jack London, as far as we know, had not even a distant practical goal ahead of him. The possibility of his going on to high school apparently was given little thought; like many of the boys and girls of his neighbourhood, he was ready to meet the world without further aid from schooling. Having no professional career in mind he should have turned after grammar school to some sort of apprenticeship, should have begun to plan, with his family's help, on a life of something beside that of a casual labourer. There is no indication that he ever did so, no sign that he planned to become a carpenter or sailor or farmer. Nor did he make any attempt to use the limited knowledge of shorthand he seems to have acquired. On the contrary, a great restlessness possessed him. He was to spend the next four years holding odd jobs, rebelling against routine responsibilities, seeking adventure both inside and outside the law. He did not break away from his family at once, but a month or two of odd jobs followed by a year of working in a cannery was enough of routine labour for him. He intended no longer to be a wage slave, a boy growing into manhood doing the meanest kind of labour to help in keeping an improvident family going. He took the most

[22]

ready form of escape. The bay was there to be made use of. One could sail on it unrestricted; one could sleep on it where one pleased; one could make a living on it by the use of brawn and cunning. Instead of going on to high school Jack London became 'Prince of the Oyster Pirates'; instead of planning for college, he became a 'blowed in the glass profesh', learning to ride the rods, steal, and beg with the best of them. For most of four years Jack London was what today is termed a juvenile delinquent. He became one not so much because the grimy world bore down too heavily upon him, not because his hand was turned against society, but because he was looking for adventure. These were his *Wanderjahre*, his period for seasoning and seeing the world.

Most of London's wildest adventures took place when he was sixteen. During the twelve hectic months of 1892 he left home; raided the oyster beds in the *Razzle Dazzle*; took his first mistress; worked at various times as a salmon fisherman, roustabout on a bay scow-schooner, and longshoreman; served as an irregular member of the upper San Francisco Bay Fish Patrol; learned to ride the rods with the 'road kids' operating out of Sacramento, who were experienced at rolling stiffs and picking pockets; spent his first three days in jail; stepped up his drinking so much that at one time he was drunk for three weeks, and at another nearly died of surfeit of alcohol in the blood at a political rally; and attempted to commit suicide by deliberately swimming to exhaustion in Carquinez Straits. To a law enforcement officer of the period he may not have differed greatly from many another unhappy youth at loose ends. Newsmen of the time reported that over five hundred young boys and girls, just out of grammar school, were roaming the Bay area streets, contracting habits of idleness and viciousness. Later Jack London was to boast that when he joined the 'road kids' he was merely expanding a career that already had its criminal aspects:

'As an oyster pirate I had already earned convictions at the hands of justice, which, if I had tried to serve them, would have required a thousand years in state's prison. To rob was manly; to beg was sordid and despicable. But I developed in the days to come all right, all right, till I came to look upon begging as a joyous prank, a game of wits, a nerve-exerciser.'[8] And to a friend he later wrote of this era in his life: 'When I was just sixteen I broke loose and went off on my own hook. Took unto myself a mistress of the same age, lived a year of wildest risk in which I made more money in one week than I do in a year now, and then, to escape the inevitable downward drift, broke away from everything and went to sea.'[9]

There were, of course, two sides to the story. It is true that oyster piracy was but 'burglary in a boat', that robbing and begging were not only dangerous but demoralizing, and that drinking heavily could lead in time to serious consequences. But there undoubtedly was adventure, too, and much of London's activity involved more excitement than harm. Sailing the *Razzle Dazzle* into the shallow south bay during the dark of the moon took skill, evading the guards at the oyster beds was a tricky business, and there was real sport in coming home on a spanking breeze to reach the market where saloon-keepers bought readily for oyster breakfasts and free lunches, caring not a whit whether the oysters came from the abandoned beds off Asparagus Island or from the inadequately guarded holdings of the monopolistic company across the bay near Redwood City.

The sympathy of the public was with the pirates, for the growers leased their tidal lands from the notoriously unpopular Southern Pacific Railroad, 'The Octopus' in local parlance. The juvenile yarns of *The Fish Patrol* tell of many an exciting moment catching poachers and fishermen using illegal nets and lines. The amateur members of the badly undermanned patrol had to be good to make a capture, considering the fact that they were unarmed and unpopular with the fishing public. They had to concentrate on Greeks and Chinese to get a conviction. They were paid according to the number of convictions that followed their raids. And riding the passenger trains, the blind baggages, rods, and gunnels, was one of the main sources of adventure for boys in a day when 'The Road' meant a railroad rather than a highway. Jack London had no intention of becoming a tramp. He learned to ride the rods 'because of the life that was in me, of the wanderlust in my blood that would not let me rest. . . . I went on "The Road" because I couldn't keep away from it; because I hadn't the price of the railroad fare in my jeans; because I was so made that I couldn't work all my life on "one same shift".'

Still, it was a good thing that he decided to go to sea to get away from the life he had been living. He was sure that crime and destruction lay ahead of him if he did not, and he was probably right. Also, it was time for him to see more water than lay in San Francisco Bay and visit stranger shores than those of Goat Island and Benicia. The sealing fleet was wintering in the bay, a considerable portion of it in Oakland Estuary; and in the local saloons Jack met skippers, mates, hunters, boat-steerers, and boat-pullers. One of the seal hunters named Pete Holt sized him up as a likely boat-puller and offered to arrange to have him ship as his helper on the next voyage out. Accordingly, on the twentieth of January, 1893, eight days after his seventeenth birthday, London signed before the shipping commissioner the articles of the *Sophia Sutherland* as an able-bodied seaman.

The three-masted *Sophia Sutherland*, one of the newest and biggest of the ships in the sealing fleet, was a schooner of 150 tons. It sailed on the twenty-third, took the southern passage in order to benefit from the north-east trades, skirting Hawaii within sight of its volcanoes, and reached the Bonin Islands (Ogassawarajima) in fifty-one days.

After ten days in the Bonins, the ship sailed north to hunt fur seals in the foggy coastal waters off Japan and Siberia for a hundred days, going perhaps as far as the Bering Sea. On her return she put in at Yokohama for a fortnight stay, after which she made San Francisco by the northern course in thirty-seven days, arriving home on the twenty-sixth of August. The voyage had gone smoothly except for an occasional blow, and a typhoon off Japan. The purpose of the trip was accomplished by spending something over three months hunting seals in dirty weather, running hazards of getting lost in the fog, skinning the seals on decks messy with blubber and blood, and packing the seal-skins into the hold. Two shore leaves, one at the Bonins and one at Yokohama, provided variety. The trip was un-eventful, except for the death of a misfit, whom London was to call the Bricklayer in notes and sketches.

To the other sailors the trip was doubtless routine, but London gained much from it. Like Richard Henry Dana, Jr., he found life at sea invigorating and benefited from its discipline. He got along with his companions, in spite of the fact that he had no right to be earning the wages of an able-bodied seaman. And he saw a great deal aboard ship and on shore leave that he was to remember when he began writing. Though he would have the readers of *John Barley-corn* think that the shore leaves at the Bonins and Yoko-hama were but glorious drunks, the sketches he wrote for the Oakland High School *Aegis* painted quite a different picture. Moreover, the first article he ever published was a vivid description of a typhoon off the coast of Japan. The article appeared in a local newspaper not long after he reached home, and many attributes of the voyage of the *Sophia Sutherland* were to contribute to the voyage of *The Ghost* in *The Sea-Wolf*. There was no Wolf Larsen aboard 'the Sophie', but there was real action upon which nar-rative imagination could work.

After giving most of his earnings to his family, Jack

London, urged on by his mother, set out to find a job which would keep him at home. There was little temptation to return to his wild life on the bay, and what little there was was effectually quenched by the discovery that many of his old companions were in jail or dead. Yet it was a poor time for getting any kind of a job, for the panic of 1893 had hit the West Coast and thousands were out of work. At that, he found a place in an Oakland jute mill, working at a burlap machine for ten cents an hour; then he decided to learn about electricity (perhaps he could resourcefully learn a trade on the job) but got no farther up the ladder than shovelling coal for long hours in a local street-railway power plant at thirty dollars a month. In his grimy misery he began to talk about 'work beasts' and to wonder if it was to be like this for him for the rest of his life. After a few months, the very depression which had made jobs hard to find paradoxically brought him the escape that his nature so much demanded. He took to the Road in earnest.

As the bitter winter of 1893–1894 wore on, unemployment and distress throughout the country became more and more acute, with more than two million men out of work and few state or federal provisions to meet the emergency. The search for jobs resulted in an increase of free traffic on the railroads, with many bona fide labourers crowding the professional hobos in freight cars and on express trains. In the Far West, the restless unemployed went so far as to organize groups of from fifty to three hundred and simply move in on the railroads to get to their destinations. The popular opposition to the Southern Pacific encouraged the men to rationalize that the railroad owed them a ride; and the railroad, sensitive to its position as scapegoat in an economy gone awry, made little attempt to prevent them.

Much the same situation existed throughout the nation. Josiah Flynt, an expert on vagabonding, estimated that there were some sixty thousand men on the move on

American railways; many of them were like Jack London, getting their Grand Tour in this fashion. Flynt noted: 'If the mood for a "trip" comes, it seems to them the most natural thing in the world to indulge it. If they had the means they would ride on Pullman cars and imagine themselves princes, but lacking the wherewithal, they take to the road.' Under the circumstances, it was too much to expect Jack London to stay home shovelling coal for his rent. He had already earned his monikers of 'Sailor Kid' and 'Frisco Kid', and his alias of 'John Drake'. He was all for getting out of Oakland and seeing the world.

The immediate occasion of his new venture was the departure from Oakland on April 6 of 'Kelly's Army', a large group of unemployed who set out to join 'General' Coxey in his march on Washington to dramatize the plight of the unfortunates. In true frontier fashion, Kelly's group, which numbered about two thousand by the time it reached Des Moines, intended to ask for huge reclamation projects for the West and chose as its means of transportation the freight cars of the Southern Pacific, which could thus atone for some of its errors of the past. The railroad chose to cooperate, knowing, as an Oakland newspaper pointed out, that 'the fever of organizing troops of men and marching towards Washington is now upon the country.' It was encouraged to do so by the communities of the West, each eager to get the 'Army' out of town. Never actually a member of Kelly's Army, Jack London started twelve hours late and did not catch up with it until it had ended its railroading at Council Bluffs, Iowa. There, while locomotives fled eastward with all rolling stock, Kelly and his men puzzled over their logistic problems. Urged by the citizens of Council Bluffs to depart, they set out by foot for Des Moines.

Jack London did not care for the walking, but there was at least food for the marchers, donated by communities along the road, and there was much to be seen. At Des

Moines, while the Army built flat-boats to go down the Des Moines River to the Mississippi, he found things better. 'We lay in camp, made political speeches, held sacred concerts, pulled teeth, played baseball and seven-up, and ate our six thousand meals per day, and Des Moines paid for it.' Once more in a boat, he had fun out-distancing the main troops on the trip down the shallow river to Keokuk, but, after five less comfortable days on the Mississippi, London 'deserted' at Hannibal, Missouri, and went back to the rods. He wanted to see the Columbian Exposition in Chicago, which he did; he wanted to visit his mother's relatives named Everhard in St Joseph, Michigan, and get cleaned up and sleep comfortably and eat good meals, which he did; and he wanted to see Niagara Falls, which he did. But his Grand Tour was interrupted at that point in a fearful way.

The records of the Erie County Penitentiary at Buffalo tell the story succinctly: 'On June 29, 1894, one John Lundon [sic], age 18: Single: Father & Mother Living, Occupation—Sailor; Religion—Atheist;—was received at the Erie County Penitentiary, for a term of 30 Days, charge of Tramp, sentenced by Police Justice Charles Piper—Niagara Falls, New York; and was released on July 29, 1894.'[10]

During his thirty days in the penitentiary Jack London, who was always tremendously sensitive to experience, saw things and felt things which for the rest of his life he insisted were not only unprintable but unthinkable. Being denied a jury trial or even an opportunity to plead his case shocked his faith in American institutions, while having his hair and small moustache clipped, donning striped prison garb, and walking in the chain gang hurt his ego. It is true that he was soon named a trusty and learned, liked his fellows, to benefit from the system of petty graft which thrived in the jail. But this amelioration of his lot did not disguise the fact that he was truly in 'the pit, the

[29]

abyss of civilization'. He met men who were vile, met more who were helpless victims of circumstance. 'Our hall was a common stews, filled with the ruck and the filth, the scum and dregs, of society—hereditary inefficients, degenerates, wrecks, lunatics, addled intelligences, epileptics, monsters, weaklings, in short, a very nightmare of humanity.' He saw fellow turn his hand against fellow. He saw a man so beaten by the guards that his spirit was broken. He saw another prisoner thrown from landing to landing to fall in a crushed heap at the bottom of the cell block, later to crawl miserably away. He found that most of his companions intended to return to crime when they were released. At first he had felt very resentful at being jailed without serious cause or due process—he was going to spend years getting even. By the time his sentence had been served, he was willing to let bygones be bygones and to admit that his respect for the law and his comprehension of the problems it faced had increased. 'All I asked, when I got out, was a chance to fade away from the landscape.'

It is a tribute to his reliance, or pluck, or perhaps stubbornness, that after emerging from the prison he did not go home at once. Rather, he continued his original plan of seeing the country, hitchhiking the trains, begging, doing odd jobs, and thriftily doling out the pennies his family managed to send him. For the rest of the summer and most of the fall he was on his way, adventuring and becoming an amateur sociologist. South through New York and Pennsylvania he went, to Harrisburg, where he swam in the Susquehanna and saw a gypsy beat his wife and children with a horsewhip; to Baltimore, where he was fascinated by the intellectual discussions indulged in by the tramps and soap-box orators in Druid Hall Park; to Washington, where he visited the national monuments, failed to get a handout, and worked for his lodging in a livery stable; to New York, where he was deeply moved by the misery of the poor in the Bowery, where he was hit with a billy by a policeman when he was doing nothing more sinister than watching a street fight; to Boston, where he argued philosophy and economics with another tramp for two days and won a policeman's friendship by telling him of life in Yokohama; to Montreal, and on in slow stages to Ottawa, after which he 'held down the Overland' to Winnipeg 'in spite of two brakemen, a conductor, a fireman, and an engineer', and travelled the remaining thousand miles to British Columbia in a coal car. A few weeks in Vancouver ended the journey except for the trip down to San Francisco on the *Umatilla*, on which he stoked coal for his passage. He did not guess that two and a half years later he would be taking the same steamer north to the Klondike.

The effect on London's thinking of this journey, a journey during which he saw the pains and disorders of American society in one of its most disturbing crises, cannot be overestimated. Many times later he wrote that the experience opened his eyes, that for the first time he realized that society was badly put together, and that, in meeting his personal problems so as to avoid becoming a victim to social disorder, he resolved in the future to use his brains and 'open the books'. Only in that way could he escape the plight of the casual labourer, 'the work beast'.

Though he had known poverty and distress in Oakland, he had never seen anything like the horrors he had come upon in the penitentiary and in the city of New York. His reaction was something like that of Henry George a generation earlier; the contrast between the comparatively affluent West and the slums of the East turned London to-wards socialism just as it had helped to make George into a single-taxer. 'The woman of the streets and the man of the gutter drew very close to me. I saw the picture of the Social Pit as vividly as though it were a concrete thing, and at the bottom of the Pit I saw them, myself above them, not far, and hanging on to the slippery wall by main strength and sweat.'[11] The young man confessed that what he saw scared him into thinking. His attention now was to turn towards educating himself in order to escape from the labouring class, to help society, and to learn how to write.

*   *   *

The first step Jack London took in order to equip himself to sell his brains rather than his brawn was to try to catch up with his formal education. As he put it in *John Barleycorn*, 'I was working to get away from work.' He was nineteen years old when he entered Oakland High School in January, 1895, three or four years older than most of his classmates. If he had good luck and could manage to support himself, help his family, and keep in school, he would be able to graduate from high school when he was twenty-two, from the university when he was twenty-six. Apparently when he returned to school he intended to follow this course. Just as certainly he was sure to become impatient with it, for he was far too mature and experienced to be content with catching up with his lost education in this way. Already he was itching to write, eager to discuss politics in the town park. By the time he would have earned a B.A. under the normal routine, he had in fact married, had fathered his first child, and had published two books and had three more in manuscript.

Looking back on his early plans after this achievement, he realized how mistaken had been his dream of getting an orthodox education. 'High school or college curriculum I simply selected from, finding it impossible to follow the rut—life and pocket book were too short,'[12] he wrote to his first publishers. By doing odd jobs and working as a janitor at the new high school building, he managed to complete one year of regular work. He barely earned college-entrance grades in mathematics, but he did well in French and history, and received an 'A' in English. In addition, he published nine stories and one short article in the student paper, the *Aegis*. Almost all the stories dealt with his sealing voyage and his hobo experiences. The short article reflected his newly developed interest in socialism. At about this time he joined the Henry Clay debating society, an Oakland group which included some Fabian socialists among its members. He discovered Marx as well as Ruskin and Morris; and he made friends with some of the Socialist Labor Party members, possibly through his interest in the soap-box oratory very actively carried on at this time in the city hall park. He is said to have done considerable soapbox talking himself during his high school days; in one letter he speaks of being 'more notorious than esteemed' [13] as a young radical. He also found time to fall in love. His experiences as an awkward youth entering a cultured home for the first time are reflected in the early parts of *Martin Eden*, when Martin becomes acquainted with Ruth Morse, fictional name for the golden-curled Mabel Applegarth.

Though *Martin Eden* was only partially autobiographical, such evidence as has survived not only supports the belief that London's social education was similar to that of his hero but that his reaction to books was much the same. And it is characteristic that most of the writers who were to mean much to London were discovered outside the classroom. Very early he had learned to rifle the public library of numerous treasures. He who had filled his seabag with books when he boarded the *Sophia Sutherland*, who had whiled away the time at Des Moines while Kelly's Army waited for transportation by reading every book he could lay his hand on, and who had often managed to read a novel while riding the rods under a freight car, did not need a schoolteacher to urge him to read. He discovered Kipling and Stevenson and Robert Browning outside the schoolroom and not only enjoyed them but used them for ideas and methods in his writing. Marx's *Communist Manifesto* came to his attention not in the schoolroom but in the city park. His greatest discovery of this period was Herbert Spencer; he probably met him much as Martin Eden did.

Martin Eden had heard Spencer quoted by 'wordy socialists and working-class philosophers' in the park in front of the city hall a number of times, but he had not really become excited about him until he listened spellbound to a seedy tramp 'with a dirty coat buttoned tightly at the throat to conceal the absence of a shirt', defend his favourite with passion. Because of the frequency with which the tramp mentioned *First Principles*, Martin drew that book out of the library. Then came the great discovery:

> Once before he had tried Spencer, and choosing the 'Principles of Psychology' to begin with, he had failed as abjectly as he had failed with Madam Blavatsky. There had been no understanding the book, and he had returned it unread. But this night, after algebra and physics, and an attempt at a sonnet, he got into bed and opened 'First Principles'. Morning found him still reading. It was impossible for him to sleep. Nor did he write that day. He lay on the bed till his body grew tired, when he tried the hard floor, reading on his back, the book held in the air above him, or changing from side to side. He slept that night, and did his writing next morning, and then the book tempted him and he fell, reading all afternoon, oblivious to everything. . . .

It seemed to London that Spencer's ideas were both scientific in derivation and comprehensive in scope, and were centred on a reassuring theory of progress derived not from theology, which he had eschewed, but from biology and physics. His writings were well suited to provide a faith for those whose creedal orthodoxy had waned, as Thomas Stevenson, like many another distraught father, found out when Robert Louis Stevenson discovered Spencer. Others with backgrounds similar to London's, such as Theodore Dreiser, Clarence Darrow, and Hamlin Garland, were easy converts. Thus, to Martin Eden and to Jack London, Spencer was great because he gave meaning to life. He reduced everything to unity. 'It was in obedience to law that the bird flew, and it was in obedience to the same law that fermenting slime had writhed and squirmed and put out legs and wings and become a bird.' It was but a step from Spencer to Darwin and Huxley, aided by interpreters like Fiske and Saleeby. The social Darwinism which emerged was to form one of the most persistent and interesting strains in London's writing; the inconsistencies and contradictions of his social Darwinism were to appear boldly in his fiction, there to reflect the inconsistencies and contradictions of the period in which he wrote.

Making such discoveries for himself, London had little reason to pinch pennies and work nights in order to finish two more years of high school. He accordingly decided in the spring of 1896 to quit the regular course and concentrate on cramming for the entrance examinations for the University of California. This he did, aided by a few weeks at Anderson's University Academy in Alameda, and well-directed help offered generously by such friends as Fred Jacobs and Bessie Maddern. In midsummer he took the examinations and did well enough to enter the university in the fall on a probationary basis. He was now 'John Griffith London, social science special of the class of '00'.

In entering the University of California in 1896 Jack London was six years behind his most important rival among Far Western novelists, Frank Norris, who had spent his undergraduate years at Berkeley from 1890 to 1894. Curiously both youths had entered the university without the ordinary secondary school preparation, for Norris had spent his high school years studying painting in Paris. Like London, he was a special student, and also like London, he left without a degree, although he spent eight semesters rather than one at Berkeley. Moreover, the two men were much alike in some of their tastes, both being apostles of adventure. They shared an oft-expressed enthusiasm for Browning, Kipling, and Stevenson and showed the influence of these writers markedly in their early works. Both extolled the frontier and the Anglo-Saxon fighting spirit, flamboyantly illustrating the latter while they grew as maudlin as spectators at football games. In their writing both showed very clearly the mingling of interests in the romantic and the realistic, with Norris discovering Zola and naturalism, London Marx and socialism, at about the same age. And both quickly grew impatient with the regulation college assignments, particularly in English courses.

Otherwise, their student lives were very different. Whereas Norris was a resident student, London continued to live in Oakland and commute by bicycle, seeing little of student life. Both twenty when they became freshmen, Norris acted younger than his age, throwing himself with glee into class high jinks and becoming such an enthusiastic fraternity man that the Fijis established a nationwide annual dinner in his name; London was in college with serious intent and wasted not a moment on the customary undergraduate foolishness. His reputation as a socialist who had been a sailor and a hobo encouraged him in a role which emphasized maturity.

Two contrasting incidents showed how different were the backgrounds of the embryo writers. Whereas Norris was suspended from the required course in military science because he refused to turn up for drill, London was humiliated before his company by an officer who objected to his appearing in a secondhand uniform he had bought for five dollars. Whereas Norris had gone to the expensive Belmont Academy as a pupil, London was shortly to work there as a hired hand in the laundry.

Most of the evidence indicates that at the time London enjoyed his short stay at the University of California, although later he came to talk much about 'the passionless pursuit of passionless knowledge' which he associated with academic life. The picture his fellow writer, James Hopper, left of him probably comes close to describing his role as student. Hopper remembered that when he first saw London on the steps of North Hall, he had under his arm 'about sixteen books, and his eyes were full of a gay fever'. With his rolling sailor gait, his open-necked shirt, his mop of curly hair 'spun of gold', his eyes like a sunlit sea, and his two missing teeth, he seemed to Hopper to be 'a strange combination of Scandinavian sailor and Greek god'.

With infectious enthusiasm, 'like a flood of sunshine', London was full of gigantic plans in his adventure into the ideal seas of learning. He intended, he said, to take all the courses in English, most of those in natural science, many in history, and 'bite a respectable chunk out of the philosophies'.[14] Hopper was a bit appalled, for he had already taken some of the courses that London looked forward to so eagerly and had found them a bit dull. Actually, during the one semester he spent at the university, London took English courses in prose style, history of literature, and composition, and courses in medieval and nineteenth-century history. He did well in the history courses but failed to complete the English. He enrolled for a second semester, still, as Anna Strunsky put it, hoping 'to read all the books, register in all the courses',[15] but the financial going was too heavy, and he withdrew on February 4, 1897, receiving an honourable dismissal.

*   *   *

Jack London was by no means defeated when he left the university; he simply turned his not inconsiderable energy to other things. He was running for the Oakland Board of Education as a Socialist-Labor candidate in the spring election. Possibly as a means of advertising his candidacy, he agreed with his socialist colleagues to challenge a city ordinance prohibiting soap-box oratory except in specifically designated parks. Accordingly, after being denied permission to speak at Tenth and Broadway, he mounted a box there on February 10 and was taken in hand by the obliging police. He asked for a jury trial and received one in the City of Oakland Police Court eight days later. Well publicized in the local press, he conducted his own defence. Possibly the jury was even more impressed by his story of his life and how he became a socialist than they were by his perfunctory attack on the constitutionality of the city ordinance. The assistant district attorney conducted but a lame prosecution, all but one juror voted for acquittal, and the city decided not to press the case further. The press was friendly and the Oakland *Times* of February 11, 1897, announced that London 'is recognized among a certain set as a leader in socialism, and is thought to be a bright fellow'. It was all good fun, and Jack London received 552 votes at the election on the eighth of March. This was several thousand votes less than it took to win, but it was five hundred more than the Socialist-Labor candidate for mayor was able to poll.

His socialist activities at the moment, though they brought his name before the public, were not his main concern. He had determined to become a writer. 'Naturally, my reading early bred in me a desire to write, but my manner of life prevented me attempting it,'[16] he once stated in an autobiographical sketch. He had attempted to get a schooling to further him in this ambition, but now he would go it on his own. He felt he might make a success as a writer, for he had always been strongly devoted to the frontier concept that a good man could accomplish anything he tackled if he were persistent enough. He was by temperament a jack-of-all-trades. In his days as a tramp, he had passed directly from the status of 'road-kid' to 'profesh', scorning to serve the apprentice period of 'gay-cat' or tenderfoot. Before the mast he had shipped as an able-bodied seaman, feeling confident that he could make his way without any of the customary training for working on a sailing schooner. When he was thrown into the penitentiary, he quickly became a trusty, learning empirically how to get his share of the graft. He later was to boast many times that he learned to become a writer without college training, without knowing another writer, without knowing anything about publishers, and hardly able when he began to write to avoid the double negative. In the frontier myth, every man was as good as the next.

He had, of course, been interested in writing for a number of years. When he had won the San Francisco *Call* contest in 1893 just after returning from his sealing voyage, he exulted that his description of a typhoon at sea had been declared the best of the hundreds of manuscripts that were sent in by young people, most of them with college training. The second prize had gone to a Stanford University student, the third to an entrant from the University of California! He had at once begun writing other articles and sending them out in the hope that they would be bought and published. For a while he had no luck, but he apparently remained sanguine. The earliest of his rejection slips at the Huntington Library is an encouraging letter— not the usual printed slip—from *Youth's Companion*, dated November 23, 1894.

During his tramp across country that year, he had not only kept extensive notes aimed at producing articles, but he had persuaded his aunt, Mary Everhard, to act as an informal agent for him. On Boston Common he had told the editor of the new *Bostonian*, Maitland Leroy Osborne, that he was seeing the world in order to get material for writing. During his high school days his sketches for the *Aegis* showed real promise, particularly the ones entitled 'One More Unfortunate' and 'Sakaicho, Hona Asi and Hakadaki'. He had failed to contribute to the University of California student publication, the *Occident*, but had published articles on political subjects in the Oakland *Times* and *Item* while attending college.[17] Now that he had left college, he was determined to put everything into an attempt to break into the writing game. And it was going to be fun.

'I decided immediately to embark on my career,' he later wrote of that writing splurge in the spring of 1897.

I had four preferences: first, music; second, poetry; third, the writing of philosophic, economic, and political essays; and, fourth, and last, and least, fiction writing. I resolutely cut out music as impossible, settled down in my bedroom, and tackled my second, third and fourth choices simultaneously. Heavens, how I wrote! Never was there a creative fever such as mine from which the patient escaped fatal results. The way I worked was enough to soften my brain and send me to a mad-house. I wrote, I wrote everything—ponderous essays, scientific and sociological, short stories, humorous verse, verse of all sorts from triolets and sonnets to blank verse tragedy and elephantine epics in Spenserian stanzas. On occasion I composed steadily, day after day, for fifteen hours a day. At times I forgot to eat, or refused to tear myself away from my passionate outpouring in order to eat.

Characteristically, he was trying to learn to type at the same time. He was using an antiquated Blickensdorfer, which wrote entirely in capitals. It was so old and stiff that London ached in back and shoulders from pounding it. 'The keys of that machine had to be hit so hard that to one outside the house it sounded like distant thunder or someone breaking up the furniture,' he recorded. 'I had to hit the keys so hard that I strained my first fingers to the élbows, while the ends of my fingers were blisters burst and blistered again.' The nature of the resulting manuscripts, manuscripts easily identified among the surviving London papers, suggests that some editors turned them down automatically because they were such a nuisance to read. It is at this time that London added notably to his collection of rejection slips.

Jack London later felt that the things he wrote during these fevered few weeks did not amount to much—'the stuff I wrote was as weird as its typing'. At least two of his stories of this period, however, were eventually published. One, 'Two Gold Bricks', appeared in the *Owl* in New York in September, 1897, just about the time London reached the headwaters of the Yukon. It is written in the slick patter made popular by Richard Harding Davis and tells about two buddies overhearing the plans of some friends to concoct funeral speeches for themselves and preserve them on phonograph records, to be used at the proper time. The buddies steal the records and so embarrass their friends by starting to play them at a party that they collect a thousand dollars each in blackmail to turn them off. 'Then we're both bricks, good gold bricks, worth ten hundred apiece,' is their closing remark.

The other story, 'A Thousand Deaths', which he unexpectedly managed to sell to the *Black Cat* for forty dollars in 1899, was much more promising. Using what would today be called a science fiction formula, it told of a scientific father who repeatedly killed and revived his son for experimental purposes until the son turned the tables by committing patricide with a charge of nitroglycerin. To Mabel Applegarth, London described this story as 'a pseudo-scientific tale, founded on hypothetical chemical, biological, and pathological laws, dealing with the diametric converse of chemical affinity and the mysteries of protoplasmic coagulation. Very sorry, but can't forward definitions.'[18] Still other attempts at this time, which never were published but have survived in their original typing, included 'The Mahatma's Little Joke', a dull sketch concerning two young men who persuaded a mahatma to exchange their souls so that they might woo each other's sister with the advantages of the propinquity provided by family life, and 'O Haru', the tale of a geisha girl, descendant of a samurai, who in her disappointment over her marriage commits hara-kiri while dancing before her enthusiastic admirers. It is heavy with local colour. The unpublished 'The Plague Ship' dealt with disease, riots, mutiny, and love aboard a vessel adrift in the tropics and was spattered with gore and punctuated with histrionics. Finally, 'The Strange Experiences of a Misogynist' is a somewhat more interesting fantasy dealing with the experience of an anti-female bachelor, who dreams that all women suddenly disappear, that society thereafter rapidly disintegrates, and that destruction from starvation faces him. Fortunately the misogynist awakes at that moment and rushes off to propose. These stories seem very amateurish and completely lack the drive and substance with which the Klondike was shortly to provide London.

London's poetry clearly shows that he had little talent in that field; the ponderous articles have by this time disappeared, or perhaps have been rewritten and published; and an autobiographical sketch describing hobo life, 'The "Road": Glimpses of the Underworld', filled with argot and localisms, survives in manuscript to illustrate how much London was to learn about writing before he published *The Road* ten years later. Undoubtedly some of the sketches he wrote at this time were among those items of hack work which he peddled during the first years of his success as a writer on the Klondike: possibly 'The Handsome Cabin Boy', 'In the Time of Prince Charley', 'A Lesson in Heraldry', and 'Their Alcove' were among them. These are trivial early yarns which London never saw fit to include in any later collection of short stories, although his standard for inclusion was not always high.

It is evident that at this time he had not found his stride as a writer, but it is also evident that he was trying desperately hard to do so. The period is important in showing that he was determined to write even before going to the Klondike.

The enthusiastic writing splurge lasted only a few weeks, for the young writer could not find the money to keep going. He had sold his schoolbooks for a song, had borrowed all he could, and had let his family help him as long as his conscience would allow him to do so. A friend found him a job in a laundry at the Belmont Academy, across the bay. When he took it he expected to get some reading done evenings, and perhaps some writing on the weekends. He also still hoped that some of his manuscripts which were going the rounds of the publishers would be accepted, and he could afford to resume his 'career', as he liked to call it. But, as he vividly tells in *Martin Eden* and *John Barleycorn*, work in the laundry proved so exhausting that for the first time in his life he had no energy left to read after he went to bed. Though he took a trunkful of books to Belmont, he returned at the close of the spring term without having read a single one. It was the longest period without reading London had known since he had discovered *Signa* and *The Alhambra* as a farm boy in Livermore. Of course he got no writing done. And now, after his high school and university experiences and after his short but intensive spurt of writing activity, he found the intellectual starvation very painful. 'When I went coal-shovelling, my mind had not yet awakened. Between that time and the laundry my mind had found the kingdom of the mind. While shovelling coal, my mind was somnolent. While toiling in the laundry, my mind, informed and eager to do and be, was crucified.'

Jack London was about to go on the adventure path again, but this time it was to lead most definitely toward his goal. It would not be long before experience and imagination would coalesce to produce the sort of writing that was in him. He was already at the threshold of his development as an artist.

*   *   *

The phenomenon which drew London north was by no means an unprecedented one. Rather, it was but a culmination of a process that had been going on for two generations, with the California gold rush its most noted predecessor. It was inevitable that prospectors would eventually search for gold on the banks of the Yukon and its tributaries—the tremendous river which drained three hundred and thirty thousand square miles between its headwaters in the Yukon Territory of Canada to its mouth in the Bering Sea. Pierre Berton, whose *The Klondike Fever* is an excellent account of an epic movement, describes the process which eventually built Dawson City as follows: 'Thus was completed a northward osmosis that had been going on since the rush to California, a kind of capillary action that saw restless men with pans and picks slowly inching their way along the mountain backbone of North America from the Sierras to the Stikines, up through Arizona, Colorado, Nevada, and Idaho, leaving behind names like Leadville, Deadwood, Pike's Peak, Virginia City, Cripple Creek, Creede, and Tombstone; up through the wrinkled hide of British Columbia, through the sombre canyons of the Fraser and the rolling grasslands of the Cariboo to the snowfields of the Cassiars, at the threshold of the sub-Arctic.'

For twenty years before the big rush there had been desultory but persistent mining activity on the Yukon. After prospectors discovered that they could reach the upper river by crossing the Chilkoot Pass in the Alaskan panhandle, they filtered in in greater and greater numbers. They had fairly good luck. A hundred thousand dollars of free gold was washed out of the sands at the junction of the Stewart and the Yukon before men discovered larger nuggets some hundred miles downstream at Fortymile. Both of these strikes were in Canadian territory, though they were developed principally by Americans, but the next big one took place even farther north and west, on American soil. Circle City, a wide-open Alaskan city which called itself 'the Paris of the north', mushroomed where the Yukon flowed into its great bend near the Arctic Circle. And it was sourdoughs from Fortymile and Circle City

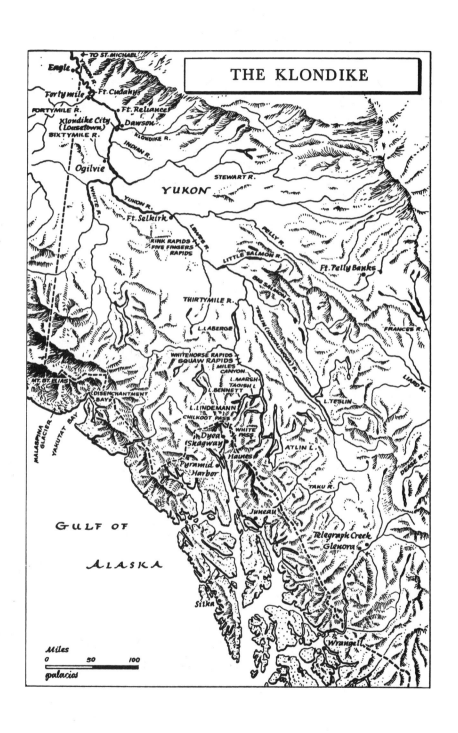

THE KLONDIKE

TO ST. MICHAEL

Eagle

Fortymile • Ft. Cudahy
FORTYMILE R. • Ft. Reliance
Klondike City • Dawson
(Lousetown)
SIXTYMILE R. KLONDIKE R.
INDIAN R.
Ogilvie

YUKON

STEWART R.

YUKON R.
Ft. Selkirk

RINK RAPIDS
FIVE FINGERS
RAPIDS
LITTLE SALMON R.
PELLY R.
Ft. Pelly Banks

THIRTYMILE R.
FRANCES R.

L. LABERGE

WHITEHORSE RAPIDS
SQUAW RAPIDS
MILES
CANYON
L. MARSH
TAGISH L.
L. TESLIN
MT. ST. ELIAS L. BENNETT
DISENCHANTMENT L. LINDEMANN
BAY CHILKOOT PASS
WHITE
PASS ATLIN L.
MALASPINA Dyea
GLACIER Skagway
YAKUTAT BAY Haines DEASE R.
Pyramid
Harbor TAKU R.

Juneau

GULF OF
Telegraph Creek
Glenora
ALASKA

Sitka

Miles
0   50   100
palacios

Wrangell

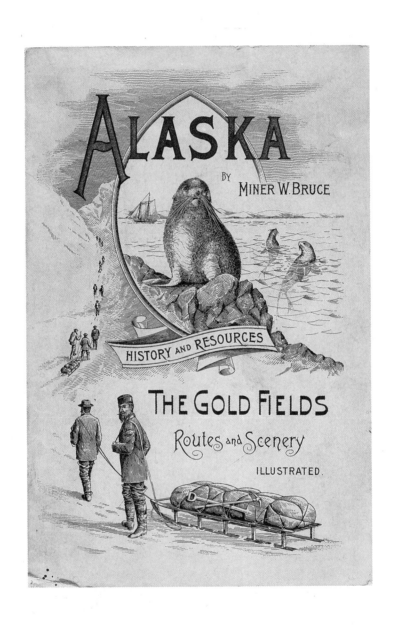

ALASKA

BY MINER W. BRUCE

HISTORY AND RESOURCES

THE GOLD FIELDS

Routes and Scenery

ILLUSTRATED.

London's handbook in the Klondike

who opened up the Klondike and built Dawson City at the point where it joined the Yukon. In doing so, they were moving back upstream and nearer the Chilkoot, the Alaskan panhandle, and Juneau. The Klondike strike was entirely on Canadian soil in an area then known as the North-west Territory, but it has always been associated in the popular mind with Alaska.

On August 17, 1896, an American prospector named George Carmack, together with his Indian 'brothers-in-law', Skookum Jim and Tagish Charlie, discovered a rich deposit of nuggets and dust on a branch of the Klondike not far above the latter's confluence with the Yukon River. This unpromising area, known among the old-timers as worthless 'moose-pasture', had long been called Rabbit Creek, but it was renamed Bonanza Creek after the population of Fortymile rushed to the new location. Soon the population of Circle City also arrived, and by the end of August all of Bonanza was staked.

It seemed that everyone was making a fortune except the Canadian Robert Henderson, who had tipped off the indolent Carmack to the fact that there might be gold in the region. As the claims multiplied, the 'pups' or smaller creeks running into the Bonanza were also prospected; one of them, christened Eldorado, proved to be fabulously rich in gold deposits. As the news spread through Alaska and the Canadian Yukon, Dawson City was developed as a centre for the new mines at the point where the swift Klondike (Indian 'Thron-diuck', meaning 'Hammer-Water') flowed into the mighty Yukon.

Dawson was a town of fifteen hundred inhabitants by the time winter was over. News of the fabulous discovery had leaked out as far as Juneau by midwinter, and by the time of the break-up of the ice on the Yukon in the spring of 1897 a thousand men had climbed the icy Chilkoot (or Chilkat), built boats at Lake Lindeman (miscalled by the Klondikers 'Lake Linderman'), and were ready to float down the Yukon to the new diggings. But the real rush had not started yet; the outside world was not to go mad until the vanguard of the lucky men who had struck it rich on Bonanza and Eldorado creeks the summer of 1896 reached the United States with their fortunes slung over their backs. The very slowness with which the world became aware of the new Pandora's box is an indication of the isolation of the Klondike country.

The prelude to the drama which so captured the imagination of people throughout the world was the departure from Dawson by the first river-boats which could get downstream, of some eighty miners, each bearing a fortune that ran from twenty-five thousand to half a million dollars per man. They transshipped to ocean vessels at St Michael, the *Portland* heading for Seattle, the *Excelsior* for San Francisco. The *Excelsior* won the race south, reaching San Francisco on July 14, 1897, and the *Portland* steamed into Seattle three days later. As the miners carried off their gold with a triumphant flourish, the excitement in the port cities grew in intensity. Forty passengers debarking from the *Excelsior* staggered down the gang-plank, no one toting less than three thousand dollars worth of nuggets and dust. So heavy was the booty they carried in bags, tin cans, and valises that they chartered the Palace Hotel bus to take them directly to the mint. Three days later a similar group of miners walked off the *Portland* in Seattle, carrying, according to the newspapers, which were getting more excited every minute, more than a ton of gold among them.

From that Sunday the press throughout the country devoted itself almost exclusively to stories about the new strike. The pattern of the press coverage was completely paradoxical. On the front pages were long columns filled with personal accounts by sourdoughs, each telling of how much gold he had found in the creeks and tailings of Bonanza and Eldorado—$5,000, $40,000, $100,000 — so it went. In contrast, the editorial pages featured articles pointing out that extreme caution was necessary: that the strike had taken place in one of the most forbidding and remote portions of the continent, that all the good diggings had already been pre-empted (for it was eleven months since the original discovery), that it was now too late in the year to try to get to the Klondike before the freeze-up closed the Yukon, that the cost for each man was so great that little chance of a profit existed. But the people at home read the news columns instead of the editorials. It seemed that the fever was not to be checked by caution. Each man, like Charlie Chaplin in *The Gold Rush*, was drawn (or pushed on) by an irresistible force. On July 25, 1897, eleven days after the *Excelsior* docked, Jack London joined the stampede to the North.

How long did it take London to decide to abandon ideas of continuing in college or learning to write in order to go to the Klondike? One account says a week, which means that he managed to get ready to board the *Umatilla* in four days. To get ready that quickly was not unusual, even for adventurers as broke as Jack was when the fever hit San Francisco. This was to be known as the poor man's gold rush. How did London manage his grubstake? First, he tried to get a job representing a newspaper but found that means overcrowded. Next he went up to the 'Hights' above Oakland to seek advice from Joaquin Miller, the bearded poet of the Sierras who was always in on adventure, for he had heard that Miller was to represent the San Francisco *Examiner* in the Yukon. He found that Miller had already departed, planning to cross the Chilkoot 'with forty pounds on his back and his face to the morning star'.

Help then came from an unexpected source. Jack's brother-in-law, J. H. Shepard, though he was in his sixties and suffering from a bad heart, offered to grubstake him if he would take him along as a partner and provide the energy and brawn to get the two men to the Klondike.

It was a mad scheme and involved mortgaging the Shepard home, but mortgaging modest homes was a commonplace event in the Klondike rush. Jack's stepsister Eliza, ever willing to help him to his heart's desire, volunteered to carry on alone the Shepard business of handling Civil War pension applications, while her elderly husband and eager brother pursued the end of the rainbow. Moreover, she saw to it that the two had first-class outfits, in spite of the fact that good outfits cost at least a thousand dollars. These contained food for winter—cereals, salt meat, coffee and sugar, etc., as well as gold pan, a Yukon stove, possibly a sled, certainly a whipsaw to make a boat. The journals were full of the 'minimum necessities'. And Jack found enough time during the hectic days of preparation to gather in a few books, their weight a small matter compared to the treasures they held. Then he was all set to go.

II · OVER CHILKOOT

IT WAS a chilly Sunday morning when Jack London brought his outfit down to the Broadway wharf in San Francisco to board the *Umatilla* for the Klondike. Though the steamer was not due to sail until nine o'clock, most of the gold seekers had come at dawn, some with elaborate outfits, including fur rugs and snowshoes, others with little more than what they wore on their backs. The docks were piled high with bacon, flour, canned goods, beans, whipsaws, sleds. . . . By scheduled sailing time more than a thousand friends, relatives, and curiosity seekers had arrived to see the ship on its way. The *Umatilla*, crack steamer of the Pacific Steamship Company, was licensed to carry 290 passengers. On this morning of July 25, 1897, she took aboard 471, sixty-one of whom had passage assured to Juneau in the Alaska panhandle. The rest would leave the ship at Puget Sound ports—Victoria, Port Townsend, or Seattle—most of them hoping to get passage farther north in one of those busy harbours. The sixty-one fortunate would transship to the *City of Topeka* at Port Townsend and continue on their way. Among this group were Jack London and his brother-in-law, J. H. Shepard.

Though the *Umatilla* was scheduled to leave at nine o'clock, it was ten-thirty before the big engines began to throb. The crowd waited silently until the ship was at right angles to the dock; then, with one accord, they sent forth such a shout as had not been heard on the San Francisco waterfront for many a year. 'God speed you!' they cried. Those on the ship sent back an answering cry, 'Hurray for Klondike!' and waved until a turn in the bay hid the

D

[49]

groups from each other. Listing heavily to port from the baggage piled hastily aboard—much was left on the dock, piles of food and duffel—the ship waddled through the Golden Gate and headed for colder water.

Most of the Klondike passengers were travelling steerage, partly because they had made their plans too late to obtain cabin passage, partly because they were almost to a man short of money, and partly because in their excitement they were willing to start roughing it early. During the short time the *Umatilla* had been in port, much had been done to expand the steerage offerings. Canvas cots and hammocks were placed in every available spot to supplement the regular three-decker bunks, now freshly separated by cretonne curtains. In its attempts to mitigate the crowded squalor, the management had even laid strips of rug on the deck. All this for twenty-five dollars per man, San Francisco to Juneau. Still, only gold excitement would in the long run counter the twin miseries of steerage sea-sickness and steerage grub.

The eight-day trip up the coast to Juneau, with the hurried transfer of passengers at Port Townsend to the *City of Topeka*, the short stopover at Victoria, with opportunity to buy goods that would pass the Tagish customs without Canadian duty, and the quiet sail up the inland waters beside tall mountains and frowning glaciers, passed slowly for the Klondikers, even though the scenery was frequently awe-inspiring. Winter seemed perilously close to the men who were gambling on getting to the Yukon before the freeze started; they were well aware that the Klondike veterans who had just come out with their booty had been highly sceptical of anyone being able to pack his outfit over the passes and float it down the river before the weather made such an approach impossible. The restless argonauts, serious almost to the point of stopping swearing, gathered in groups to watch amateur boxing matches on deck, to sing beside the piano, or to play poker at a five-cent limit.

Hours were spent examining outfits, each man sure that he had just the right goods for the job.

Conversation turned often to the problems of debarking at Dyea, to the relative difficulties of the old Dyea and the new Skagway trails, and to the persistent question of how much duty the passengers would have to pay to get their outfits to Dawson. If they bought goods at Victoria, they would probably have to pay American customs to cross the strip of Alaskan soil between tidewater and the summit of the Chilkoot Pass. On the other hand, they knew they would have to pay Canadian customs on American-purchased goods after they clambered over the escarpment into the Yukon basin. To add to the confusion, the location of the boundary was still a matter of dispute between the Canadian and American governments. Accordingly, all sorts of rumours were heard aboard ship about how stiff the Canadian customs at Lake Tagish would be. What a shame the strike had to be inside Canada when it was so obviously an American gold rush!

Jack London, aware that Shepard had suffered a mild heart attack brought on by excitement shortly before boarding the *Umatilla*, knew that it would be to his interests to join up with two or three younger men to face the long trek ahead. The forming of such groups was one of the principal occupations aboard ship. It was probably not long after the *Umatilla* passed out of the Golden Gate that London and Shepard joined up with three other argonauts to make up a party. The passenger list gives the names of these as J. M. Sloper, Jim Goodman, and F. C. Thompson. Merritt Sloper was forty years old and weighed about a hundred pounds. He had come 'direct from adventure in South America' and was not only cheerful and brave but very resourceful, with a knowledge of carpentry and sailing which would come in handy when it came to making a boat and shooting the rapids. Jim Goodman, 'Big Jim', knew something about hunting and mining and would

[51]

obviously be able to outpack most men on the trail. Fred Thompson, a slender, red-whiskered young man, may have had no experience in roughing it, but he was temperamentally fitted to be an organizer and recorder. It was Thompson who kept the diary, and it is that diary which is the principal source of information on the itinerary which London followed in going into the Klondike.

Fortunately somewhat detailed, Thompson's diary will serve as the backbone of this account of London's journey from San Francisco to Dawson. To it will be attached the flesh, excerpts from London's fiction, both tales and novels, which reflect his memory of the experience. Even though frequently overdramatized, London's accounts capture the feeling of the rush at the same time that they illustrate his creative talent working from personal observation.

How London and his companions covered the final leg of their sea journey, from Juneau up the natural fjord called the Lynn Canal to Dyea, is not at all clear. During the rush, most of the coastal steamers carried their passengers all the way to Skagway or Dyea. In his diary, however, Thompson refers several times to Juneau as the destination of the *City of Topeka*. After three days' stop there he writes: 'Thursday, Aug. 5. 11 a.m. left Juneau for Dyea with Indians and Canoes.' Possibly this cryptic entry means that the party of five, doubtless accompanied by others, were carried with their outfits to Dyea in one of the big dugout canoes with which the Indians long had negotiated these sheltered waters. This theory is supported by the fact that Thompson notes that it took two days to cover the 150 miles involved. Jack London makes nothing of this interesting venture in his fiction, though in *A Daughter of the Snows* he does describe: 'A pair of seventy-foot canoes, loaded with outfits, gold-rushers, and Indians . . . under full sail.'

Whether he reached Dyea by steamer or canoe, he was confronted when he arrived on Saturday, August 7, 1897, by a scene of confusion which disheartened many of the men who were in a hurry to get on their way over the mountains. Dyea had no wharfs nor any adequate harbour—it was located on a beach with a thirty-foot tide at the mouth of a mountain torrent. There were no adequate facilities for landing goods or men, and there were no shelters for goods or men after they reached the beach.

The ships, boats, and scows which came up the Dyea Inlet rarely provided any help in disembarking and unloading. They stood off from shore some quarter mile while their skippers fretted to start on their return voyages. During high tide, which was the only practical time to operate, passengers were besieged by boatmen eager to take them off for exorbitant figures. These robbers would also transport outfits, once those outfits were located by the owners in the scrambled mess in the hold, but usually the prospective miner had to help not only in loading but also in rowing. Accidents were not infrequent, and a dunking in the ice-cold water was neither comfortable nor safe, though the horses, which were forced to swim, usually survived. Whether London debarked from a ship or merely stepped ashore from a canoe, he made much of the difficult unloading conditions in his fiction. In *A Daughter of the Snows*, for instance, he dramatized them to the hilt.

Everybody was in everybody else's way; nor was there one who failed to proclaim it at the top of his lungs. A thousand goldseekers were clamouring for the immediate landing of their outfits. Each hatchway gaped wide open, and from the lower depths the shrieking donkey-engines were hurrying the misassorted outfits skyward. On either side of the steamer, rows of scows received the flying cargo, and on each of these scows a sweating mob of men charged the descending slings and heaved bales and boxes about in frantic search. Men waved shipping receipts and shouted over the steamer-rails to them. Sometimes two and three identified the same article, and war arose. The 'two-circle' and the 'circle-and-dot' brands caused endless jangling, while every whipsaw discovered a dozen claimants.

Frona Welse, the heroine of the novel, found that rowing in to shore was no time to admire the dark valley shrouded in mist leading to Eldorado. At every dip of the small boat in which she debarked, the glacier-fretted mountains rose and fell like great billows heaving along the skyline. There was an occasional glimpse of the teeming beach towards which they were heading and other glimpses of a score or so of steamships lying at anchor. 'From each of these, to the shore and back again, flowed a steady stream of scows, launches, canoes, and all sorts of smaller craft.' She eventually reached the sandspit, crowded with heterogeneous piles of merchandise and buzzing with men. In *Smoke Bellew* the hero 'landed through the madness of the Dyea beach congested with the thousand-pound outfits of thousands of men'. There was a constant scramble to drag the outfits above high-water line and a constant vigilance to keep outfits together. When they got their breath, the newcomers examined Dyea, their base of operations.

Before the rush Dyea had consisted of a trading post, established by Healy and Wilson, made up of one building devoted to residence, trading, and post-office. Several hundred yards north of this, along the bank of the Dyea (Taiya) River, was a crowded, smelly village inhabited by Siwash Indians who spoke the Tlingit dialect of Athabascan. The men were short and heavy-set, Mongolian of feature with drooping black moustaches; the dumpy women painted their faces with chocolate or black pigment. As the rush hit the sandspit, the Indians in the area got word that white men needed them to pack over the divide, and the village soon became a big encampment of natives from far and near. Sexual promiscuity and heavy drinking were the evils which accompanied the vigorous effort on the parts of all members of the Indian families to help in the portage. By early August the beach was covered higgledy-piggledy by the tents and outfits of ten thousand argonauts, and the town had reached the edge of the Indian village.

Naturally, the aim of Jack London, as well as of all the other arrivals who did not get faint-hearted and reship for home, was to get out of Dyea as soon as possible. Their principal problem was to figure out how to transport their supplies over the glacier-fretted escarpment which separated salt and fresh water. The Dyea River could be navigated for some six miles by Indian canoe or small boat tugged up the river-bank. This left eight miles of stiff climb up a canyon and three-quarters of a mile of forty-five-degree scramble over a 3,600-foot saddle, the Chilkoot Pass, to reach the rim of the Yukon saucer. This was the trail which had long been used by the Indians and the Alaskan and Yukon sourdoughs. It was easier to negotiate in winter than in summer because during the cold season sleds drawn by dogs or men could be used to the base of the steep climb, and the slope of snow and ice of the final stretch was easier to climb on foot than the rain-swept rocks and mudholes of summer.

The greatest difficulty to large-scale movement over the Chilkoot was the fact that it was practically impossible to use horses or other pack animals to get over the saddle. For this reason, a new route had recently been opened up some seven miles south along the coast, where the Skagway River debouched on the inlet and where the boom town of Skagway appeared overnight. Though the Skagway was not navigable and this route to the headwaters of the Yukon was a few miles longer, White Pass, as it was called, was only 2,885 feet in elevation, and the approach to it was not so steep as that to the Chilkoot. In another year it was to be chosen as the route of the railroad from Skagway to Lake Bennett. For a while during the fall of 1897 a considerable number of the argonauts stopped at Skagway, planning to pack over the White Pass with horses and mules. However the rains, together with the heavy, uncontrolled traffic, soon made this route well-nigh impassable, and it became known as the 'Dead-Horse Trail'. By the time London reached the beach, nearly all the Klondikers were resigned to packing their outfits across the Chilkoot or hiring them packed by the Indians. London discovered, as did Smoke Bellew, that 'This immense mass of luggage and food, flung ashore in mountains by the steamers, was beginning slowly to dribble up the Dyea Valley and across Chilkoot. It was a portage of twenty-eight miles, and could be accomplished only on the backs of men.'

One could hire an Indian packer by bargaining for him in the Siwash village or by fortunately running across an unengaged man among the tents or on the trail, but the favoured spot for making arrangements with the packers was in front of Healy's store, where the scales for weighing outfits were located. With the demand far exceeding the supply, rates on packing had been going up steadily from the eight cents a pound which was standard before the rush began. The results are dramatized in London's first novel, *A Daughter of the Snows*.

Before the store, by the scales, was another crowd. An Indian threw his pack upon the scales, the white owner jotted down the weight in a note-book, and another pack was thrown on. Each pack was in the straps, ready for the packer's back and the precarious journey over the Chilcoot. . . . The tenderfoot who was weighing up consulted his guide-book. 'Eight cents,' he said to the Indian. Whereupon the Indians laughed scornfully and chorused, 'Forty cents!' A pained expression came into his face, and he looked about him anxiously. . . . He was busy reducing a three-ton outfit to terms of cash at forty dollars per hundredweight. 'Twenty-four hundred dollars for thirty miles!' he cried. 'What can I do!'

Frona shrugged her shoulders. 'You'd better pay them the forty cents,' she advised, 'else they will take off their straps.'

The man thanked her, but instead of taking heed went on with his haggling. One of the Indians stepped up and proceeded to unfasten his pack-straps. The tenderfoot wavered, but just as he was about to give in, the packers jumped the price on him to forty-five cents. He smiled after a sickly fashion, and nodded his head in token of surrender. But another Indian joined the group and began whispering excitedly. A cheer went up, and before the man could realize it they had jerked off their straps and departed, spreading the news as they went that freight to Lake Linderman was fifty cents.

Jack London and his friends were also tenderfeet and doubtless heard themselves called by the Siwash equivalent of that term, 'cheechakos', as they held a council alongside their piled-up outfits. But they had no intention of paying fifty cents a pound to get their things over the hill. They decided to take them by water as far as navigation permitted and then reconsider the portage problem. Accordingly, they bought a boat for ten dollars and spent the following four days rowing and towing their outfits up the river. Much of the labour was done by dragging the boat from the bank; several trips were necessary in order to get all the goods up the six-mile stretch. By Thursday, August 12, they were past Finnegan's Point and were ready to start the most difficult part of the journey, the packing of their outfits 'across the rubble-covered flats, up the dark canyon to Sheep Camp, past the over-hanging and ever-threatening glaciers to the Scales, and from the Scales up the steep pitches of ice-scoured rock where packers climbed with hands and feet'.[1]

After two days of this arduous labour, during which time the team advanced two miles, Thompson wrote, '8 miles from Dyea—very warm. Creek raised several feet. Sent 3,000 lb. to Summit 14 miles by Indian pack train paying 22 cents per lb.' Whether any of the goods so portaged came from London's outfit is not known. Probably he carried most of his goods over himself.

London put an extraordinary amount of emphasis in his fiction and autobiographical comments on the task of packing over the Chilkoot and the techniques followed by the successful packer. Extraordinarily given to boasting about his physical prowess, he felt that in learning to pack in competition with the Siwash Indians he had accomplished a notable feat. In *John Barleycorn* he writes: 'I was twenty-one years old, and in splendid physical condition. I remember, at the end of the twenty-eight-mile portage across Chilkoot from Dyea Beach to Lake Linderman, I was packing up with the Indians and outpacking many an Indian. The last pack into Linderman was three miles. I back-tripped it four times a day, and on each forward trip carried one hundred and fifty pounds. This means that over the worst trails I daily travelled twenty-four miles, twelve of which were under a burden of one hundred and fifty pounds.' This performance fitted in well with his theory of Anglo-Saxon supremacy.

In fact, the ordeal of packing was the major one faced by men crossing the escarpment. And, as each man was taking in enough supplies to keep him going for a year, this was no mean job. London thoroughly enjoyed exploiting it in his fiction, as in *A Daughter of the Snows*.

Time had rolled back, and locomotion and transportation were once again in the most primitive stages. Men who had never carried more than parcels in all their lives had now become bearers of burdens. They no longer walked upright under the sun, but stooped the body forward and bowed the head to the earth. Every back had become a pack-saddle, and the strap-galls were beginning to form. They staggered beneath the unwonted effort, and legs became drunken with weariness and titubated in diverse directions till the sunlight darkened and bearer and burden fell by the way. Other men, exulting secretly, piled their goods on two-wheeled go-carts and pulled out blithely enough, only to stall at the first spot where the great round boulders invaded the trail. Whereat they generalized anew upon the principles of Alaskan travel, discarded the go-cart, or trundled it back to the beach and sold it at fabulous price to the last man landed. . . . And so, in gasping and bitter sweat, these sons of Adam suffered for Adam's sin.

[58]

In *Smoke Bellew* he enlarged on the difficulties of learning to pack properly. At first, Smoke thought it would be easy. 'He picked out a sack of flour which he knew weighed an even hundred pounds. He stepped astride it, reached down, and strove to get it on his shoulder. His first conclusion was that one hundred pounds were real heavy. His next was that his back was weak. His third was an oath, and it occurred at the end of five futile minutes, when he collapsed on top of the burden with which he was wrestling.' The task of getting over the summit began to look formidable. Though there were four in Bellew's party, one would have to stay in camp and do the cooking:

. . . so to each of the three young men fell the task of carrying eight hundred pounds one mile each day. If they made fifty-pound packs, it meant a daily walk of sixteen miles loaded and of fifteen miles light—'Because we don't back-trip the last time,' Kit explained the pleasant discovery. Eighty-pound packs meant nineteen miles travel each day; and hundred-pound packs meant only fifteen miles.

'I don't like walking,' said Kit. 'Therefore I shall carry one hundred pounds.' He caught the grin of incredulity on his uncle's face, and added hastily: 'Of course I shall work up to it. A fellow's got to learn the ropes and tricks. I'll start with fifty.'

He did, and ambled gaily along the trail. He dropped the sack at the next camp-site and ambled back. It was easier than he had thought. But two miles had rubbed off the velvet of his strength and exposed the underlying softness. His second pack was sixty-five pounds. It was more difficult, and he no longer ambled. Several times, following the custom of all packers, he sat down on the ground, resting the pack behind him on a rock or stump. With the third pack he became bold. He fastened the straps to a ninety-five-pound sack of beans and started. At the end of a hundred yards he felt that he must collapse. He sat down and mopped his face.

'Short hauls and short rests,' he muttered. 'That's the trick.'

Sometimes he did not make a hundred yards, and each time he struggled to his feet for another short haul the pack became undeniably heavier. He panted for breath, and the sweat streamed from him. Before he had covered a quarter of a mile he stripped off his woollen shirt and hung it on a tree. A little later he discarded his hat. At the end of half a mile he decided he was finished. He had never exerted himself so in his life, and he knew that he was finished. As he sat and panted, his gaze fell upon the big revolver and the heavy cartridge-belt.

'Ten pounds of junk!' he sneered, as he unbuckled it.

He did not bother to hang it on a tree, but flung it into the underbrush. And as the steady tide of packers flowed by him, up trail and down, he noted that the other tenderfeet were beginning to shed their shooting-irons.

Whether 'cheechako' London had a shooting-iron to shed is not known, but he did shed nearly everything else, packing on the hot trail in nothing but his red underwear.

No doubt he was remembering his own aches and pains when he wrote of Smoke Bellew's experience for the first days out. 'He had become a work animal. He fell asleep over his food, and his sleep was heavy and beastly, save when he was aroused, screaming with agony, by the cramps in his legs. Every part of him ached. He tramped on raw blisters; . . . His shoulders and chest, galled by the pack-straps, made him think, and for the first time with under-standing, of the horses he had seen on city streets.' In time Smoke caught his second wind, however, and learned by using a head strap and by taking long hauls and long rests as the Indians did that he would survive after all. 'Thus [like Jack London] he was soon able to bend along with a hundred pounds in the straps, fifteen or twenty more lying loosely on top the pack and against his neck, an ax or a pair of oars in one hand, and in the other the nested cooking-pails of the camp.'

Packing was not only arduous, it often became danger-ous because of the difficulty of the terrain as the Klon-dikers made their way up the precipitous, dark canyon formed by the Dyea River in its rush from glaciers to the sea. If one took the stream trail, as London did, and thus avoided the long climbs over the shoulders on the upper trail, there were a number of places where the threatening water had to be crossed, either by fording or passing over improvised bridges. Here the peril of falling and being drowned because of the weight of the pack became only too real. Thus, Old Tarwater in 'Like Argus of the Ancient Times' comes upon the unfortunate Anson on the morning trail. 'He beheld a little man weighing no more than a hundred, staggering along a foot-log under all of a hundred pounds of flour strapped on his back. Also, he beheld the little man stumble off the log and fall face-downward in a quiet eddy where the water was two feet deep and proceed quietly to drown. It was no desire of his to take death so easily, but the flour on his back weighed as much as he and would not let him up.'

' "Thank you, old man," he said to Tarwater, when the latter had dragged him up into the air and ashore.'

Smoke Bellew also tells about packers who had fallen so that they could not rise without help, but the most dramatic incident of this sort is to be found in *A Daughter of the Snows*. Frona Welse is passed near a ford of the Dyea by six strapping Scandinavians, each packing a hundred pounds and all harnessed to a go-cart which carries fully six hundred more. 'Their faces were as laughing suns, and the joy of life was in them.' As they approached the ford they passed a dismal sight which gave them pause for the moment. 'A drowned man lay on his back on the sand-bar, staring upward, unblinking, at the sun. A man, in irritated tones, was questioning over and over, "Where's his pardner? Ain't he got a pardner?" Two more men had thrown off their packs and were coolly taking an inventory of the dead man's possessions. One called aloud the various articles, while the other checked them off on a piece of dirty wrapping-paper. Letters and receipts, wet and pulpy, strewed the sand. A few gold coins were heaped carelessly on a white handkerchief. Other men, crossing back and forth in canoes and skiffs, took no notice.'

After hesitating for a moment, the blond giants with their heavy go-cart stepped into the ford and splashed onward. Paying no attention to warning cries, they got nearly across the ford.

The water had sunk to the knees of the two foremost men, when a strap snapped on one nearest the cart. His pack swung suddenly to the side, overbalancing him. At the same instant the man next to him slipped, and each jerked the other under. The next two were whipped off their feet, while the cart, turning over, swept from the bottom of the ford into the deep water. The two men who had almost emerged threw themselves backward on the pull-ropes. The effort was heroic, but, giants though they were, the task was too great and they were dragged, inch by inch, downward and under.

Their packs held them to the bottom, save him whose strap had broken. This one struck out, not to the shore, but down the stream, striving to keep up with his comrades. A couple of hundred feet below, the rapid dashed over a toothed-reef of rocks, and here, a minute later, they appeared. The cart, still loaded, showed first, smashing a wheel and turning over and over into the next plunge. The men followed in a miserable tangle. They were beaten against the submerged rocks and swept on, all but one. Frona, in a canoe (a dozen canoes were already in pursuit), saw him grip the rock with bleeding fingers. She saw his white face and the agony of the effort; but his hold relaxed and he was jerked away, just as his free comrade, swimming mightily, was reaching for him. Hidden from sight, they took the next plunge, showing for a second, still struggling, at the shallow foot of the rapid.

A canoe picked up the swimming man, but the rest disappeared in a long stretch of swift, deep water. For a quarter of an hour the canoes plied fruitlessly about, then found the dead men gently grounded in an eddy. A tow-rope was requisitioned from an up-coming boat, and a pair of horses from a pack-train on the bank, and the ghastly jetsam hauled ashore. Frona looked at the five young giants lying in the mud, broken-boned, limp, uncaring. They were still harnessed to the cart, and the poor worthless packs still clung to their backs. The sixth sat in the midst, dry-eyed and stunned. A dozen feet away the steady flood of life flowed by, and Frona melted into it and went on.

[62]

In addition to the treacherous ford, there was the place farther up the canyon where men crossed the stream on a thin, swaying log. Smoke Bellew, already aware of 'the ominous pounding of his heart against his eardrums and the sickening totteriness of his knees', heard about this hazard well in advance.

A companion warned him: ' "Wait till you hit the Canyon. You'll have to cross a raging torrent on a sixty-foot pine tree. No guide-ropes, nothing, and the water boiling at the sag of the log to your knees. If you fall with a pack on your back, there's no getting out of the straps. You just stay there and drown."

' "Sounds good to me," he retorted; and out of the depths of his exhaustion he almost meant it.

' "They drown three or four a day there," the man assured him. "I helped fish a German out of there. He had four thousand in greenbacks on him." '

Frona Welse had trouble with the same log (which was eighty feet long this time!), illustrating in her braving its perils the hardihood of the Anglo-Saxon challenged by the Indian.

The trail dipped through a precipitous morass to the river's brink. A slender pine tree spanned the screaming foam and bent midway to touch the water. The surge beat upon the taper trunk and gave it a rhythmical swaying motion, while the feet of the packers had worn smooth its wave-washed surface. Eighty feet it stretched in ticklish insecurity. Frona stepped upon it, felt it move beneath her, heard the bellowing of the water, saw the mad rush—and shrank back. She slipped the knot of her shoe-laces and pretended great care in the tying thereof as a bunch of Indians came out of the woods above and down through the mud. Three or four bucks led the way, followed by many squaws, all bending in the headstraps to the heavy packs. Behind came the children burdened according to their years, and in the rear half a dozen dogs, tongues lagging out and dragging forward painfully under their several loads.

The men glanced at her sideways, and one of them said something in an undertone. Frona could not hear, but the snicker which went down the line brought the flush of shame to her brow and told her more forcibly than could the words. Her face was hot, for she sat disgraced in her own sight; but she gave no sign. The leader stood aside, and one by one, and never more than one at a time, they made the perilous passage. At the bend in the middle their weight forced the tree under, and they felt for their footing, up to the ankles in the cold, driving torrent. Even the little children made it without hesitancy, and then the dogs, whining and reluctant but urged on by the man. When the last had crossed over, he turned to Frona.

'Um horse trail,' he said, pointing up the mountain side. 'Much better you take um horse trail. More far; much better.'

But she shook her head and waited till he reached the farther bank; for she felt the call, not only upon her own pride, but upon the pride of her race; and it was a greater demand than her demand, just as the race was greater than she. So she put foot upon the log, and, with the eyes of the alien people upon her, walked down into the foam-white swirl.

Jack London had not been born in Dyea, as had Frona Welse, nor had he gone in as strenuously as his heroine for swinging clubs, boxing, fencing, chinning a bar, making high dives, and walking on his hands, but he also had 'the race' to push him on, and he could double his arm until the biceps knotted. He and his companions were doubtless sorry they had come, but not sorry enough to turn back. Struggling up the six miles of the dark, narrow canyon, a passage described by one traveller as 'one grand splash, slide, and stumble', they had little spirit for admiring the snow peaks, which rose precipitously on either side, for enjoying the spruce, birches, and elders which made their trail tortuous, or fishing for the salmon and grayling that abounded in the stream. They could envy the 'stolid, mule-footed Indians' with heavy packs yet not accept their stoicism. They moved 'with thousands of men, each back-tripping half a ton of outfit, retracing every mile of the trail twenty times . . . driven desperately on by the near-thrust of winter, and lured madly on by the dream of gold.'[2] Each morning saw the snow-line dropping down the mountains, and each morning Jack London, like Smoke Bellew of his fiction, doubtless felt the pack on his shoulders weighing on him like the Old Man of the Sea on the neck of Sindbad the Sailor.

It took London and his companions ten days, from August 12 to August 21, to pack up the canyon from the head of navigation to Sheep Camp, thus covering the stretch of the trail which proves so exciting in his fiction. London's companion Fred Thompson described the scramble up the slit in the mountains in his sketchy diary, necessarily less spirited than London's novels. Two days of packing quenched the fires of Shepard's gold fever; 'Mr Shepard left us today for his home at Oakland, Cal. having got rumatism very bad.' Like many another, London's brother-in-law was unfit and too discouraged to continue. He left his outfit for London to dispose of and headed down the trail for Dyea. The next day there breezed into camp an old man named Tarwater, from Santa Rosa, whom London was to use, retaining his very name, as the seventy-year-old hero of 'Like Argus of the Ancient Times' (hereinafter referred to as 'Argus'). Thompson does not record whether Tarwater sang doggerel to the doxology, like his fictional counterpart, but he does note—'took him as passenger exchanging board and passage for his work'. Other entries add that Tarwater was helpful at cooking, repairing shoes, packing. This is about all the information the diary throws on this leg of the journey except that the companions were tired and footsore, that they had difficulty crossing the stream on logs—'. . . crossed the river 3 times on logs, one tied across the other are very hard to walk with the water rushing underneath with 100 lb. on your back'—that they struggled past a spot on the trail ironically called 'Pleasant Camp'; and that the excessively warm weather had been replaced by cold and drizzle by the time they reached Sheep Camp, 'a very tough hole'.

Sheep Camp lay at the upper end of Dyea Canyon, not

far below the timberline. Once there had been enough forage to pasture a few sheep, but now every blade of grass was gone and the scattered dwarf spruce and elders were disappearing under the need for firewood. Still, it was a habitable place, a place to gather strength before tackling the final four miles to the Summit up a bare gorge over a stony trail. A tent city had grown up, its life spasmodic and feverish. Here men rested their feet and listened to rumours; some gave up hope, sold their outfits, and turned back; a few went mad or committed suicide.

Although most of the people in Sheep Camp were transients, catching their breath for the last climb, there was a sort of local inhabitant who hung out there. Usually he was a sailor or lumberman who had decided to make his Klondike strike by packing up outfits for other men, earning as much as twenty-six dollars a day. Or he was a saloon keeper or gambler, well aware of the gain to be made from discouraged men. Addison Mizner, who, with his brothers Wilson and William, reached Sheep Camp a couple of months after London, tells of 'The Big Tent Saloon', the centre of activity. Tappan Adney, correspondent for *Harper's Weekly* describes the makeshift taverns: '. . . a tent, a board counter a foot wide and six feet long, a long man in a Mackinaw coat, and a bottle of whiskey make a saloon here.' Faro and craps were the popular games; lawlessness was in the air, as was the case frequently on the Alaskan side of the Chilkoot.

More than one inhabitant of Sheep Camp was like the Montana Kid whom London presents in 'At the Rainbow's End'. The Klondike rush had drawn many such misfits into the wilderness. 'True, the new territory was mostly barren; but its several hundred thousand square miles of frigidity at least gave breathing space to those who else would have suffocated at home. Montana Kid was such a one.' Lacking the energy and purpose to be a successful miner, he cast about him in search of quick harvests. Between the beach and the passes were scattered many thousands of passionate pilgrims. These pilgrims Montana Kid proceeded to farm. At first he dealt faro in a pine-board gambling shack; but disagreeable necessity forced him to drop a sudden period into a man's life, and to move on up trail. Then he effected a corner in horse-shoe nails, and they circulated at par with legal tender, four to the dollar, till an unexpected consignment of a hundred barrels or so broke the market and forced him to disgorge his stock at a loss. After that he located at Sheep Camp, organized the professional packers, and jumped the freight ten cents a pound in a single day. In token of their gratitude, the packers patronized his faro and roulette layouts and were mulcted cheerfully of their earnings. But his commercialism was of too lusty a growth to be long endured; so they rushed him one night, burned his shanty, divided the bank, and headed him up the trail with empty pockets.

After running whisky across the line, terrorizing the camp at Bennett, and stealing a sled, he finally went on his way towards Dawson.

London and his companions did not find much to please them at Sheep Camp. All were teetotalers except Jack, and he was pretty much on the wagon. Rain rather than whisky was their concern. On Sunday they rested as best they could, with everything a sea of mud, while Tarwater repaired shoes. Monday, 'rain and . . . mud . . . cold'. Tuesday. 'Rain most of night, boys dont feel much like packing but must keep moving.' Wednesday, Aug. 25. '. . . raining this morning, but moved to Stone House.' Without much rest possible they had started on that final stony climb, thinking always of reaching the Summit. Beyond Sheep Camp they struggled up a nearly bare gorge on a rapidly rising trail. Soon the alders and spruce disappeared altogether, and they began camping without firewood. The way climbed over boulders and across bogs; the mountainsides rose steep, hard, and bold to prodigious heights. A mile or so above Sheep Camp they came to 'Stone House', named for one of the huge boulders which had tumbled down the cliffs in one of numerous massive slides. A little farther on glaciers overhung the trail and seemed on the verge of crashing down on those below. This whole stretch of gorge was, in fact, the most dangerous portion of the trail; yet even here, without wood for cook fires or tent poles, people camped among the huge ice-worn boulders. Two weeks after London, Thompson, Sloper, Goodman, and Tarwater packed through here, sleeping cold in the mud, a heavy landslide crashed down the mountain, killing one man, injuring several others, destroying many tents and outfits, and wiping out the main trail. The following spring, an even greater mass of ice and snow swept down the three-thousand-foot mountainside and covered ten acres, burying more than sixty Klondikers in an icy tomb.

Although London heightened the tension of camping below the glaciers in his 'Siwash', he faithfully reflected the nightmares of those who travelled this road in the fall of 1897.

A snort of the gale dealt the tent a broad-handed slap as it hurtled past, and the sleet rat-tat-tatted with snappy spite against the thin canvas. . . . The trio peered out. It was not a heartening spectacle. A few water-soaked tents formed the miserable foreground, from which the streaming ground sloped to a foaming gorge. Down this ramped a mountain torrent. Here and there, dwarf spruce, rooting and grovelling in the shallow alluvium, marked the proximity of the timber line. Beyond, on the opposing slope, the vague outlines of a glacier loomed dead-white through the driving rain. Even as they looked, its massive front crumbled into the valley, on the breast of some subterranean vomit, and it lifted its hoarse thunder above the screeching voice of the storm. . . . Another tremendous section of the glacier rumbled earthward. The wind whipped in at the open doorway, bulging out the sides of the tent till it swayed like a huge bladder at its guy ropes. The smoke swirled about them, and the sleet drove sharply into their flesh.

And here came to a climax the morbid tragedy of dying

horses which had plagued the men from the moment they hit Dyea Beach. Hundreds of horses, mules, and burros had been imported by the argonauts to carry their outfits, and almost to an animal they met destruction. Forage was almost nonexistent, and the cost of oats and hay was very high. To keep a horse alive on the other side of the Summit meant using all the animal's energy to pack in its own food. Many horses were sick and decrepit, unfit to be used for any purpose even before they were shipped north. Most of the men on the trail knew nothing of how to take care of them and cared little about what happened to them. There was an acute shortage of horseshoes and nails, with a shoe selling for ten dollars, nails for twenty-five cents each. Lame and starving, the horses blundered on. Wet blankets, saddles not cinched right, saddles that did not fit, loads that were unequally balanced took their toll. The horses were constantly slipping and falling on the glacial rocks, often landing on their backs in the many mudholes on the trail. Many were shot in order to put them out of their miseries; others were allowed to die of pain and exhaustion.

The worst trouble with horses occurred on the White Pass (Skagway) trail, not on the Chilkoot; Thompson notes in his diary that when they reached Lake Bennett, where the two trails converged, they heard that enough horses had died on the Skagway trail to cover it end to end with the animals' rotting bodies. But no doubt the impressions London used in picturing this condition on the White Horse trail, in 'Which Make Men Remember', were based on his observations on the Chilkoot, where some horses were driven to the very foot of the Pass.

The horses died like mosquitoes in the first frost, and from Skaguay to Bennett they rotted in heaps. They died at the Rocks, they were poisoned at the Summit, and they starved at the Lakes; they fell off the trail, what there was of it, or they went through it; in the river they drowned under their loads, or were smashed to pieces against the boulders; they snapped

[69]

their legs in the crevices and broke their backs falling backwards with their packs; in the sloughs they sank from sight or smothered in the slime, and they were disembowelled in the bogs where the corduroy logs turned end up in the mud; men shot them, worked them to death, and when they were gone, went back to the beach and bought more. Some did not bother to shoot them, stripping the saddles off and the shoes and leaving them where they fell. Their hearts turned to stone— those which did not break—and they became beasts, the men on Dead Horse Trail.

In 'Trust' London has one of his characters fall into a mudhole full of dead horses on the Chilkoot Trail. The hero was making his way out of Klondike, bringing his partner's gripsack with him.

Part way down, the stars clouded over again, and in the consequent obscurity he slipped and rolled and slid for a hundred feet, landing bruised and bleeding on the bottom of a large shallow hole. From all about him arose the stench of dead horses. The hole was handy to the trail, and the packers had made a practice of tumbling into it their broken and dying animals. The stench overpowered him, making him deathly sick, and as in a nightmare he scrambled out. Half-way up, he recollected Bondell's gripsack. It had fallen into the hole with him; the pack-strap had evidently broken, and he had forgotten it. Back he went into the pestilential charnel-pit, where he crawled around on hands and knees and groped for half an hour. Altogether he encountered and counted seventeen dead horses (and one horse still alive that he shot with his revolver) before he found Bondell's grip. Looking back upon a life that had not been without valour and achievement, he unhesitatingly declared to himself that this return after the grip was the most heroic act he had ever performed. So heroic was it that he was twice on the verge of fainting before he crawled out of the hole.

Undaunted by rain, threatening glaciers, or dead horses, London's party struggled on from Stone House as the valley made a sudden turn to the right and the trail climbed over great boulders for a couple of miles before it reached the foot of the precipitous slope which led to the Summit.

Canyon Dyea Trail, six miles of 'splash, slide, and stumble'

Our faithful friends on the summit of Chilkoot Pass

RIGHT:
Chilkoot Pass,
c. 1894
(from *Alaska* by
Miner W.
Bruce)

BELOW:
Chilkoot Pass,
c. 1898 after
Yukon gold
discovery

Thompson notes that it took them five days, from Wednesday, August 25, to Monday, August 30, to make that last trek. Their last camp was at the Scales, the name given to the boulder-strewn terrace at the foot of the steep wall of gray rock. 'We camped on the cold rocks with ice-cold water running underneath then gathered what brush and moss we could find spread it on our rocky floor in tent, ate our scanty supper and we had barely wood enough to get breakfast with as we had to pack it 2 miles, spread our blankets and tried to get some sleep laying on the soft side of many sharp stones.' The next morning they tackled the Chilkoot.

The celebrated climb involved moving up what appeared from below to be almost a cliff but what actually had an average slope of about 45 degrees. At the foot of the rise lay many boulders; the face was composed of one bench above another, separated by shale; and many trails zigzagged up the face to meet at the summit, which was nearly always shrouded in mist. The climb was about three-fourths of a mile in length. The pass was more difficult to negotiate in the summer, when London surmounted it, than in the winter, because nothing could be dragged on sleds during the warmer weather, rocks were harder on feet than packed snow, and the return journey, which had to be made a number of times, could not effectively be accomplished by sliding. In the winter one simply whizzed down a chute and started up again with another load. Still, though men frequently had to scramble over rocks on hands and feet, as if they were going up the Great Pyramid, they did not usually find this last and most famous part of the crossing as tough as several of the sections lower down the trail. That the climb was not too strenuous for London and his companions is indicated by the fact that on that Tuesday, August 31, Thompson recorded, after spending the night at the foot of the pass: 'Got our goods all over the Summit and . . . to Crater Lake.'

The comparative ease of the final climb was also attested to by the fact that London paid so little attention to it in his stories. His most detailed description is in *A Daughter of the Snows*, but even in this case Frona spends more time marvelling at the sight of the men climbing than she does in getting over herself.

The midday sun beat down upon the stone 'Scales'. The forest had given up the struggle, and the dizzying heat recoiled from the unclothed rock. On either hand rose the ice-marred ribs of earth, naked and strenuous in their nakedness. Above towered storm-beaten Chilcoot. Up its gaunt and ragged front crawled a slender string of men. But it was an endless string. It came out of the last fringe of dwarfed shrub below, drew a black line across a dazzling stretch of ice, and filed past Frona where she ate her lunch by the way. And it went on, up the pitch of the steep, growing fainter and smaller, till it squirmed and twisted like a column of ants and vanished over the crest of the pass. Even as she looked, Chilcoot was wrapped in rolling mist and whirling cloud, and a storm of sleet and wind roared down upon the toiling pigmies. The light was swept out of the day, and a deep gloom prevailed; but Frona knew that somewhere up there, clinging and climbing and immortally striving, the long line of ants still twisted towards the sky.

Not long afterward, Frona 'blew through the gap of the pass in a whirlwind of vapour'. It was this harassing weather in the gap that London stressed most in his fiction. Perhaps it was the detail he remembered most distinctly. Tarwater, like Frona, 'blew across Chilcoot Pass'. And Smoke Bellew reached 'the crest of the divide in the thick of a driving snow-squall'. The latter was forced to spend the night on the Summit. This was no place to camp—no stream, no wood, no shelter—but many men stopped there. 'When he had paid off the Indians and seen them depart, a stormy darkness was falling, and he was left alone, a thousand feet above timber-line, on the backbone of a mountain. Wet to the waist, famished and exhausted, he would have given a year's income for a fire and a cup of coffee. Instead, he ate half a dozen cold flap-jacks and crawled into the folds of the partly unrolled tent. . . . In the morning, stiff from his labours and numb with frost, he rolled out of the canvas, ate a couple of pounds of uncooked bacon, buckled the straps on a hundred pounds, and went down the rocky way. Several hundred yards beneath, the trail led across a small glacier and down to Crater Lake.'

The trip from the Summit to Lake Lindeman was neatly summarized in 'Argus': 'From Happy Camp to Long Lake, from Long Lake to Deep Lake, and from Deep Lake up over the enormous hog-back and down to Linderman, the man-killing race against winter kept on. Men broke their hearts and backs and wept beside the trail in sheer exhaustion. But winter never faltered. The fall gales blew, and amid bitter soaking rains and ever-increasing snow flurries, Tarwater and the party to which he was attached piled the last of their outfit on the beach.'

It was Wednesday, September 8, 1897, when the London party reached Lake Lindeman, head of small-boat navigation on the Yukon. It had taken eight days to move from the Summit the nine miles down the string of volcanic lakes and swift streams to the head of Lake Lindeman. Here were pleasant fields and a community of tents. And here the second stage of the trek was to begin.

III · 'INTO THE TEETH
OF THE NORTH'

THE rest of the way to Dawson City was downhill. The
problem the Klondikers now faced was comparatively
simple; they must build or buy boats, then float, sail, row,
or drag those boats nearly six hundred miles down the
string of lakes and connecting rivers which form the upper
reaches of the Yukon. A good sailor in a well-built boat
found nothing about the journey markedly hazardous.
The principal danger came at the several rapids on the
upper river, particularly those at White Horse, but these
could always be avoided by portage.

The main error made by landlubbers unused to river
travel was to attempt to keep going when boats leaked, the
weather turned bad, nerves became frayed, and fatigue
impaired judgement. The urge to get downstream as soon
as possible was very strong. Not only did the tug of gold
pull the adventurers on, but the approach of winter meant
danger that the river would freeze over, leaving them
stranded where they were caught in the ice. There they
would probably remain for the winter, unless they were
fortunate enough to get sleds and dogs to transport their
outfits after the river trail was opened. As the freeze-up
frequently came as early as mid-October, London and his
companions felt as if they were racing against an implacable Nature. To them the journey was a 'perilous traverse
of half a thousand miles of lakes and rapids and box canyons, driving squarely into the teeth of the north'.

For Klondikers coming over the Chilkoot Trail, Lake
Lindeman was the logical starting point for the run down-

river. Not only were there spruce trees near at hand with which to build boats, but from this point, except for a short portage between Lakes Lindeman and Bennett and possibly one at White Horse, men could take their craft the entire distance to Dawson City without removing the carefully packed duffel. The route they followed carried them through five narrow lakes: Lindeman (six miles long), Bennett (twenty-four miles), Tagish (nineteen miles), Marsh (nineteen miles), and Laberge (thirty-one miles). These were connected by stretches of river which varied from the smooth neck of water joining Bennett and Tagish, known then as Caribou Crossing, today shortened to Carcross, to the rough sixty-mile nightmare which lay between the lower lakes, Marsh and Laberge—the stretch which contained midway the much-feared Box Canyon and White Horse Rapids.

Once the lakes were behind them, the argonauts floated down an ever-widening river. Thompson's diary shows that London's party spent nearly two weeks at Lake Lindeman building a boat, four days running the four lakes to White Horse, one day getting through Box Canyon and the rapids, more than a week covering the thirty miles of river to Laberge and crossing that formidable, wind-swept lake, and a final week making the 330 additional miles to the mouth of the Stewart River, some eighty miles above Dawson, where they ended their voyage on October 9, 1897. There is not a scrap of evidence to indicate that they at any time met serious trouble. Their experience was something like that faced by forty-niners crossing the plains. In both gold rushes, most men won their way past the many hazards by careful planning, persistence, or good luck. Yet the river journey was full of danger and excitement—the hardships were challenging, the excitement of participating in a race was ever-present, and the catastrophes which came to the unlucky few dramatized the success of those who won through handily. As London turned to this part of his Klondike experience for matter for fiction, he naturally stressed the dramatic and unusual; his picture is not, however, a false one—merely a heightened one.

Where the Chilkoot trail reached Lake Lindeman there was an encampment of perhaps a hundred and fifty tents, which belonged to men who were building boats or backtracking the last of their outfits from the Summit. Here the men were cheerful, confident that they were really going to get to Klondike, given to singing and cheering. A half-dozen sawpits where Klondikers sawed the spruce trees into rough boards were in constant use, and from six to ten boats set off each day, to an accompaniment of cheers and revolver shots. If you had enough money and were persistent, you could possibly buy a boat, as Rasmunsen did for six hundred dollars in 'The One Thousand Dozen'. Or you might buy passage in a boat, probably for less than a thousand dollars, the sum the mysterious heroine paid Sitka Charley to ride in his Peterborough canoe in 'The Sun-Dog Trail'. But if you were like London and his friends, you built a boat.

Surprisingly, little record of the interesting art of Yukon boat-building is to be found in the stories. In 'The One Thousand Dozen' London mentioned the 'fresh-whipsawed boats departing for Dawson', but the theme in this story stressed desperate haste. Nothing is said about the primitive method of whipsawing the logs, with one man above, keeping the saw on the chalked line, and one below in a pit getting the sawdust in his eyes. Nor does London tell anything about smoothing up the rough-hewn planks, fitting them together for bottom and sides, or caulking the resulting craft with oakum and tar, if you had some in your pack, or moss from underfoot and pitch from the trees if you did not.

A great anxiety brooded over the camp where the boats were built. Men worked frantically, early and late, at the height of their endurance, calking, nailing, and pitching in a frenzy of haste for which adequate explanation was not far to seek. Each day the snow-line crept farther down the bleak, rock-shouldered peaks, and gale followed gale, with sleet and slush and snow, and in the eddies and quiet places young ice formed and thickened through the fleeting hours. And each morn, toil-stiffened men turned wan faces across the lake to see if the freeze-up had come. For the freeze-up heralded the death of their hope—the hope that they would be floating down the swift river ere navigation closed on the chain of lakes.

A closer parallel to London's own experience is found in the account in the highly autobiographical 'Argus'. 'There was no rest. Across the lake, a mile above a roaring torrent, they located a patch of spruce and built their saw-pit. Here, by hand, with an inadequate whipsaw, they sawed the spruce-trunks into lumber. They worked night and day. Thrice, on the night-shift, underneath in the saw-pit, Old Tarwater fainted. By day he cooked as well, and, in the betweenwhiles, helped Anson in the building of the boat beside the torrent as the green planks came down.' In this account, the pace has been stepped up to emphasize Tarwater's grit, but many of the details ring true.

Thompson notes that the day the party reached Lindeman it joined with another party in plans to make two boats. Jack London and Merritt Sloper went five miles upstream to cut lumber, having as companions 'Bill, Dave, and Jud'. Apparently they built their boats near the spot where they cut their logs. Sloper had had experience in building boats, and London had had much experience in sailing them. Thompson and Tarwater remained at Lindeman to pack the rest of the supplies down from the mountain trail where they had been cached. Nothing is said of Jim Goodman; perhaps he went hunting, as this was his forte. During the next ten days the two parties which had gone upstream completed the *Belle of the Yukon* and the *Yukon Belle*. The latter, which was to carry London, his three partners and Tarwater downstream, together with more than five thousand pounds of outfit, was twenty-seven feet long and, according to London, one of the best boats on the river (the *Belle of the Yukon* was no doubt its principal rival).

On September 19, London and Sloper 'lined [lowered by rope] the rough-made boat down the mountain torrent, nearly losing it a dozen times, and rowed across the south end of Lake Linderman' to the base camp.

Then, while the others carved four oars, Jack London made and installed the mast and sail, presumably a good big square sail planned to catch as much of the wind as the skiff could take. It had the potentialities and also the dangers of the rig described in 'The One Thousand Dozen': '. . . the Yankee closed with the remaining rival, a brawny son of the sea and sailor of ships and things, who promised to show them all a wrinkle or two when it came to cracking on. And crack on he did, with a large tarpaulin squaresail which pressed the bow half under at every jump.' With such a sail, there was always a danger of capsizing. But what was the use of coming north if you weren't willing to take a gamble?

At the base camp the two parties who had built boats together were now ready to start their long voyage. Tarwater was to ride in London's boat, the *Yukon Belle*, at least as far as Stewart River. In the *Belle of the Yukon* there were, in addition to 'Bill, Dave, and Jud', a 'poetically inclined' Charles Rand, who produced some doggerel on the trip that Thompson included in his diary, and a Mrs Hirschberg, who was sturdy enough to wield the steering oar in some fairly ticklish spots. Thompson tells us nothing of her appearance, background, or character; he merely speaks of her as 'a passenger with the other crowd', who could cook well. Did she wear men's clothes, as many of the women on the Klondike trail did, or were her skirts down around her ankles, daringly high above the shoe tops? Was she tough or was she retiring, a dance-hall girl or a restaurant cook? Many women made the trek that winter to the Klondike, and many women appear in London's stories. They were, by and large, 'men's women', although they ranged from the proper matron to the breezy hussy.

It was Tuesday, September 21, when the boats took off, with Jack London at the steering oar of the *Yukon Belle*. Probably there were the customary shouts of encouragement and salvos of revolver shots from the onlookers. Certainly there was no such trouble as that described in *Smoke Bellew*, although getting under way in heavily-loaded, rough-hewn boats could not have been easy.

One boat, already loaded, was just starting, and Kit paused to watch. The wind, which was fair down the lake, here blew in squarely on the beach, kicking up a nasty sea in the shallows. The men of the departing boat waded in high rubber boots as they shoved it out toward deeper water. Twice they did this. Clambering aboard and failing to row clear, the boat was swept back and grounded. Kit noticed that the spray on the sides of the boat quickly turned to ice. The third attempt was a partial success. The last two men to climb in were wet to their waists, but the boat was afloat. They struggled awkwardly at the heavy oars, and slowly worked off shore. Then they hoisted a sail made of blankets, had it carry away in a gust, and were swept a third time back on the freezing beach.

The *Yukon Belle* was a better boat than this, its occupants were better sailors, and the weather, though there had been frost for two weeks, was hardly this bitter as yet.

Lindeman is a lovely lake, narrow between towering mountains, six miles long with a dogleg in the middle. London described it in *Smoke Bellew*: 'Lake Linderman was no more than a narrow mountain gorge filled with water. Sweeping down from the mountains through this funnel, the wind was irregular, blowing great guns at times and at other times dwindling to a strong breeze.' The breeze must have been with them that morning, for the *Yukon Belle* was soon at the end of the lake, the temporary end of navigation. The outlet stream dropped abruptly through a gorge on its way to Lake Bennett, three-quarters of a mile below. It was one continuous cascade over a narrow, rocky bed.

'It was the custom to line the empty boats down and to portage the cargoes across. Even then, many empty boats had been wrecked,' London wrote in 'Argus'. In that story he has Liverpool, his fictional self, run the boat down filled with cargo (the season was too late for caution), but in real life this would have been a foolhardy trick, almost certain to end in disaster. Actually Thompson's diary tells that London and his friends 'portaged' their boats (lowered them by rope?) themselves and paid $27.50 each to have their outfits packed to Bennett. This was doubtless better than taking two days to carry the outfits on their shoulders down the sandy path through the pines, as did Smoke Bellew. But London's cash must have been disappearing fast; twice coming down from the Summit to Lindeman he and his partners had paid steep ferrying charges to get their goods across the small glacial lakes which pocketed the mountain. They paid thirty dollars at Crater Lake and a like amount at Long Lake; at Deep Lake they were able to rent a boat for eight dollars, four dollars of which they were able to recoup by carrying the outfits of another party across.

At the head of Lake Bennett, where a shack and tent town and even a sawmill had sprung up, they lingered only long enough to get the news. This was plentiful, as Bennett was the junction point of the trails from Dyea and Skagway. The news consisted almost entirely of stories of dead horses on the White Pass trail and accounts of food shortages in Dawson City and the Klondike diggings. The conditions downriver were not encouraging. There were, in fact, far too many Klondikers like Tarwater slipping into the Yukon without grub to keep them going through the long winter months. In 'Argus' this concern plays a prominent part.

[80]

Community of tents at Lake Lindeman

One Mile River between Lindeman and Bennett

Shack and tent town on Lake Bennett

"Ho" for Klondike, Lake Bennett

The days grew shorter. The wind shifted into the north and blew unending gales. In the mornings the weary men crawled from their blankets and in their socks thawed out their frozen shoes by the fire Tarwater always had burning for them. Ever arose the increasing tale of famine on the Inside. The last grub steamboats up from Bering Sea were stalled by low water at the beginning of the Yukon Flats hundreds of miles north of Dawson. In fact, they lay at the old Hudson Bay Company's post at Fort Yukon inside the Arctic Circle. Flour in Dawson was up to two dollars a pound but no one would sell. Bonanza and Eldorado Kings, with money to burn, were leaving for the Outside because they could buy no grub. Miners' Committees were confiscating all grub and putting the population on strict rations. A man who held out an ounce of grub was shot like a dog. A score had been so executed already. . . . The Northwest Mounted Police, stationed at the foot of Lake Marsh where the gold-rushers entered Canadian Territory, were refusing to let a man past who did not carry with him seven hundred pounds of grub. In Dawson City a thousand men, with dog-teams, were waiting the freeze-up to come out over the ice. The trading companies could not fill their grub-contracts, and partners were cutting the cards to see which should go and which should stay and work the claims.

On September 22, the *Yukon Belle* sailed down beautiful Lake Bennett at a fast clip, passing her companion, the *Belle of the Yukon*, and many other boats. The account in 'Argus' probably comes fairly close to describing the argonauts' experiences. 'A shift of gale to the south gave them a fair wind down Lake Bennett, before which they ran under a huge sail made by Liverpool. The heavy weight of outfit gave such ballast that he cracked on as a daring sailor should when moments counted. A shift of four points into the south-west, coming just at the right time as they entered upon Caribou Crossing, drove them down that connecting link to lakes Taggish and Marsh. In stormy sunset and twilight they made the dangerous crossing of Great Windy Arm, wherein they beheld two other boat-loads of gold-rushers capsize and drown.' Thompson noted in his diary: ' . . . sailed down Bennett with a very strong fair wind which made our boats hum passed everything in sight—wind was fair and very strong all day and waves 3 or 4 feet high making our boats hard to steer but we went flying and camped about 5 o'clock p.m. on the shores of Lake Taggish—a good many boats swamped on Bennett.' Years later Charmian London wrote that Jack vividly remembered two boats capsizing and their occupants drowning on that day on Lake Bennett.

London later utilized these disasters in his short story, 'The One Thousand Dozen', in which his hero, Rasmunsen, races northward with a boat-load of eggs in order to take advantage of the high scarcity price in Dawson. 'Bennett was a twenty-five-mile lake, narrow and deep, a funnel between the mountains through which storms ever romped. Rasmunsen camped on the sand-pit at its head, where were many men and boats bound north in the teeth of the Arctic winter. He awoke in the morning to find a piping gale from the south, which caught the chill from the whited peaks and glacial valleys and blew as cold as north wind ever blew.'

There were other boat-loads of eggs on hand, their owners eager to reach Dawson first. Rasmunsen raced his rivals down the lake, straining at the steering-oar while his passengers chopped ice from their oars. 'The iron-bound shores were in a lather of foam, and even down the middle the only hope was to keep running away from the big seas. To lower sail was to be overtaken and swamped. Time and again they passed boats pounding among the rocks, and once they saw one on the edge of the breakers about to strike. A little craft behind them, with two men, jibed over and turned bottom up.' One of his rival egg merchants was stranded on a rock. Another with a square-sail too large for his boat capsized: '. . . the black tarpaulin swooped from sight behind a big comber. The next wave rolled over the spot, and the next, but the boat did not reappear.' Eventually Rasmunsen reached Caribou Crossing with his eggs intact—everything else had been thrown overboard. The next day he patched up his boat and headed on into Tagish. 'A cruel east wind blew in his teeth from Tagish, but he got the oars over the side and bucked manfully into it, though half the time he was drifting backward and chopping ice from the blades. According to the custom of the country, he was driven ashore at Windy Arm; three times on Tagish saw him swamped and beached; and Lake Marsh held him at the freeze-up.'

On Thursday morning London and his friends while floating down the sluggish six-mile stream connecting Tagish and Marsh saw the red British flag on the right bank and pulled over to the Canadian customs. Though they had been in Canadian territory ever since reaching Chilkoot Summit, they were meeting Canadian authority for the first time. Here at Tagish Post the customs officer, supported by a detachment of North-west Mounted Police, stopped all boats coming from the south, thus meeting all emigrants from the converging trails. The customs officer must have been very lenient, for he collected only $21.50 for the five thousand pounds aboard the boat and let Tarwater through without an outfit. Thompson boasts that they got by so cheaply 'by scheming', and that others 'not onto their job' had to pay a good deal more.

That night, after again passing many boats, they camped on the shores of Lake Marsh and the next day entered the section of the upper Yukon (then called the Lewes) which was known as the Sixtymile River. Thompson makes clear that the party was feeling fine. 'Sailed from Marsh Lake to the Lewis River, arriving at the river about noon, cooked our dinner on the boat, and drifted and rowed down the river, having a very pleasant afternoon,—found good camp for the night on the river bank. Jim shot 2 pheasants.' The next day was in marked contrast. 'Sat. Sept. 25. Up bright and early, snowing and cold, started down river again,—got very cold so went ashore and built

[83]

a fire, got warm and had something to eat. Jim went out to try and shoot a Moose but saw nothing,—started down river again snowing stopped.'

By noon they had navigated half of the sixty-mile stretch of ever-swifter water which joined Marsh and Laberge. They were about to reach the most feared passage on the journey downriver, the twin hazards of Box Canyon and White Horse Rapids. Suddenly the narrowing canyon seemed to come to an abrupt end, an illusion caused by a sharp turn in the gorge; the men saw a red flag and a sign on the bank, 'Canyon ahead'; and moments later they had drawn their boat up to the little beach at the head of Box Canyon. Like every other Klondiker on his way down the river to Dawson, they had to decide whether to risk their boats, their cargo, and their necks in running the canyon and rapids below it or to take several days to portage their outfits around the obstructions which faced them.

The urge to take a chance and run the canyon and rapids was furthered by concern over the snow and cold which had hindered them that morning. Also, a good many other Klondikers were taking their boats through, frequently with full loads. The many stories of boats capsizing and men drowning in the rapids but added zest to the venture.

At the Box Canyon, or Miles Canyon, as it was officially called, the river ran for nearly a mile through a trough which narrowed down to a mere slit in the plateau. This trough was walled by perpendicular basaltic rock in hexagonal formation. Midway in the trough was a widening out where a whirlpool churned slowly around. The whole striking phenomenon could be seen from the top of the walls, where hundreds of men watched boats dashing through. London and his companions joined the onlookers to survey a scene which he described in *Smoke Bellew*: 'The Box Canyon was adequately named. It was a box, a trap. Once in it, the only way out was through. On either side arose perpendicular walls of rock. The river narrowed to a fraction of its width and roared through this gloomy passage in a madness of motion that heaped the water in the centre into a ridge fully eight feet higher than at the rocky sides. This ridge, in turn, was crested with stiff, up-standing waves that curled over yet remained each in its unvarying place. The canyon was well feared, for it had collected its toll of dead from the passing gold-rushers.'

The party, acting democratically, took a vote and found itself unanimously in favour of running the canyon with the full load. Thompson describes the event with somewhat more detail than he usually uses in his diary: '. . . came to Box Canyon, which we shot after taking a look at it with everything in our boat—Jack at stern, Sloper at bow, Jim and myself at the oars—[Tarwater obviously walked around in order not to burden them with his weight.] The ride was a swift one as the river at the point narrows to about 30 feet and the water dashes and rolls through this narrow box with walls from 50 to 100 feet high at a great speed making it rather dangerous to enter, but as our boat was large and strong we did not feel alarmed to make the run, and as it was we made the run in 3 minutes otherwise it would have taken us 4 days to pack around.'

London told the story at greater length in an article entitled 'Through the Rapids on the Way to Klondike', written two years later and published in an obscure magazine, and recently reprinted in *Jack London's Tales of Adventure* edited by Irving Shepard.

Lashing the steering oar so that it could not possibly escape, I allotted my comrades their places; for I was captain. Merritt Sloper, direct from adventures in South America and who knew a little of boating, took his position in the bow with a paddle. Thompson and Goodman, landlubbers who had never rowed before this trip, were stationed side by side at the oars. . . .

'Be sure to keep on the Ridge,' cried the men on the bank as we cast off.

The water, though swift, had a slick, oily appearance until we dashed into the very jaws of the Box, where it instantly took on the aspect of chaos broken loose. Afraid that the rowers might catch a crab or make some other disastrous fumble, I called the oars in.

Then we met it on the fly. I caught a glimpse of the spectators fringing the brink of the cliffs above, and another glimpse of the rock walls dashing by like twin lightning express trains; then my whole energy was concentrated in keeping to the Ridge. This was serrated with stiff waves, which the boat, dead with weight, could not mount, being forced to jab her nose through at every lunge. For all the peril, I caught myself smiling at the ridiculous capers cut by Sloper, perched in the very bow and working his paddle like mad. Just as he would let drive for a tremendous stroke, the stern would fall in a trough, jerking the bow clear up, and he would miss the water utterly. And at the next stroke, perhaps, the nose would dive clean under, almost sweeping him away—and he only weighed one hundred pounds. But never did he lose his presence of mind or grit. Once, he turned and cried some warning at the top of his lungs, but it was drowned in the pandemonium of sound. The next instant we fell off the Ridge. The water came inboard in all directions, and the boat, caught in a transverse current, threatened to twist broadside. This would mean destruction. I threw myself against the sweep till I could hear it cracking, while Sloper snapped his paddle short off.

And all this time we were flying down the gutter, less than two yards from the wall. Several times it seemed all up with us; but finally, mounting the Ridge almost sidewise, we took a header through a tremendous comber and shot into the whirlpool of the great circular court.

Ordering out the oars for steerage-way, and keeping a close eye on the split currents, I caught one free breath before we flew into the second half of the canyon. Though we crossed the Ridge from left to right and back again, it was merely a repetition of the first half. A moment later the *Yukon Belle* rubbed softly against the bank. We had run the mile of canyon in two minutes by the watch.

After the successful passage, London and Sloper returned to the eddy at the head of the canyon and ran through the twenty-two-foot skiff belonging to a 'Mr and Mrs Ret'.

Thompson's notes imply that this was done out of goodness of heart, an assumption which is supported by an incident in *Smoke Bellew* in which Kit Bellew and Shorty (who is much like Sloper) return to take through a boat and outfit belonging to a man named Breck, who was travelling with his wife and young nephew as his only companions. Breck had appeared so helpless that the two had been glad to take his boat through Miles Canyon while Breck and his family walked around.

After running the stranger's boat through, Kit and Shorty met his wife, a slender, girlish woman whose blue eyes were moist with gratitude. Breck himself tried to hand Kit fifty dollars, and then attempted it on Shorty.

'Strangers,' was the latter's rejection, 'I come into this country to make money outa the ground an' not outa my fellow critters.'

Breck, the stranger, rummaged in his boat and produced a demi-john of whiskey. Shorty's hand half went out to it and stopped abruptly. He shook his head.

'There's that blamed White Horse right below, an' they say it's worse than the Box. I reckon I don't dast tackle any lightning.'

The White Horse Rapids, reached after negotiating some three miles of rough water known as the Squaw Rapids, was in fact even more formidable than Miles Canyon. Particularly when the water was as low as it was in September, the jagged rocks which caused the white waves named after flying horses' manes were a fearful menace to adventurers in small boats. Many travellers, probably the majority, took the advice of Miner Bruce in his *Alaska*, a book which London carried with him and constantly consulted, to portage their outfits and even their boats around the rough water. Many others ran the rapids, most of them without disaster. Some were not so fortunate. One such case played a prominent part in *Smoke Bellew*, in which London plays up the danger to the hilt.

Kit Bellew and his companions had walked down to look at the bad water before attempting passage through it.

The river, which was a succession of rapids, was here deflected toward the right bank by a rocky reef. The whole body of water, rushing crookedly into the narrow passage, accelerated its speed frightfully and was up-flung into huge waves, white and wrathful. This was the dread Mane of the White Horse, and here an even heavier toll of dead had been exacted. On one side of the Mane was a corkscrew curl-over and suck-under, and on the opposite side was the big whirlpool. To go through, the Mane itself must be ridden.

'This plumb rips the strings outa the Box,' Shorty concluded.

As they watched, a boat took the head of the rapids above. It was a large boat, fully thirty feet long, laden with several tons of outfit, and handled by six men. Before it reached the Mane it was plunging and leaping, at times almost hidden by the foam and spray.

Shorty shot a slow, sidelong glance at Kit and said: 'She's fair smoking, and she hasn't hit the worst. They've hauled the oars in. There she takes it now. God! She's gone! No; there she is!'

Big as the boat was, it had been buried from sight in the flying smother between crests. The next moment, in the thick of the Mane, the boat leaped up a crest and into view. To Kit's amazement he saw the whole long bottom clearly outlined. The boat, for the fraction of an instant, was in the air, the men sitting idly in their places, all save one in the stern, who stood at the steering-sweep. Then came the downward plunge into the trough and a second disappearance. Three times the boat leaped and buried itself, then those on the bank saw its nose take the whirlpool as it slipped off the Mane. The steersman, vainly opposing with full weight on the steering-gear, surrendered to the whirlpool and helped the boat to take the circle.

Three times it went around, each time so close to the rocks on which Kit and Shorty stood that either could have leaped on board. The steersman, a man with a reddish beard of recent growth, waved his hand to them. The only way out of the whirlpool was by the Mane, and on the third round the boat entered the Mane obliquely at its upper end. Possibly out of fear of the draw of the whirlpool, the steersman did not attempt to straighten out quickly enough. When he did, it was too late.

Alternately in the air and buried, the boat angled the Mane and was sucked into and through the stiff wall of the corkscrew on the opposite side of the river. A hundred feet below, boxes and bales began to float up. Then appeared the bottom of the boat and the scattered heads of six men. Two managed to make the bank in the eddy below. The others were drawn under, and the general flotsam was lost to view, borne on by the swift current around the bend.

A comparison of this passage of *Smoke Bellew* with London's account of his actual experiences in running the rapids, as described in 'Through the Rapids on the Way to Klondike', furnishes an excellent example of the way in which he turned fact of his own passage into the fiction of his novel.

When we struck the 'Mane', the *Yukon Belle* forgot her heavy load, taking a series of leaps almost clear of the water, alternating with as many burials in the troughs. To this day I cannot see how it happened, but I lost control. A cross current caught our stern and we began to swing broadside. Then we jumped into the whirlpool, though I did not guess it at the time. Sloper snapped a second paddle and received another ducking.

It must be remembered that we were travelling at racehorse speed, and that things happened in a tithe of the time taken to tell them. From every quarter the water came aboard, threatening to swamp us. The *Yukon Belle* headed directly for the jagged left bank, and though I was up against the steering sweep till it cracked, I could not turn her nose downstream. Onlookers from the shore tried to snapshot us, but failed to gauge our speed or get more than a wild view of angry waters and flying foam.

The bank was alarmingly close, but the boat still had the bit in her teeth. It was all happening so quickly, that I for the first time realized I was trying to buck the whirlpool. Like a flash I was bearing against the opposite side of the sweep. The boat answered, at the same time following the bent of the whirlpool, and headed upstream. But the shave was so close that Sloper leaped to the top of a rock. Then, on seeing we had missed by a couple of inches, he pluckily tumbled aboard, all in a heap, like a man boarding a comet.

Though tearing like mad through a whirlpool, we breathed

freer. Completing the circle, we were thrown into the 'Mane', which we shot a second time and safely landed in a friendly eddy below.

In his diary Thompson adds: 'Jack and Sloper then went back and ran boat through for Mr and Mrs Ret in safety— Pitched camp below White Horse, had our supper and went to bed with our minds easy.' Though London does not mention in his article that for a second time they had performed this act of kindness, he makes it into a vivid passage in *Smoke Bellew*. In the novel Kit and Shorty hesitated to tackle the White Horse in the small and balky Breck boat (the Ret boat was only twenty-two feet long), but the deep distress of the slim young wife once more persuaded them. Also, desperate measures were in order. 'A long, gray twilight was falling, it was turning colder, and the landscape seemed taking on a savage bleakness.' Once more they went through the 'smother, leaping and burying and swamping', to emerge

breathless, wet through, the boat filled with water almost to the gunwale. Lighter pieces of baggage and outfit were floating inside the boat. A few careful strokes on Shorty's part worked the boat into the draw of the eddy, and the eddy did the rest till the boat softly touched the bank. Looking down from above was Mrs Breck. Her prayer had been answered, and the tears were streaming down her cheeks.

'You boys have simply got to take the money,' Breck called down to them.

Shorty stood up, slipped, and sat down in the water, while the boat dipped one gunwale under and righted again.

'Damn the money,' said Shorty. 'Fetch out that whisky. Now that it's over I'm getting cold feet, an' I'm sure likely to have a chill.'

Perhaps the most often repeated story about Jack London's experiences in the Klondike is the one that he stayed on at the White Horse Rapids long enough to earn a sizeable sum piloting boats through the rapids. For instance, Irving Stone in *Sailor on Horseback* writes: 'Instantly

ABOVE:
Box Canyon, or
Miles Canyon,
a much feared
passage on the
journey down-
river to the
Klondike

LEFT:
Shooting White
Horse Rapids,
another feared
passage

London's party took a week to conquer Lake Laberge

Jack was deluged with offers to take other boats through. He charged twenty-five dollars a boat, remained for several days, and earned three thousand dollars for his party. There was another five thousand dollars to be had, but it was already mid-September.' And any visitor to booming White Horse, the present-day capital of the Yukon Territory which was built below the falls, will be told that London made a considerable sum by running boats through the rapids. Under these circumstances, it is ironical that the only boat other than his own which Jack ran through was taken through for kindness rather than gain.

Thompson's diary contains information which should forever put an end to the story that London stopped over to earn a grubstake at White Horse. After a good night's rest, 'with our minds easy', the occupants of the *Yukon Belle* started on the next leg of their journey. 'Sunday Sept. 26. Broke camp and went down the river to Lake LeBarge, here we found a north wind blowing, so camped for the night.' As the section of the Sixtymile River joining Lakes Marsh and Laberge which they covered that cold Sunday was thirty miles long, it is not likely that Jack London spent any time running boats through the rapids before they started. It is also significant that there is no record in his writings, in his notes, or in the biographies by Charmian London and Joan London that he ever piloted for money at White Horse.

Navigating the thirty miles down Lake Laberge proved to their surprise to be the most difficult hurdle to be overcome by London and his friends on their way into Klondike—much more of a problem than Box Canyon and the White Horse Rapids put together. The persistent north winds, the cold water, and the abrupt shores all added to their troubles. This was to become in time the frozen bottom of hell in the saga of the Klondike; it was a locality fixed in legend by Robert Service when the Canadian Kipling was working as a bank clerk in the village of White Horse a decade after the Klondike rush had passed by. (There had been no bank or village when London was there; in Service's day White Horse was the important point where travellers transferred from the White Pass Railroad to the Yukon River steamers.) Service used Lake Laberge for the setting of his famous sourdough ballad, 'The Cremation of Sam McGee'. McGee's partner, looking for a means of cremating Sam, found it in the firebox of an abandoned boat on the edge of the frozen lake. He built a roaring fire in the firebox, put in the body of his friend, who had suffered from northern cold in life, and returned after a while assuming, 'I guess he's cooked, and it's time I looked.' There was Sam, sitting up in the flames, chortling, 'Since I left Plumtree, down in Tennessee, it's the first time I've been warm.'

It took the *Yukon Belle* nearly a week to conquer Lake Laberge. Its crew spent Monday and Tuesday in camp, waiting for the freezing, bitter wind to die down. There was little current on the lake to carry them down it, and to sail into the teeth of the wind was next to impossible. To add to their problems, it was apparent that they would have trouble finding coves where they could stop for the night, as most of the banks were abrupt and hostile; as far as they could see there were steep cliffs and bald headlands of rounded limestone, patched with groves of small dark spruce. Finally, on Wednesday morning the occupants of the two boats—for the *Belle of the Yukon* was now with them—set out in desperation to row down the lake, only to run into a blinding snowstorm. Still, they managed to make progress by rowing all day, 'got dinner on boat and pulled into a very nice harbour for camp at night.'

'Thurs. Sept. 30. Got up very early and made a start but as we rounded a point struck a very heavy sea and a hard storm, finding that we could not make any headway pulled into a little cove under a rock for shelter where we remained nearly all day in a blinding snow storm. At

4 o'clock p.m. we pulled about one mile farther and found another harbour where we pulled in and camped—at this point we found several boats laid up.' Friday, the storm was so heavy that they barely stirred from camp; Jim Goodman went out to hunt but soon returned discouraged. Saturday they made it at last—but not without a final effort. 'Up very early and made start across the lake to the river—rowed nearly all the way as the Lake was calm and no wind blowing so we could not use our sails—we entered the river (which is called Thirtymile River) about 3 o'clock p.m.'

Difficult though their passage had been, London greatly intensified the struggle when he based fiction on it. Here it is that winter seems most clearly on the heels of the argonauts. In 'Argus' he makes the freeze-up the antagonist and stays up all night.

Inside the mouth of the river, just ere it entered Lake Le Barge, they found a hundred stormbound boats of the argonauts. Out of the north, across the full sweep of the great lake, blew an unending snow gale. Three mornings they put out and fought it and the cresting seas it drove that turned to ice as they fell in-board. While the others broke their hearts at the oars, Old Tarwater managed to keep up just sufficient circulation to survive by chopping ice and throwing it overboard.

Each day for three days, beaten to helplessness, they turned tail on the battle and ran back into the sheltering river. By the fourth day, the hundred boats had increased to three hundred, and the two thousand argonauts on board knew that the great gale heralded the freeze-up of Le Barge. Beyond, the rapid rivers would continue to run for days, but unless they got beyond, and immediately, they were doomed to be frozen in for six months to come.

'This day we go through,' Liverpool announced. 'We turn back for nothing. And those of us that dies at the oars will live again and go on pulling.'

And they went through, winning half the length of the lake by nightfall and pulling on through all the night hours as the wind went down, falling asleep at the oars and being rapped awake by Liverpool, toiling on through an age-long nightmare

[93]

while the stars came out and the surface of the lake turned to the unruffledness of a sheet of paper and froze skin-ice that tinkled like broken glass as their oar-blades shattered it.

As day broke clear and cold, they entered the river, with behind them a sea of ice.

Smoke Bellew and his companions have an even harder time conquering Laberge. Here, London brings to a climax a feud between Kit (Smoke) Bellew and Shorty on one side, and their dude employers, Sprague and Stine, weak-souled and weak-kneed sons of wealthy fathers, on the other. Several times the dudes insist on returning to camp; finally, in a showdown, Bellew and Shorty take command, forcing the weaklings to row in spite of themselves.

Sprague hesitated, gave a short hysterical laugh, put the revolver away, and bent his back to the work.

For two hours more, inch by inch, they fought their way along the edge of the foaming rocks, until Kit feared he had made a mistake. And then, when on the verge of himself turning back, they came abreast of a narrow opening, not twenty feet wide, which led into a land-locked enclosure where the fiercest gusts scarcely flawed the surface. . . . They landed on a shelving beach, and the two employers lay in collapse in the boat, while Kit and Shorty pitched the tent, built a fire, and started the cooking.

Stine and Sprague were not to rest for long, however; Kit and Shorty decided they would have to get out that night or stay for the winter. They woke the reluctant dudes by bringing half the tent down on them, and started out again.

They broke their way through the thin ice in the little harbour, and came out on the lake, where the water, heavy and glassy, froze on their oars with every stroke. The water soon became like mush, clogging the stroke of the oars and freezing in the air even as it dripped. Later the surface began to form a skin, and the boat proceeded slower and slower.

Often afterward, when Kit tried to remember that night and

failed to bring up aught but nightmare recollections, he wondered what must have been the sufferings of Stine and Sprague. His one impression of himself was that he struggled through biting frost and intolerable exertion for a thousand years, more or less.

Morning found them stationary. Stine complained of frosted fingers, and Sprague of his nose, while the pain in Kit's cheeks and nose told him that he, too, had been touched. With each accretion of daylight they could see farther, and as far as they could see was icy surface. The water of the lake was gone. A hundred yards away was the shore of the north end. Shorty insisted that it was the opening of the river and that he could see water. He and Kit alone were able to work, and with their oars they broke the ice and forced the boat along. And at the last gasp of their strength they made the suck of the rapid river. One look back showed them several boats which had fought through the night and were hopelessly frozen in; then they whirled around a bend in a current running six miles an hour.

This is a fictionalized account of the nightmare that London and his companions dreamed as they fought their way across Laberge.

The Thirtymile River below Laberge (still another section of what is now called the Yukon) was not without its dangers, for there were many rocks to create rough water. This was the section of the river which after the freeze-up abounded in ice bridges, perilous traps for sleds and men on the winter trail. But though it was uncomfortably rough, its current was fast and the boats moved along briskly. Soon they were in smoother water at the junction with the Hootalinqua, which runs down from placid Lake Teslin. They floated on through dense fog, in bitter cold, on past Cassiar Bar and the Big Salmon, and on Tuesday reached the Little Salmon, one hundred miles below Laberge, where they stopped to visit the Indian village. The Indians at Little Salmon were, according to Thompson, 'a tough looking set'. About all they wore were large rings in their noses and ears; they had plenty of money, and asked high prices for the fish, meat, and moccasins they pressed on all travellers. Jack and his friends refused to buy.

This was Monday of the last week on the river; by Saturday the party would be ensconced in cabins at the mouth of the Stewart River. Though winter was pressing on, there was now less snow on the ground than they had seen above Laberge, and the weather was pleasant except for the early morning fogs. There was more than a touch of Indian summer in the air. With their destination almost literally around the bend, with all major obstacles passed, they must have felt a bit like a character in 'The Men of Forty-Mile' who commented on the beauty of the Yukon valley at the change of seasons.

'Last fall, a year gone, 'twas Sitka Charley and meself saw the sight, droppin' down the riffle ye'll remember below Fort Reliance. An' regular fall weather it was—the glint o' the sun on the golden larch an' the quakin' aspens; an' the glister of light on ivery ripple; an' beyand, the winter an' the blue haze of the North comin' down hand in hand. It's well ye know the same, with a fringe to the river an' the ice formin' thick in the eddies —an' a snap an' sparkle to the air, an' ye a-feelin' it through all yer blood, a-takin' new lease of life with ivery suck of it. 'Tis then, me boy, the world grows small an' the wandther-lust lays ye by the heels.'

The only thing to worry them now was the steady increase of ice on the river. Thompson mentions that when they passed the mouths of the Big Salmon and the Little Salmon, those tributaries were carrying much slush ice into the Yukon; and they were to see even more ice at the junction with the Pelly. London described their downstream progress, Yukon stove and all, in 'Argus': 'All of which came to pass; and the boat, in the grip of the current, like a river steamer with smoke rising from the two joints of stove-pipe, grounded on shoals, hung up on split currents, and charged rapids and canyons, as it drove deeper into the Northland winter. The Big and Little Salmon rivers were throwing mush-ice into the main river as they passed, and, below the riffles, anchor-ice arose from the river bottom and coated the surface with crystal scum. Night and day the rim-ice grew, till, in quiet places, it extended out a hundred yards from shore.'

It was this 'anchor' ice which proved so novel to the cheechakos on the Yukon. It apparently was no part of the rim-ice which formed along the side of the river in the fashion normal in more southern climates. The anchor ice appeared to form on the bottom, break loose, and float to the top. Though London and his friends did not know the term 'permafrost', they had learned that the land in the Arctic regions remained perpetually frozen a little distance below the surface, no matter how strongly the sun shone on the muskeg and water above. For this reason, many of them accepted the theory that the river froze first on the bottom and filled with ice *upwards*. Others scoffed at this theory, insisting that river conduct could never so reverse itself. The ensuing argument nearly caused a duel in 'The Men of Forty-Mile', one of London's best short stories, in which one sourdough insists that he has seen the anchor ice ' "clingin' an' clusterin' to ivery rock, after the manner of the white coral" ', while another sticks to his premise: ' "But facts is facts, an' they ain't no gittin' round 'em. It ain't in the nature of things for the water furtherest away from the air to freeze first." '

By three o'clock on Tuesday October 5, 1897, they reached the famed Five Finger Rapids. These rapids were caused by five immense rocks thrusting themselves upwards from the river bed, breaking the channel into six streams. Only one of these, the passage farthest to right, was easily negotiable, but everyone on the river knew that, and the *Yukon Belle* had no trouble. (There was enough clearance here so that within a year stern-wheelers were to pass upstream at this point with the help of a cable and winch.) Nor did they have any trouble running the six-mile-long Rink Rapids, a few miles farther on. Once more sticking to the right side, they raced down through what could be called mildly rough water. In between the two rapids they saw activity on the left bank, where the Dalton Trail, an alternate Klondike route which started overland from a point on the peninsula opposite Dyea, now known as Haynes, reached the river. Here men were slaughtering cattle driven up the trail for hungry Klondikers; some meat they sold to passers-by for fifty to seventy-five cents a pound, but most of it they shipped downriver by raft to Dawson, where it would fetch twice that amount. That night London and his friends had a comfortable camp six miles below Rink Rapids; the weather was still mild.

On Wednesday they made sixty miles, taking full advantage of the daylight. (They never ran at night, as many of the other Klondikers did.) The principal event of the day was the half-hour stop at Fort Selkirk, situated at the confluence of the Yukon and Pelly rivers. On the left bank, almost on the spot of the original Hudson's Bay fort that had been destroyed by Indians, was an Indian trading post maintained in a desultory fashion by the Alaska Commercial Company. Near at hand were perhaps a hundred Indian huts; the Indians normally trapped the area and traded skins with the factor. Here for the first time London probably saw and heard wild Indian dogs, huskies, and half-tamed wolves, which were famous on the river for raiding boats for food. (On the other hand, he may have seen some Indian dogs at Lake Laberge, for it is there that, in *The Call of the Wild*, he has Buck and his companions attacked by a pack of savage Indian dogs.) At Fort Selkirk, the voyagers signed the informal register kept by the trading company. Thompson was No. 4845; this figure represented the number of Klondikers who had signed during the previous two months, but it did not represent all of the men who had passed that point, for many went by without stopping for Indians, dogs, or

[98]

register, no food being available at the little store.

Thus, though London came early in the fall rush of 1897, he was by no means one of the first. And it is to be remembered this was really the second stampede to the Klondike; the first had come not long after Discovery was staked on Bonanza Creek by Carmack on August 17, 1896, fifteen months before. At that time most of the sourdoughs in the area, from Fortymile, Sixtymile, Circle City, Fort Yukon, and other camps in Alaska and Canada, had deserted these towns to stake the branches and pups which ran into the Klondike. London came with the second wave (the first from the Outside), stimulated by the arrival of the gold-laden ships from the Klondike in midsummer of 1897. The third wave, or what is usually called the Klondike rush, reached Dawson the following spring, after the thaws. Thus London was too late to be a genuine sourdough but early enough to be ahead of the big rush.

On Friday, October 8, 1897, the *Yukon Belle* separated from the *Belle of the Yukon*, with Tarwater, who wished to go on to Dawson, transferring to the latter boat. This was the split-up; London and his friends decided to stop at the mouth of the Stewart, eighty miles above Dawson, and winter there, while the voyagers in the other boat continued down the Yukon. Thompson's notes for Friday read in part:

Put our passenger aboard our sister boat BELLE OF YUKON which was bound for Dawson City when [*sic*] Mr Tarwater wanted to go, we intending to stop at Stewart River, bid goodbye to the party and our sister boat and parted. Sat. Oct. 9 Started down river again as we could find no sign of game, passed 32 mounted police in boats bound for Dawson. Arrived at Stewart River about 3 o'clock p.m. took possession of a Cabin on island between the mouth of Stewart River and mouth of Henderson Creek and went into camp. On our arrival here we found several old Hudson Bay Cabins, but no people. This is a good place and we think shall make it our headquarters.

This island figures extensively in London's fiction, in

which he sometimes calls it 'Upper Island' and sometimes 'Split-up Island'. The latter name reflected the habit that parties from the Outside had of dividing there and going several ways. Some irritable Klondikers even cut their boats in two when splitting up at this point.

The decision of London and his companions to stay at the Stewart rather than to proceed to Dawson was entirely reasonable. At Stewart River they would not be as crowded as at Dawson nor as likely to face the rigours of the food shortage that was threatening that community. Once the Yukon froze over and the winter trails were established, they could travel easily to Dawson on the ice. Far more emigrants were living along the creeks than in the hovels and tents of Dawson, where fuel was high and housing almost impossible to find. Moreover, if London's party wished to prospect or to do winter mining, they could find no more promising area open than the Stewart and its environs. The Stewart had been a lodestone for sourdoughs before the Klondike was opened up, and many old-timers still considered it a better bet in the long run than the lower river, with its heavily populated diggings. In fact, Bruce's *Alaska*, London's handbook, highly recommended this area. The discovery of the empty cabins—possibly left by Harper and Ladue of the Alaska Commerical Company rather than Hudson's Bay—might have been the clincher. Shelter, fuel, and gold possibilities combined to make the selection excellent.

It was October 9, four days before the date traditionally associated with the freeze-up of the river. The London party had made the trip from Dyea in two months and two days, the river trip from Lindeman in a little less than three weeks. It was not bad time, although it was not by any means outstanding. They had arrived with good outfits and a fair amount of food. They had been able to get along without cutting each other's throats. It was wise to settle in now.

IV · GOLD CREEK
AND GOLD TOWN

GOLD is what they had come for, and, if they wished to do any prospecting before deep winter set in, it was now or never. Plans to search for a strike up the Stewart were quickly abandoned when an old-timer assured the new party that the Stewart was half-frozen and that for some days to come movement up it would be impractical. More promising hunting lay in the opposite direction. Some three or four miles down the Yukon a small stream, Henderson Creek, flowed into the river from the right; rumour had it that there might be gold in its sands. On Monday, October 11, Jim Goodman, the only experienced placer miner in the group, set out to see if he could find any likely looking ground on the Henderson. By evening he was back with word that he had got some good colours.

Tuesday bright and early Jim Goodman and Jack London, accompanied by two other gold-seekers referred to by Thompson as 'Charles and Elma', set out for the Henderson, where they spent three days prospecting. Thompson and Sloper remained at the cabin, baking yeast bread, biscuits, and pies, sharpening tools, making a sled. Their domesticity was given a note of excitement when, on Wednesday the thirteenth of October, so much slush ice came in from the Stewart that Thompson felt it likely the Yukon was freezing up and that boat traffic downriver was at an end for the season. This was the date which tradition had set as a likely one for the closing. But boats continued on that day, the next, and the next—in fact, in 1897 boats continued to get through to Dawson until early

November. By the time the boys returned from Henderson, Thompson and his companions were ready to take their chances on getting down to Dawson by boat and returning later on the ice. They could thus file gold claims, see old friends, and get the lay of the land.

How much gold London and Goodman found on the Henderson during those October days is hard to say. They had some success, according to Thompson's diary. 'Boys got back from Henderson, staked 8 claims.' How the claims were to be divided up is not clear. But we do know from the mining records in Dawson that Jack London filed papers for a claim, 'more particularly described as placer mining claim No. 54 on the Left Fork ascending Henderson Creek in the aforesaid Mining Division.'[1] 'I solemnly swear that I have discovered therein a deposit of Gold,' London was to affirm before the Gold Commissioner in Dawson.

How much of a thrill was it to see that gold, how much of a pan did he wash out? Did he actually find only 'fool's gold', as one persistent yarn maintains? Certainly the story told by Thompson in his old age to Irving Stone that London had been so misled is not very persuasive. In the first place, stories of this sort are stock-in-trade for making famous men look like fools. In addition, Thompson was not with London when he staked on the Henderson, and the experienced Goodman, who was, was not likely to make such an error. Later on in the winter London was to lie grinning in his bunk while Thompson would daydream about how much wealth they would get from the creek in the following summer. He probably grinned because he knew that, though there was pay dirt there, it was not rich enough to make strenuous effort pay off. Two years later, after London had returned to Oakland, he wrote to a friend in the Klondike asking about Thompson, who was still pursuing the will-o'-the-wisp in the Northland: he imagined him 'with wilder schemes than ever in his head; and smoking good cigars while doing nothing'.[2]

Still, there must have been a thrill even in the act of panning for gold in the wilderness, and the sight of a streak was enough to make the world seem rosy. In his fiction, London has his hero in *Burning Daylight* enjoy the thrill of discovery to the fullest.

One day in December Daylight filled a pan from bedrock on his own claim and carried it into his cabin. Here a fire burned and enabled him to keep water unfrozen in a canvas tank. He squatted over the tank and began to wash. Earth and gravel seemed to fill the pan. As he imparted to it a circular movement, the lighter, coarser particles washed out over the edge. At times he combed the surface with his fingers, raking out handfuls of gravel. The contents of the pan diminished. As it drew near to the bottom, for the purpose of fleeting and tentative examination, he gave the pan a sudden sloshing movement, emptying it of water. And the whole bottom showed as if covered with butter. Thus the yellow gold flashed up as the muddy water was flirted away. It was gold—gold-dust, coarse gold, nuggets, large nuggets. He was all alone. He set the pan down for a moment and thought long thoughts. Then he finished the washing, and weighed the result in his scales. At the rate of sixteen dollars to the ounce, the pan had contained seven hundred and odd dollars. It was beyond anything that even he had dreamed.

No such reality for London. The job for the moment was to stake, then to file in Dawson, and then decide whether to work the claim or not. To set or blaze the two centre stakes and four corner stakes was not a difficult matter, and a notice assured those to come after him that London laid claim to five-hundred feet of stream bed, from rimrock to rimrock, '260,000 square feet', as he was to estimate in Dawson.

London's gold claim may not have been based, however, on any extensive prospecting or panning for colours. London may not, in fact, have seen any colour in his pan at all. As Harold A. Innis has pointed out in *Settlement and the Mining Frontier*, with the proliferation of claims on the Yukon much land was staked on pure speculation. The saying went, 'All the prospecting tools a man needs now is an axe and a lead-pencil', and the phrase 'pool-room prospecting' became a commonplace. In June, 1897, there were eight hundred claims on record in Dawson; by January, 1898, there were five thousand; and that number had increased to seventeen thousand by September, 1898. The majority of these claims were forfeited because of failure to work on them. This was the case with London's claim; the records show it reverted to the Crown after his departure, was taken out again by a man named Ritchie in 1901, who kept it registered until 1904, when he in turn abandoned it. Today the area where the claim lay is being profitably worked by gold dredges.

Innis points out some of the reasons that very few Klondikers became successful miners; London was certainly one of the vast majority.

The rich creeks were staked in the main by miners who were in the Yukon before the strike at Bonanza and who had the advantage of experience with the peculiar problems of the district. The art of handling frozen ground and of sinking shafts to the bedrock of creeks and drifting across the channel to discover the pay streak had been developed, as we have seen, before the discovery of the Klondike. On the other hand, 'so much more is being learned that it may truthfully be said that it has taken the second year at Klondike to develop the Yukon placer expert.' Work began as soon as the frost dried up the surface water of the creeks. Wood to the extent of possibly 30 cords of pine, spruce, and birch was cut during the summer in preparation for burning and thawing. The upper layer of muck was picked or thawed and shovelled out. When the shaft of about 4 feet × 6 feet reached an inconvenient depth for shovelling, a rope windlass was erected and the dirt hoisted up by bucket. By placing the windlass at the top of cribbing above the shaft labour in disposing the dump was reduced, the latter being gradually piled up around the cribbing. After penetration through the muck, gravel was reached and it was necessary to depend on thawing. Dry and green wood were hauled to the shaft on dog sleds, split to a required fineness and taken to the bottom. A layer of finely split dry spruce was covered by heavier pieces of very dry wood and in turn by green wood. The latter was intended to lengthen the time of burning and to hold in heat. Candles were necessary to raise the temperature of the pine and to light it.

And so the story goes. It took a month to cut down to bedrock, perhaps another month to drift across the streak. Thawed earth had to be panned for gold to see if you were on the right trail. (Twenty-five cents a pan was considered very rich gravel, while ten cents a pan corresponded to an adequate wage in the States.) These operations were restricted to four or five months, say November to March. After that, the moderation of temperature made the mining unsafe. When warm weather finally arrived, you washed your dump in sluice boxes, if you were fortunate enough to have the use of a good stream of water. Usually this involved going in with others to build a diversion dam and flume. All this took a good deal of faith, confidence in one's luck, and persistence. What chance that it would be done by amateurs on soil showing poor pickings a few miles up the Henderson?

The boys were back from their prospecting by Friday evening, and on Saturday afternoon at 1.45 p.m., October 16, 1897, Thompson, London, 'Charles and Elma' started downriver by boat for Dawson. They had with them enough stores to last for about three weeks, together with tent, blankets, and other camping equipment. 'Went to get news, mail &c. and post ourselves on the country in general, also to file our claims on Henderson,' Thompson noted. They made 22 miles before stopping for the night at the old station of Sixtymile, at the mouth of the tributary by that name which flowed into the west side of the Yukon; here were many empty cabins, a post store with no food to sell, and a good many boats headed for Dawson pulled up for the night.

Saturday, with two additional passengers, they made the final fifty-mile run to Dawson, stopping en route to cut some firewood, knowing that wood was scarce in the boom-town. They camped that night three miles short of their goal so that they would reach their destination in the morning with a day to get settled in. On Monday, October 18, they floated around a bend to see the famous Klondike flow in from their right. Klondike City, better known as Louse Town, lay before them just short of the noted tributary. Dawson City was on a spongy flat below a slide-scarred mountain on the far side of the shallow gold stream. The Yukon, unconcerned with man's paltry efforts, continued to move with majesty between steep hills as it swept past Dawson towards its big bend above the Arctic Circle.

They beached the *Yukon Belle* at Louse Town, where Thompson stayed with the outfits, while London and his new companions crossed the Klondike by ferry, climbed up the sixteen-foot bank which formed the south edge of Dawson, and set out to look for a camping place. While he waited, Thompson ran across some of the travellers from the *Belle of the Yukon* (Charles Rand, Dave Sullivan, and William Odette) and learned that Tarwater had nearly drowned 'crossing the Klondyke River with his pack on his back'. That pack did not contain much food, and Dawson was far from hospitable to men without outfits. Already, along with many others, Tarwater had been urged to continue downriver to Fort Yukon. By evening the party had encountered Louis W. Bond, who was known to some of them, and had set up camp by the Bond cabin.

London was to remain in Dawson somewhat over six weeks, leaving for Split-up Island on the third of December and arriving there on the seventh of December. During this period he had plenty of opportunity to get impressions of the gold city, which was to appear frequently in his fiction. His movements can no longer be followed in Thompson's diary, which ends on October 18. His reactions can, however, be built up to some extent from his fiction.

Dawson City that fall was no place to pick up one's spirits. It was cold, often shrouded in fog, its ramshackle shanties and leaky cabins inhabited by some five thousand restless and nearly panic-stricken sourdoughs and cheechakos. The shortage of food, which had created many rumours on the Chilkoot trail and which had driven Tarwater downriver, was the most pressing topic of the moment. As early as August, Inspector Charles Constantine of the North-west Mounted Police had written Ottawa, '. . . the outlook for grub is not assuring for the number of people here—about four thousand crazy or lazy men, chiefly American miners and toughs from the coast towns.'[3] The prospect had got worse rather than better since then. River steamboats bringing food to the Klondike had first been shoaled in slack water and then frozen in at Fort Yukon, three hundred and fifty miles downriver; two steamboats that had got past Fort Yukon had been held up at Circle City and robbed of their supplies by desperate men even worse off than those in Dawson. About two weeks before London arrived, Inspector Constantine had posted a notice on Front Street:

'. . . For those who have not laid in a winter's supply to remain longer is to court death from starvation, or at least the certainty of sickness from scurvy and other troubles. Starvation now stares everyone in the face who is hoping and waiting for outside relief. . . .'[4]

In *A Daughter of the Snows* London pictures a tense Dawson City, the authorities fearful of the food shortage, making plans for getting as many people as possible out of town. The head of one of the big trading companies has just issued orders to scale down filling of warehouse requisitions to half the amount stipulated so that the food would last longer. A steamer is about to set off downriver with three hundred Klondikers willing to face short rations at Fort Yukon rather than starve in Dawson, where newcomers who had packed over the Chilkoot were frantically selling their outfits to buy dogs to trek back up again as soon as the ice was firm. Distressed Klondikers had

[107]

posted many notices on the front of the big warehouse building: 'Dogs lost, found, and for sale occupied some space, but the rest was devoted to notices of sales of outfits. The timid were already growing frightened. Outfits of five hundred pounds were offering at a dollar a pound, without flour; others, with flour, at a dollar and a half.'

During the six weeks London spent in Dawson matters seemed at a standstill, with everyone awaiting the closing of the river. The weather of late October was fitful and changeable; finally, when the freeze, which would make sledding possible both to the mines and upriver to the Stewart and on to the Chilkoot and Dyea, seemed about at hand, a warm Chinook came along to prolong the suspense. The birches and aspens along the Yukon and on the slopes of Moosehide Mountain back of Dawson had long since turned fiery yellow-red and dropped their leaves; their ashen trunks had stood naked in the autumn winds for nearly two months. The Arctic hare and ptarmigan had turned from brown to white, the bears had gone into caves for their winter sleep, and the grey days had grown very short indeed before the longed-for freeze-up finally arrived. At last, one morning at the end of the first week in November men woke to find the river frozen.

Naturally, the freeze-up was more dramatic if you were making your way downriver in a desperate attempt to reach Dawson before you were caught in the ice! London's description of Smoke Bellew and his companions making this final effort gives a vivid picture of one of the most characteristic phenomena of the Arctic regions.

The sky was clear, and in the light of the cold, leaping stars they caught occasional glimpses of the loom of mountains on either hand. At eleven o'clock, from below, came a dull grinding roar. Their speed began to diminish and cakes of ice to up-end and crash and smash about them. The river was jamming. One cake, forced upward, slid across their cake and carried one side of the boat away. It did not sink, for its own cake still upbore it, but in a whirl they saw dark water show for an instant within a foot of them. Then all movement ceased. At the end of half an hour the whole river picked itself up and began to move. This continued for an hour, when again it was brought to rest by a jam. Once again it started, running swiftly and savagely, with a great grinding. Then they saw lights ashore, and, when abreast, gravity and the Yukon surrendered, and the river ceased for six months.

It was on November 5 that Dawson woke to find the river frozen. It was on this same day, according to the books in the gold-records office, that Jack London filed claim for his gold strike on Henderson Creek. This cost him ten dollars for a mining licence and fifteen dollars for filing his first claim. That he had waited eighteen days after reaching the capital of the North-west Territory before filing strongly suggests that he didn't put much faith in the claim. Or he may have been waiting to win the twenty-five dollars in a faro game. Or he may have been too busy talking to Klondikers and seeing the sights in Dawson. The last seems the most unlikely explanation for his delay, for the resources offered by Dawson gossip and sights were soon exhausted. London still had another month to look around before going back to Split-up Island.

The year-old mining centre of Dawson, which sprawled over the triangle formed by the Klondike and Yukon rivers and the abrupt Moosehide Mountain (the latter named for the scar on its side), was as raw and ugly as that scar on the hill behind it. Its principal buildings, none of them known for their pleasing architecture, stretched along Front Street parallel to the Yukon. Of these, the ones most often mentioned by London in his fiction were the Catholic hospital at the upper end of town, where the remarkable Father Judge helped many sick and wounded, the barracks of the North-west Mounted Police at the lower end, and the establishments of the two rival trading companies which formed the heart of the town. These companies were all-important, for they brought supplies into the region and owned the Yukon steamers.

'The Company' was the original Alaska Commercial Company (A.C. Company), which had long held a monopoly in the Yukon Valley. Its rival was the North American Trading and Transportation Company (N.A.T. & T.), newer and more popular. This latter enterprise, financed, like the A.C., in the United States, was headed in Dawson by John J. Healy, hunter, trapper, soldier, prospector, whisky-trader, editor, guide, Indian scout, and sheriff. After establishing a trading post at Dyea, Healy had moved into the Yukon Valley, when Fortymile was still the focus of men's hopes and Dawson had not yet been dreamed of. With his cowlick and his goatee and his ramrod figure, the crusty, powerful Healy probably served as the original of London's Jacob Welse, father of the heroine and leading exponent of Anglo-Saxon individualism in *A Daughter of the Snows*. According to London, Welse was 'an economic missionary, a commercial St Paul', who 'preached the doctrines of expediency and force.' Devoted to the doctrine that 'competition was the secret of creation', he fought the economic fight with no holds barred and still found time in his softer moments to read Browning and to love his daughter, who was truly a 'man's woman' if there ever was one.

The commercial store in London's books, whether it be the A.C. Company or the N.A.T. & T., was a large building constructed of logs with brown moss stuffed between them, trimmed with rough, unstained boards. Along the length of the building ran a long counter with the gold scales perhaps more prominent than the piles of furs and the mining equipment. The shelves ordinarily used for canned goods were nearly bare, and there was little flour, no sugar, in sight. Huge red-hot wood-burning stoves made the room inhabitable; whiskbrooms hung near the door so that visitors could brush the snow from moccasins and parkas to keep the room decent. A dim light came through small-paned windows, real glass windows, a luxury in the Yukon.

Prices were high at the trading companies during the

fall of 1897, but the really formidable inflation was found in the restaurants, such as Shavovitch's, which appeared often in London's fiction. Five dollars for a meal of beans, apples, bread, and coffee was a standard price. London later played up shortages of sugar and eggs in his fiction; probably he himself did little eating in restaurants in Dawson, for he and Thompson had brought provisions with them from Split-up Island just to avoid such a contingency.

The saloons were another thing. Naturally, many scenes in London's stories take place in saloons, for this was the customary place for Klondikers to foregather. Here they escaped the cold, they drank, they heard the latest news and took part in arguments, and they met the girls. London's stories mention the Eldorado, the Monte Carlo, the Elkhorn, the Moosehorn, the M & G, and the M & M. Probably the last was Pete McDonald's M & N Saloon and Dancehall, where the gambling was usually for heavy stakes and it cost a dollar a go to dance with the silk-clad girls. The dances were so short that McDonald was able to pack in as many as 125 dances in a single night's entertainment.

That London would spend a fair amount of time in the saloons is to be taken for granted. One of the few bits of direct evidence on this point is to be found in Edward E. P. Morgan's *God's Loaded Dice*, one of many books of reminiscences by Klondikers. Of London he writes:

I first met London in a Dawson bar in the late fall of 1897.... London was surely prospecting, but it was at bars that he sought his material. I believe that he had staked a claim, and it is probable that his hatred of capitalism did not extend to acquiring wealth for himself, but I never saw him working one, never met him on the trail, and do not remember ever having seen him except in some Dawson bar.... I remember him as a muscular youth of little more than average stature, with a weather-beaten countenance in which a healthy colour showed, and a shock of yellow hair, customarily unkempt and in keeping with his usual slovenly appearance. It seemed to me that whenever I saw him at the bar he was always in conversation

[111]

with some veteran sourdough or noted character in the life of Dawson. And how he did talk.

It is to be noted that Morgan dictated this account when he was an old man, and thus his evidence does not weigh very heavily. However, he acknowledges that London at the time 'was only a youth who had not yet made a name for himself', showing clearly that he could distinguish between the famous London and the unknown one he had met on the Yukon. Other old-timers have often been unable to make this distinction. In talking in 1954 to sourdoughs then living at Dawson, I found a number who maintained that they could remember London but only one who convinced me that he had actually met him. One 'acquaintance' admitted unguardedly that he reached Dawson after London had left; another swore that he had seen him write *The Call of the Wild* in a local cabin; and still another averred that London had been sent downriver after a miners' meeting because he had failed to replace the firewood in a mountain shack, thus breaking one of the cardinal rules of Northland living. But John Korbo, who came in in the spring of 1897, convinced me that he had in fact known London. He remembered that a friend had called him into a saloon to settle an argument with a pleasant chap named 'London' and that they had talked on for many minutes without coming to a conclusion. This sounds entirely likely, entirely typical, and fits in very well with Morgan's testimony.

In the bars of Dawson City, London had plenty of opportunities of both seeing and hearing old-timers as they expressed the brag of the country. Nowhere else was the line as clearly drawn between sourdough and chee-chako, a distinction explained in detail in *White Fang*. The wolf-pup was making his first contact with civilization, in Fort Yukon. 'A small number of white men lived in Fort Yukon. These men had been long in the country. They called themselves Sour-doughs, and took great pride in so classifying themselves. For other men, new in the land, they felt nothing but disdain. The men who came ashore from the steamers were newcomers. They were known as *chechaquos*, and they always wilted at the application of the name. They made their bread with baking-powder. This was the invidious distinction between them and the Sour-doughs, who, forsooth, made their bread from sour-dough because they had no baking-powder.' The sourdoughs were proud of their adaptability to famine and cold, con-temptuous of the complaining cheechako. 'Aw, you tender-feet make me tired,' explodes Dave Harney in *Scorn of Women*. 'I never seen the beat of you critters. Better men than you have starved in this country, an' they didn't make no bones about it neither—they was all bones I calkilate. What do you think this is? A Sunday picnic? Jes' come in, eh? An' you're clean scairt. Look at me—old-timer, sir, a sour-dough, an' proud of it! I come into this country before there was any blamed Company, fished for my breakfast, an' hunted my supper. An' when the fish didn't bite an' they wa'n't any game, jes' cinched my belt tighter an' hiked along, livin' on salmon-bellies and rabbit tracks an' eatin' my moccasins.'

Dave Harney could have added that the sourdoughs were also famous for gambling away their fortunes in just such bars as London was frequenting. In *Burning Daylight* the hero, who had not hesitated to gamble fifty thousand dollars in a poker game in Circle City before the Klondike was discovered, was appalled at the waste he saw displayed in Dawson.

He watched the lavish waste of the mushroom millionaires, and failed quite to understand it. According to his nature and out-look, it was all very well to toss an ante away in a night's frolic. That was what he had done the night of the poker-game in Circle City when he lost fifty thousand . . . as a mere ante. When it came to millions, it was different. Such a fortune was a stake, and was not to be sown on bar-room floors, literally sown, flung broadcast out of the moosehide sacks by drunken millionaires who had lost all sense of proportion. There was McMann, who ran up a single bar-room bill of thirty-eight thousand dollars; and Jimmie the Rough, who spent one hundred thousand a month for four months in riotous living, and then fell down drunk in the snow one March night and was frozen to death; and Swiftwater Bill, who, after spending three valuable claims in an extravagance of debauchery, borrowed three thousand dollars with which to leave the country. . . .

Besides drinking, talking, and gambling, there were singing and dancing to be found in the Monte Carlo and Eldorado, the Orpheum and the Tivoli. The saloon-*cum*-dance hall which plays the most prominent part in London's stories is the grandiloquently named Opera House, which was burned up the night before Thanksgiving in 1897, along with most of the rest of Dawson, in a fire that started when an M & N dance-hall girl threw a lamp at her rival. Whether London was in the M & N when the lamp was thrown or in the Opera House when the customary Thanksgiving eve masked ball came to an end, he certainly was in town when the flames spread to most of Dawson's buildings. In his fiction he used the Opera House not as the scene of a holocaust but a place to hold community dances, parties which are featured in *A Daughter of the Snows* and 'The Wife of a King'.

A passage from *A Daughter of the Snows* presents Opera House society in all its rough grandeur.

The crowded room was thick with tobacco smoke. A hundred men or so, garbed in furs and warm-coloured wools, lined the walls and looked on. But the mumble of their general conversation destroyed the spectacular feature of the scene and gave to it the geniality of common comradeship. For all its *bizarre* appearance, it was very like the living-room of the home when the members of the household come together after the work of the day. Kerosene lamps and tallow candles glimmered feebly in the murky atmosphere, while large stoves roared their red-hot and white-hot cheer.

On the floor a score of couples pulsed rhythmically to the

swinging waltz-time music. Starched shirts and frock coats were not. The men wore their wolf- and beaver-skin caps, with the gay-tasselled ear-flaps flying free, while on their feet were the moose-skin moccasins and walrus-hide muclucs of the north. Here and there a woman was in moccasins, though the majority danced in frail ball-room slippers of silk and satin. At one end of the hall a great open doorway gave glimpse of another large room where the crowd was even denser. From this room, in the lulls in the music, came the pop of corks and the clink of glasses, and as an undertone the steady click and clatter of chips and roulette balls.

This party ended in a fist-fight.

In *Scorn of Women* London uses the masked ball, this time held in Pioneer Hall, as a device for a confrontation between his two heroines, a dance-hall girl and the leader of Dawson society, insisting that they are sisters under the skin and both devoted to noble purposes.

Almost without exception, the dance-hall girls in London's Klondike fiction are treated kindly, not to mention gallantly. Lucile in *A Daughter of the Snows* quotes Browning by the yard and hides a very sensitive heart; and Freda Moloof in *Scorn of Women* owns a grand piano, hires a maid, and plots to save a 'good girl' from disaster. A leading character in *A Daughter of the Snows* expresses a completely romantic view of the girls: ' "Butterflies, bits of light and song and laughter, dancing, dancing down the last tail-reach of hell. Not only Lucile, but the rest of them. Look at May, there, with the brow of a Madonna and the tongue of a gutter-devil. And Myrtle—for all the world one of Gainsborough's old English beauties stepped down from the canvas to riot out the century in Dawson's dance-halls. And Laura, there, wouldn't she make a mother? Can't you see the child in the curve of her arm against her breast!" ' This is a far cry from Addison Mizner's acid comments on Dawson 'beauties' in his *The Many Mizners*: 'Glass-eyed Annie sang beautifully; Myrtle Drummond had charm; diamond-toothed Gertie was tough, but attractive; over-flowing Flora, who looked like mud squeezing up from between your toes, had lovely eyes; but, most of the rest—my Gawd—what sights. . . . I remember once asking an invalid friend of mine, who had a cook named Jennie, aged seventy-five, with one tooth and cock-eyes, "How long do you stay in this lonely spot?" "Until Jennie begins to look good to me," he replied.'

Jack London did not say in his fiction that many of these girls could be had for the hour or for the night at very fancy prices, nor does he mention the more common whores who lived in the cribs in Paradise Alley or in the swampland well back of the business district known as 'Hell's Half Acre', or the lowest of the low who were relegated to Louse Town. From his books you would never suspect that prostitution existed. (He was writing in the early nineteen hundreds.)

Death was another matter—it stalked grim and final in many of London's stories. When one thinks of dwellings in Dawson, he does not remember the house owned by a dancer with its gilt French clock, bearskin rugs and sturdy furniture, 'luxurious, comfortable, picturesque, emphasizing the contact of civilization and the wilderness',[5] but the 'sody-bottle window' cabin in which the protagonist of 'The One Thousand Dozen' killed himself. 'He re-entered the cabin and drew the latch in after him. The smoke from the cindered steak made his eyes smart. He stood on the bunk, passed the lashing over the ridge-pole, and measured the swing-off with his eye. It did not seem to satisfy, for he put the stool on the bunk and climbed upon the stool. He drove a noose in the end of the lashing and slipped his head through. The other end he made fast. Then he kicked the stool out from under.'

There was also the attempted suicide of the dance-hall girl called 'the Virgin', who was saved in the nick of time by Burning Daylight. In 'The League of the Old Men' there was the man frozen sitting upright on a sled in the main street where the men passed to and fro. 'They thought the man was resting, but later, when they touched him, they found him stiff and cold, frozen to death in the midst of the busy street. To undouble him, that he might fit into a coffin, they had been forced to lug him to a fire and thaw him out a bit.'

The task of disposing of the dead did not cease with thawing them out to get them into coffins. There was the long haul up the hill back of town to the graveyard. The hero and heroine climb that hill in *A Daughter of the Snows*, and incidentally discover what a task it is to transport a Dawson corpse to its last resting place.

At their feet, under the great vault of heaven, a speck in the midst of the white vastness, huddled the golden city—puny and sordid, feebly protesting against immensity, man's challenge to the infinite! Calls of men and cries of encouragement came sharply to them from close at hand, and they halted. There was an eager yelping, a scratching of feet, and a string of ice-rimed wolf-dogs, with hot-lolling tongues and dripping jaws, pulled up the slope and turned into the path ahead of them. On the sled, a long and narrow box of rough-sawed spruce told the nature of the freight. Two dog-drivers, a woman walking blindly, and a black-robed priest, made up the funeral cortege. A few paces farther on the dogs were again put against the steep, and with whine and shout and clatter the unheeding clay was hauled on and upward to its ice-hewn hillside chamber.

Of the hardest task of all, to dig a grave in the permafrost, London tells in 'The Unexpected'. 'The ground was frozen. It was impervious to a blow of the pick. They first gathered wood, then scraped the snow away and on the frozen surface built a fire. When the fire had burned for an hour, several inches of dirt had thawed. This they shovelled out, and then built a fresh fire. Their descent into the earth progressed at the rate of two or three inches an hour. It was hard and bitter work. The flurrying snow did not permit the fire to burn any too well, while the wind cut through their clothes and chilled their bodies.' Eight hours of hard work found the graves completed. 'They were shallow, not more than two feet deep, but they would serve the purpose.'

Always in the consciousness of men in Dawson City was the cold, indifferent environment; the low hills of scrub fir and birch around them; the abrupt bluffs across the Yukon which hemmed them in; the clear sky when the thick fog which so often rose from the river was not pressing upon them; the breathless air, for weeks unmoving under the stable Arctic high; the vivid, unfeeling stars. Joaquin Miller, who also was spending the winter in a Dawson cabin, described the oppressive stillness as 'this vast white silence, as if all earth lay still and stark dead in her white shroud waiting the judgment day.' He complained that the sun was skulking behind the broken Klondike steeps, that he had not seen its cheery face for days and did not expect to see it again for weeks. 'Let me not be caught here again,' he moaned, 'for caught I am like a wary old rat in a trap.'[6]

In this inhuman natural theatre, the aurora borealis, melodramatic though it was, did not seem out of place. Time and again London etched the scene, its vocal accompaniment furnished by the howling of uneasy dogs. A typical example is found in *A Daughter of the Snows*.

It was a clear, cold night, not over-cold—not more than forty below—and the land was bathed in a soft, diffused flood of light which found its source not in the stars, nor yet in the moon, which was somewhere over on the other side of the world. From the southeast to the northwest a pale-greenish glow fringed the rim of the heavens, and it was from this the dim radiance was exhaled.

Suddenly, like the ray of a search-light, a band of white light ploughed overhead. Night turned to ghostly day on the instant, then blacker night descended. But to the south-east a noiseless commotion was apparent. The glowing greenish gauze was in a ferment, bubbling, uprearing, downfalling, and tentatively thrusting huge bodiless hands into the upper ether. Once more a cyclopean rocket twisted its fiery way across the sky, from horizon to zenith, and on, and on, in tremendous flight, to horizon again. But the span could not hold, and in its wake the black night brooded. And yet again, broader, stronger, deeper, lavishly spilling streamers to right and left, it flaunted the midmost zenith with its gorgeous flare, and passed on and down to the further edge of the world. Heaven was bridged at last, and the bridge endured!

At this flaming triumph the silence of earth was broken, and ten thousand wolf-dogs, in long-drawn unisoned howls, sobbed their dismay and grief.

They were not all northern dogs in Dawson that winter, though huskies and malemutes were in the majority. It was a winter for dogs, this and the winter of early 1898, when Yukon transportation depended almost wholly upon them. Later horses took their place, and the dogs became a picturesque rarity. But in 1897 dogs of all sorts had been sent up from Canada and the States. Many of them were too small or too weak to be of much use, but some drivers found that the best of the large 'outside' dogs suited the sudden needs of the area as well as the native huskies. Jack London had come to know one of these imports, a cross between a St Bernard and a Scotch collie, owned by Louis Bond, near whose cabin he had camped when he first reached Dawson. Louis Bond was the son of Judge Bond of Santa Clara, California, who was to appear as Judge Miller in *The Call of the Wild*, while Louis Bond was to lend some of his traits to Stanley Prince in *The Son of the Wolf*. Louis' dog, still to be seen in old photographs, was the original of Buck, both in breed and in temperament.

When the fictional Buck reached Dawson after sledding over the Klondike trail during the same winter that London spent in the North, he found Dawson City a regular capital city of dogland.

Here were many men, and countless dogs, and Buck found them all at work. It seemed the ordained order of things that dogs should work. All day they swung up and down the main street in long teams, and in the night their jingling bells still went by.

[119]

They hauled cabin logs and firewood, freighted up to the mines, and did all manner of work that horses did in the Santa Clara Valley. Here and there Buck met Southland dogs, but in the main they were the wild wolf husky breed. Every night, regularly, at nine, at twelve, at three, they lifted a nocturnal song, a weird and eerie chant, in which it was Buck's delight to join.

With the aurora borealis flaming coldly overhead, or the stars leaping in the frost dance, and the land numb and frozen under its pall of snow, this song of the huskies might have been the defiance of life, only it was pitched in minor key, with long-drawn wailing and half-sobs, and was more the pleading of life, the articulate travail of existence. It was an old song, old as the breed itself—one of the first songs of the younger world in a day when songs were sad. It was invested with the woe of unnumbered generations, this plaint by which Buck was so strangely stirred. When he moaned and sobbed, it was with the pain of living that was of old the pain of his wild fathers, and the fear and mystery of the cold and dark that was to them fear and mystery. And that he should be stirred by it marked the completeness with which he harked back through the ages of fire and roof to the raw beginnings of life in the howling ages.

It is not unlikely that, as Jack London idled through the weeks of early winter in Dawson City, he saw more than one prized dog put through the test of breaking out a heavily-laden sled from the frozen snow crust. Thus he would have the background detail for the magnificent scene in which Buck lives up to the confidence of his master, John Thornton, by starting a sled loaded with twenty fifty-pound sacks of flour. Thornton had accepted a wager from a Bonanza King that his dog, a hundred and fifty pounds of 'grit and virility', could not possibly budge such a load. The sourdoughs and cheechakos at the Eldorado poured out into the snow (it was sixty degrees below zero) to watch the trial of strength. Every reader of *The Call of the Wild* remembers the passage:

Buck threw himself forward, tightening the traces with a jarring lunge. His whole body was gathered compactly together in the tremendous effort, the muscles writhing and knotting like live things under the silky fur. His great chest was low to the ground, his head forward and down, while his feet were flying like mad, the claws scarring the hard-packed snow in parallel grooves. The sled swayed and trembled, half-started forward. One of his feet slipped, and one man groaned aloud. Then the sled lurched ahead in what appeared a rapid succession of jerks, though it never really came to a dead stop again . . . half an inch . . . two inches . . . . The jerks perceptibly diminished; as the sled gained momentum, he caught them up, till it was moving steadily along.

It is less likely that London saw any dog like White Fang, half-husky and half-wolf, exhibited in Dawson for fifty cents a head, penned in a cage as a 'Fighting Wolf'. White Fang, captive from the remote 'Northland Wild', was beginning his journey from raw nature to civilization, where he eventually would be won over by the love of man. But Beauty Smith, the primordial bully who was exhibiting White Fang, was hardly calculated to hasten this process. In Dawson, he pitted White Fang against any animal that would fight him. The fights took place outside town in order to avoid interference from the Mounties, or 'Yellow-Legs'; it is possible that London, with his interest in the primordial, saw more than one such fight while he was in the Klondike. White Fang conquered the best of the native dogs, fought successfully with a lynx (later London was to be attacked as a 'nature fakir' by Teddy Roosevelt for pitting a lynx against a dog), but was nearly killed by a tenacious bulldog, from which he was rescued near death by an outraged bystander, who was to provide him with the warmth and generosity of a good human master.

Arguing in bars like the Moosehorn, gambling in dives like the Eldorado, dancing at masked balls in the ill-fated Opera House, watching men test their dogs on Front Street or fight them on the far side of the Yukon—these occupations might well have provided relief from the dull routine of cooking beans and bacon and sourdough bread, scraping out ice from the cabin or tent, chopping wood, mending torn clothes, and dragging heavy buckets of water up from ice holes in the river. There were two of these last which figured in London's fiction, one down near the barracks, where the Klondike joined the Yukon, the other at the north end of town near the hospital and the sawmill. During the late fall, men raised water through these holes; as the winter tightened its grip, they found the holes frozen and were forced to chop ice for their water supply, now toting it up the steep bank in sacks rather than in buckets.

Did London ever walk the dozen miles up the Klondike to the Bonanza diggings or continue even farther to the fabulous Eldorado placer claims or to those on the Hunker? Did he see anything of the burrowing operations that were going on on the banks of these streams back of Dawson, talk to any of the miners who were piling up frozen tailings for the spring thaw? A description in *Burning Daylight* strongly suggests that he saw something of the mines.

Six thousand spent the winter of 1897 in Dawson, work on the creeks went on apace, while beyond the passes it was reported that one hundred thousand more were waiting for the spring. Late one brief afternoon, Daylight, on the benches between French Hill and Skookum Hill, caught a wider vision of things. Beneath him lay the richest part of Eldorado Creek, while up and down Bonanza he could see for miles. It was a scene of a vast devastation. The hills, to their tops, had been shorn of trees, and their naked sides showed signs of goring and perforating that even the mantle of snow could not hide. Beneath him, in every direction, were the cabins of men. But not many men were visible. A blanket of smoke filled the valleys and turned the gray day to melancholy twilight. Smoke arose from a thousand holes in the snow, where, deep down on bed-rock, in the frozen muck and gravel, men crept and scratched and dug, and ever built more fires to break the grip of the frost. Here and there, where new shafts were starting, these fires flamed redly. Figures of men crawled out of the holes, or disappeared into them, or, on raised platforms of hand-hewn timber, windlassed the thawed gravel to the surface, where it immediately froze. The wreckage of the spring washing appeared everywhere—piles of sluice-boxes, sections of elevated flumes, huge water-wheels—all the debris of an army of gold-mad men.

On the way to the Klondike

Gold mining in the Yukon

As Daylight looked on this scene, he thought some of the thoughts London expressed in his article 'Economics in the Klondike', an essay devoted to the thesis that not all the gold in the Yukon equalled the outlay in cash of the individuals who pursued it. And the rape of nature compounded the deficit. Daylight 'looked at the naked hills and realized the enormous wastage of wood that had taken place. From this bird's-eye view he realized the monstrous confusion of their excited workings. It was a gigantic inadequacy. Each worked for himself, and the result was chaos. In this richest of diggings it cost one dollar to mine two dollars, and for every dollar taken out by their feverish, unthinking methods another dollar was left hopelessly in the earth. Given another year, and most of the claims would be worked out, and the sum of the gold taken out would no more than equal what was left behind.'

This was the mood of a later day, however. At the moment, London was more likely to have thrown his enthusiasm into one or more of the stampedes which periodically emptied Dawson of its inhabitants in a mad dash to still another creek. Almost every commentator on the Klondike rush remarks on these stampedes, recognized as largely futile but tremendously exciting. After all, with the many rich creeks near Dawson fully staked, it was not out of character to rush farther away in hopes there would be some reward for the ardours of reaching the Klondike and the discomforts of living there.

London includes three stampedes in his fiction, but two of them, the substance of the early story, 'Thanksgiving on Slav Creek' and the chapter in *Smoke Bellew* entitled 'The Stampede to Squaw Creek', prove on close examination to be the same event, retold to fit *Smoke Bellew* long after Dawson had become a ghost town. It is a typical stampede, starting in the middle of the night. The word has gone round of a rich find on a creek thirty miles up the Yukon, and each man is keeping the information to himself or merely confiding it to a partner. All of Dawson is awake, though, as the lights from windows suggest. Soon men are slipping out with light stampede-packs (sure signs of a secret abroad), scuttling for the river, where they slide down a thirty-foot ice chute and pile up at the bottom. Crossing the frozen river, a confusion of jam-packed ice cakes, proves to be such a difficult task that men light candles to find their way, candles which burn steadily in the windless air. Fireflies are now dancing all over the river. 'It was a mile across the jams to the west bank of the Yukon, and candles flickered the full length of the twisting trail. Behind them, clear to the top of the bank they had descended, were more candles.'

Across the river the stampeders turned south along the sled trail to Dyea. For the rest of the night they pushed on in the cold. Frequently the faster men floundered through the snow up to their waists in order to pass the more stolid hikers on the hard-packed trail. Morning came with its pink dawn to find half of Dawson up a frozen creek, not a worthwhile prospect in sight. The next day saw the stampeders back in their cabins and tents, joking about what suckers they had been. It was not all fun, however; gradually news of disaster along the trail seeped back to Dawson. 'Nor did they learn till afterward the horrors of that night. Exhausted men sat down to rest by the way and failed to get up again. Seven were frozen to death, while scores of amputations of toes, feet and fingers were performed in the Dawson hospitals on the survivors. For the stampede to Squaw Creek occurred on the coldest night of the year. Before morning the spirit thermometers at Dawson registered seventy degrees below zero.' Exaggeration was inherent in the story. Probably no men froze, but they might have. Here was excitement, at least, in what one writer has called the world of 'the young, strong, and stupid'.[7] Such a stampede was fit punctuation for a winter in Dawson.

V · SPLIT-UP ISLAND

RELIABLE biographical information on London's return up the Yukon to Split-up Island is particularly meagre. Charmian London, presumably relying on a section of Thompson's diary which has since disappeared from the London papers, states in her biography that London and Thompson left Dawson on December 3, 1897, and reached Upper Island (Split-up Island) on December 7. We do not know for certain whether the two men covered the eighty miles of the river trail with a dog team or less romantically packed on their backs. They may even have pulled small sleds, as was the custom with Klondikers who owned no dogs.

Nor do we know why they left Dawson when they did, nor, for that matter, why they had lingered in Dawson so long. We do know, however, that as the darkest period of the winter approached, many Klondikers left Dawson to go upriver to camps near the mouths of the Stewart, the White, and the Pelly, or on to Lake Bennett, or even to Dyea. Dawson was only two degrees below the Arctic Circle, and any move upriver carried one farther south. Dawson meant famine and sickness; it meant verminous blankets and a surfeit of rotgut. Many emigrants were glad to leave as soon as feasible after the freeze-up.

In early winter men made their way up the river trail under severe handicaps. Not until later in the season was there to be a well-packed trail over the ice, which had frozen late and was still thin and treacherous in many spots. This is probably the reason that the first Dawson mail did not get through to Dyea until late in February. The mild autumn came definitely to an end on November 29, however, when the temperature dipped to sixty-seven degrees below zero. Under such severe cold, the trees cracked like pistol shots with the freezing and expanding sap, the touching of metal tore the skin from naked fingers, and the frost frequently seared the lungs of unwary travellers who unduly exerted themselves. London's characters frequently tested these low temperatures by noting how their spit behaved! The hero in 'To Build a Fire' uses this method: 'As he turned to go on, he spat speculatively. There was a sharp, explosive crackle that startled him. He spat again. And again, in the air, before it could fall to the snow, the spittle crackled. He knew that at fifty below spittle crackled on the snow, but this spittle had crackled in the air. Undoubtedly it was colder than fifty below—how much colder he did not know.' Though it brought perils, the cold spell firmed the ice on the river and made travel possible.

Even so, the five-day hike up to the mouth of the Stewart was no child's play. Camping out for four nights must have made even the trail look attractive! A few glimpses of the physical features of that section of the Yukon trail appear in London's fiction, particularly in *Smoke Bellew*. The trail on leaving Dawson crossed among up-ended ice cakes to the far bank of the river and clung close to the western bluffs beside the river for perhaps fifty miles. 'Within a few feet of the west bank, the trail swerved to the south, emerging from the jam upon smooth ice. The ice, however, was buried under several feet of fine snow. Through this the sled-trail ran, a narrow ribbon of packed footing barely two feet in width. On either side one sank to his knees and deeper in the snow.' In coldest weather this snow was not much like the snow the emigrants had known at home, London points out in *Burning Daylight*. 'Quite different was it from the ordinary snow known to those of the Southland. It was hard, and fine, and dry. It was more like sugar. Kick it, and it flew with a hissing noise like sand. There was no cohesion among the particles, and it could not be moulded into snow-balls. It was not composed of flakes, but of crystals—tiny, geometrical frost-crystals. In truth, it was not snow, but frost.'

This was pretty much the character of the trail except for heavy ice jams at the mouth of the Sixtymile, creating 'a chaos of up-ended ice-cakes'. At several points, where the ice extended smooth from shore to shore, there were many tracks packed through the snow; at others, there was only one narrow slit. Near the Stewart River area, the trail grew once more difficult. 'It was at this point that the Dyea trail, baffled by ice-jams, swerved abruptly across the Yukon to the east bank.'[1] And it was here that London and Thompson left the trail to rejoin their companions in the cabin on Split-up Island.

The island on which London spent the winter was one of a number which clustered on the west bank of the Yukon just below the mouth of the Stewart. Flat and low-lying, these islands had been created by the alluvial detritus brought in by the large tributary. Here the Yukon splayed out into a confusing tangle of channels. There were camps on a number of islands during the winter of 1897–1898, and in time the entire cluster came to be known as Stewart City or Stewart River. When London returned to this vicinity in December of 1897, it must have looked and felt very much like the scene he described in 'A Day's Lodging': 'He travelled on the frozen surface of a great river. Behind him it stretched away in a mighty curve of many miles, losing itself in a fantastic jumble of mountains, snow-covered and silent. Ahead of him the river split into many channels to accommodate the freight of islands it carried on its breast. These islands were silent and white. No animals nor humming insects broke the silence. No birds flew in the chill air. . . . The world slept, and it was like the sleep of death.' The smoke from chim-

neys, the twinkling of slush lamps after dark, and the
occasional shout of a man or bark of a dog must easily
have been absorbed in the surrounding whiteness. The
same impression of isolation is stressed when the locality
again appears in 'The Great Interrogation': 'To the sky-
line of the four quarters ... stretched the immaculate
wilderness. .... The land seemed bound under the unreality of the unknown, wrapped in the brooding mystery
of great spaces.' This land was to figure as the setting of
many stories in *The Son of the Wolf* and *The God of His
Fathers*, as well as of the latter part of *A Daughter of the
Snows*.

In the settlements on the islands, men moved about during the two or three hours of grey daylight, carrying ice
chopped from the river in sacks over their shoulders,
dragging in branches to burn in their Yukon stoves, passing from cabin to cabin to borrow or lend or swap, or seek
companionship. Life inside these primitive log huts was
similar to that pictured vividly in 'The End of the Story'.

The table was of hand-hewn spruce boards, and the men who
played whist had frequent difficulties in drawing home their
tricks across the uneven surface. Though they sat in their under-
shirts, the sweat noduled and oozed on their faces; yet their feet,
heavily moccasined and woollen-socked, tingled with the bite
of the frost. Such was the difference of temperature in the small
cabin between the floor level and a yard or more above it.
The sheet-iron Yukon stove roared red-hot, yet, eight feet away,
on the meat-shelf, placed low and beside the door, lay chunks
of solidly frozen moose and bacon. The door, a third of the way
up from the bottom, was a thick rime. In the chinking between
the logs at the back of the bunks the frost showed white and
glistening. A window of oiled paper furnished light. The lower
portion of the paper, on the inside, was coated an inch deep
with the frozen moisture of the men's breath.

This was what it was like inside a cabin. Some of these
cabins had been built and abandoned by the Alaska Commercial Company and possibly the Hudson's Bay Com-

pany. Others were thrown up hastily by the newcomers. Some of the Klondikers braved the winter in tents, in which the rigours of cabin life were merely exaggerated.

It was very cold without, but it was not over-warm within. The only article which might be designated furniture was the stove, and for this the men were frank in displaying their preference. Upon half of the floor pine boughs had been cast; above this were spread the sleeping-furs, beneath lay the winter's snowfall. The remainder of the floor was moccasin-packed snow, littered with pots and pans and the general *impedimenta* of an Arctic camp. The stove was red and roaring hot, but only a bare three feet away lay a block of ice, as sharp-edged and dry as when first quarried from the creek bottom. The pressure of the outside cold forced the inner heat upward. Just above the stove, where the pipe penetrated the roof, was a tiny circle of dry canvas; next, with the pipe always as centre, a circle of steaming canvas; next a damp and moisture-exuding ring; and finally, the rest of the tent, sidewalls and top, coated with a half-inch of dry, white, crystal-encrusted frost.[2]

In one of the half-dozen articles he wrote on his experiences in the Yukon country, 'Housekeeping in the Klondike', London gives an idea of the cabin he lived in on Split-up Island as well as of his practice as a cook when that assignment rotated to him.

It is no sinecure, being cook in the Klondike. Often he must do his work in a cabin measuring ten by twelve on the inside, and occupied by three other men besides himself. When it is considered that these men eat, sleep, lounge, smoke, play cards, and entertain visitors there, and also in that small space house the bulk of their possessions, the size of the cook's orbit may be readily computed. In the morning he sits up in bed, reaches out and strikes the fire, then proceeds to dress. After that the centre of his orbit is the front of the stove, the diameter the length of his arms. Even then his comrades are continually encroaching upon his domain, and he is at constant warfare to prevent territorial grabs.

It is fitting that London stressed cooking in his account of housekeeping, because this was about the principal routine activity going on in the cabins. We are told that though the cook seemingly had little opportunity for variety in his cuisine, being largely restricted to the three 'B's' of the Klondike—bread, beans, and bacon—he actually could avoid hopeless monotony if he were resourceful and an adept at swapping. Bacon grease was a great help, for it not only furnished fuel for the slush lamps, oil for greasing the paper windows, and lubricant for the tools, but with it a good cook could make excellent gravy as well as oil-saturated doughnuts, popular with the men who went on trail, for they resisted freezing except at very low temperatures. Usually a man carried them inside his shirt, next to his skin! London assures us that bacon grease was to the white man what blubber and seal oil were to the Eskimo. If a cook could get hold of some chili peppers, he could even make the pork and beans more palatable. Jack gives an interesting glimpse of the logistics of the Northland in describing the way in which pork and beans were handled. 'For instance, previous to the men going out for a trip on trail, he cooks several gallons of beans in the company of numerous chunks of salt pork and much bacon grease. This mess he then moulds into blocks of convenient size and places on the roof, where it freezes into bricks in a couple of hours. Thus the men, after a weary day's travel, have but to chop off chunks with an axe and thaw out in the frying pan.' If the cook incorporates some chili peppers in the 'mess', he will produce 'a dish which even the hungry arctic gods may envy.'

If the men were that easily pleased by an attempt to spice up the beans, it is certain they were even more impressed when a cook managed to do something to alleviate the agonies of the shortage of sugar. Klondikers apparently missed sugar more than any other element absent in their diet, and in more than one story London has his characters employ elaborate subterfuges in order to obtain the favoured ingredient. 'Man can endure hardship and horror with equanimity, but take from him his sugar, and he raises his lamentations to the stars.' Two effective ways to alleviate the problem, according to London, were to serve stewed dried peaches with the mush and to cook prunes with the rice. Of course, this assumed that the Klondiker still had some dried fruit among his supplies. If there were only dried apples left, he could concoct synthetic vinegar by using some of the apples, a bit of water, and brown paper from the bacon wrappings. But of course, the sourdough bread would be the *pièce-de-résistance* of his menu. And this brought a good deal of variety, for there was nothing so fickle as the dough in a miner's cabin.

London assures us that sourdough bread was deceptively easy to make. 'Make a batter and place it near the stove (that it may not freeze) till it ferments or sours. Then mix the dough with it, and sweeten with soda to taste—of course replenishing the batter for next time.' This sounds simple enough, but the cook soon found that varying conditions inevitably affected his bread. It was never twice the same.

If the batter could only be placed away in an equable temperature, all well and good. If one's comrades did not interfere, much vexation of spirit might be avoided. But this cannot be; for Tom fires up the stove till the cabin is become like the hot-room of a Turkish bath; Dick forgets all about the fire till the place is a refrigerator; then along comes Harry and shoves the sourdough bucket right against the stove to make way for the drying of his mittens. Now heat is a most potent factor in accelerating the fermentation of flour and water, and hence the unfortunate cook is constantly in disgrace with Tom, Dick, and Harry. Last week his bread was yellow from a plethora of soda; this week it is sour from a prudent lack of the same . . . .

Some cooks aver they have so cultivated their olfactory organs that they can tell to the fraction of a degree just how sour the batter is. Nevertheless they have never been known to bake two batches of bread which were at all alike. But this fact casts not the slightest shadow upon the infallibility of their theory. One and all, they take advantage of circumstances, and meanly crawl out by laying the blame upon the soda, which was dampened 'the time the canoe overturned', or upon the flour, which they got in trade from 'that half-breed fellow with the dogs'. The pride of the Klondike cook in his bread is something which passes understanding.

As for the rest of housekeeping, it consisted principally of shovelling out the ice as it accumulated on the floor. Even though one brushed off all the snow from his clothes before entering the cabin or just after passing through the door (a whisk broom was usually hanging near at hand for this purpose), his breath alone would add measurably to the ice as the day wore on. In addition to keeping the ice down as much as possible, one frequently changed the boughs beneath his bunk, if he wished to sleep well. What he did for a bath London does not make clear. And there was often mending of clothes to be done as well as carving and carpentering within the cabin.

Keeping track of the temperature and the time were absorbing occupations. To supplement the spit test and such thermometer readings as could be made outdoors, men frequently attempted to judge from within the cabin by noting the rapidity with which the ice-coating grew on window and cabin wall. London describes a novel way of keeping track of time in a country where reliable watches were hard to find. Before going to bed the responsible Klondiker wanders outside and studies the clear heavens. 'Having located the Pole Star by means of the Great Bear, he inserts two slender wands in the snow, a couple of yards apart and in line with the North Star. The next day, when the sun on the southern horizon casts the shadows of the wands to the northward and in line, he knows it to be twelve o'clock, noon, and sets his watch and those of his partners accordingly. As stray dogs are constantly knocking his wands out of line with the North Star, it becomes his habit to verify them regularly every night.'

If men had been made like some of their animal brethren, they would be able to hibernate for the months of the dead of winter, when there was little point in staying awake. Certainly this would have been a fine occupation for the Klondikers on Split-up Island, who were not mining and had little prospects of mining, and who already had a fairly clear notion that the Far North held nothing for them. In their bones most of them knew they were merely biding their time until they could go back home without too much effort. Under the circumstances, a good thing to do was to sleep as much as possible, and sleep was one of the principal activities on the islands below the mouth of the Stewart.

There was also a remedy for boredom at the opposite extreme, the blowing off of steam, an inevitable conco-mitant of being cooped up under such unnatural con-ditions. The most pleasant way of doing this was by having a party, a genial affair when Malemute Kid (the central character of the tales in *The Son of the Wolf*) and his friends went about it. The principal attribute of such a party was a powerful drink, home-concocted and called 'hooch', a word made current by the Klondikers, who borrowed it from the Tlingit's 'hoochino'. The occasion described in the opening of 'To the Man on Trail' was a Christmas celebration.

'Dump it in.'
'But I say, Kid, isn't that going it a little too strong? Whiskey and alcohol's bad enough; but when it comes to brandy and pepper-sauce and'—
'Dump it in. Who's making this punch, anyway?' And Malemute Kid smiled benignantly through the clouds of steam. 'By the time you've been in this country as long as I have, my son, and lived on rabbit-tracks and salmon-belly, you'll learn that Christmas comes only once per annum. And a Christmas without punch is sinking a hole to bedrock with nary a pay-streak.'
'Stack up on that fer a high cyard,' approved Big Jim Belden, who had come down from his claim on Mazy May to

[133]

spend Christmas, and who, as every one knew, had been living the two months past on straight moose-meat. 'Hain't fergot the *hooch* we-uns made on the Tanana, hev yeh?'

'Well, I guess yes. Boys, it would have done your hearts good to see that whole tribe fighting drunk—and all because of a glorious ferment of sugar and sourdough.'

This was something like the liquid dynamite that Stevens distilled from flour, molasses, and sugar in a still made from a kerosene can and a copper kettle, in 'A Hyperborean Brew'.

To turn from story to fact, we know nothing of London's mixing a punch or constructing a still that winter, and it is doubtful that there were drinks to be had at Christmas in a cabin where Thompson, Sloper, and Goodman were all teetotallers. According to *John Barleycorn*, London was almost equally abstemious during his stay on Split-up Island. In their cabin, 'steaming cups of tea', not whisky toddies, were offered to visitors.

There were other ways of amusing oneself than drinking convivially, however. Jack played a good deal of cribbage and whist, and there is some evidence that he found a chess-board and opponents to help him enjoy his favourite game. There was no roulette or faro here, as there was down in Dawson; and if there was any gambling it was probably for small stakes, as there was little money or dust in the camp. There was reading, of course, and London probably did a great deal of this. He did so in spite of very real handicaps; the short day filtered very little light through greased-paper windowpanes coated with frost. Candles were precious, as they cost a dollar and a half each; kerosene lamps were used sparingly; the usual recourse was to the slush lamp, or 'bitch', which burned bacon grease, giving little light and much smoke, and added its oily smog to the woodsmoke and the fumes of strong tobacco from even stronger pipes. 'When the candles give out, the cook fills a sardine-can with bacon grease, manu-

[134]

factures a wick out of the carpenter's sail-twine, and behold! the slush lamp stands complete,' London wrote in his housekeeping article. 'It goes by another and less complimentary name in the vernacular, and, next to sourdough bread, is responsible for more men's souls than any other single cause of degeneracy in the Klondike.'

Books were reasonably hard to come by. Undoubtedly London brought some with him, but he could not have brought many, as it was folly to attempt the Chilkoot with too heavy an outfit unless you could afford to pay Indians to pack it over. According to one of his companions, Emil Jensen, London treasured Darwin's *Origin of Species* and Milton's *Paradise Lost* as his two most prized books that winter. He was also able to borrow a copy of Kipling's *The Seven Seas* for his friend to read when the latter found Darwin and Milton too stiff for him. Jensen remembered that nearly everyone on the island had brought in at least one book, some two or three; Jeremiah Lynch in his *Three Years in the Klondike* testified that he ran into a Yukon miner who had lugged in the six volumes of Gibbon's *Decline and Fall of the Roman Empire* and spent his spare time reading them over and over. Though Dawson with its lending library cached in a bank was too far away for practical aid, no doubt London found as much to read as he had light for. And he could always recite poetry when he ran out of books, as he had an excellent memory and had long delighted in memorizing his favourite poems.

His favourite recreation, however, was talking and arguing, an activity of which he never tired. All his acquaintances who have recorded their impressions of London on Split-up Island have stressed his enthusiasm for these discussions. One remembers him sitting on the edge of his bunk, gesticulating with hands stained by smoke from the cigarettes he rolled so skilfully, trying to persuade a partner who was getting dinner that there was no scientific proof of the existence of God. Another recalls him lying in a bunk and listening to a judge and a surgeon argue about Darwinism; eventually he rose up and entered the argument by quoting exactly the passage which made clear the issue between them. According to still another, he would sit by the fire with eyes glowing as he expounded Herbert Spencer's ideas to his friends. This same friend also says that London was always eager for an argument over socialism. At other times he pursued the answers to such questions as 'What is truth?' or 'Is there justice in this world?' He never grew angry during these discussions; he would frequently listen eagerly for a long time, then with a gay laugh come in with his point. He was the youngest in the group and a great favourite, remembered for his winning smile and his 'irrational generosity'. The friend, Bert Hargrave, adds a vivid picture of London's appearance during these discussions: 'In appearance older than his years; a body lithe and strong; neck bared at the throat; a tangled cluster of brown hair that fell low over his brow and which he was wont to brush back impatiently when engaged in animated conversation; a sensitive mouth, but lips, nevertheless, that could set in serious and masterful lines; a radiant smile, marred by two missing teeth (lost, he told me, in a fight on shipboard); eyes that often carried an introspective expression; the face of an artist and a dreamer, but with strong lines denoting will power and boundless energy.'[3] To the writer of this description, London was a genius, fully justifying the judgement of the habitually silent French-Canadian, Louis Savard: ' "You mak' ver' good talk, but zat London he too damn smart for you." '

When London wrote, 'It was in the Klondike I found myself. There nobody talks. Everybody thinks. You get your true perspective,'[4] he was telling only half the truth, for he had forgotten the talking in the light of the total experience. Talk he did, but most important of all, he listened and observed during those months in the draughty

[136]

cabins near the mouth of the Stewart; he stored up memories, thought ideas through, felt the stirrings of a creative artist. As the winter moved on, he appeared to gain sustenance from the shadow, to develop warmth in the time of deep cold. Emil Jensen stresses this development in his memories of the future writer: 'To him, there was in all things something new, something alluring, something worth while, be it a game of whist, an argument, or the sun at noonday glowing cold and brilliant above the hills to the south. He was ever on tiptoe with expectancy, whether silent with wondering awe, as on a night when we saw the snows aflame beneath a weird, bewildering sky or in the throes of a frenzied excitement while we watched a mighty river at flood tide, and the ice "go out" in the moonlight.'[5]

London's later correspondence with old Klondikers such as Georges Dupuy, Everett Barton, Clarence Buzzini, and Cornelius Gepfert, as well as his notes for Yukon stories, Fred Thompson's diary, W. B. Hargrave's letters to Charmian London, and Emil Jensen's unpublished manuscript, 'With Jack London at Stewart River', all mention names of comrades on Split-up Island so that it is possible to build up a fairly sizeable roster of acquaintances. As might be expected, these are almost to a man cheechakos rather than sourdoughs, for what would sourdoughs be doing wintering on Upper Island? There were, first of all—and known to us in most detail—London's original partners, red-whiskered Fred Thompson, big Jim Goodman, and bantam-weight Merritt Sloper. Of these, Sloper figured most prominently in London's writing. He not only gave him the most attractive role in 'Like Argus of the Ancient Times', but paid tribute to his pluck and skill in 'Through the Rapids on the Way to Klondike' and presented him as a character under his real name in 'In a Far Country'. In the last he is the epitome of Anglo-Saxon grit.

Sloper rose to his feet. His body was a ludicrous contrast to the healthy physiques of the Incapables. Yellow and weak, fleeing from a South American fever-hole, he had not broken his flight across the zones, and was still able to toil with men. His weight was probably ninety pounds, with the heavy hunting-knife thrown in, and his grizzled hair told of a prime which had ceased to be. . . . And all this day he had whipped his stronger comrades into venturing a thousand miles of the stiffest hardship man can conceive. He was the incarnation of the unrest of his race, and the old Teutonic stubborness, dashed with the quick grasp and action of the Yankee, held the flesh in the bondage of the spirit.

Yet it was with the peppery Sloper, rather than with the pompous Thompson or the pious Goodman, that London eventually quarrelled, thus precipitating his shift from one set of companions to a new set and a new cabin. According to Charmian London, the tiff arose over Jack London's misuse of Sloper's ax in chopping ice from the water hole. London drove the ax through the ice into the gravel, badly dulling its edge. Such an event, however, seems too trivial to have caused a serious quarrel; it must have been the culmination of a series of small irritations of the sort that sooner or later broke up almost all living combinations in the Yukon. Common housekeeping in close quarters was hardly designed to soothe men's nerves. Perhaps Jack, as Charmian states, was also too openhanded and hospitable to suit his partners, insisting that each visitor stay for dinner even though the beans and dried fruit ran short in the cache. If it hadn't been one thing, it would have been another.

The intolerable tensions which built up among idle men cooped together in isolated areas were portrayed very effectively in 'In a Far Country'. It is true that the two main characters are weaklings, quite unlike London and Sloper, but the troubles arising from their being thrown constantly together were similar to difficulties which developed in many a Northland cabin. 'The intense frost could not be endured for long at a time, and the little cabin crowded them—beds, stove, table, and all—into a space of ten by twelve. The very presence of either became a personal affront to the other, and they lapsed into sullen silences which increased in length and strength as the days went by. Occasionally, the flash of an eye or the curl of a lip got the better of them, though they strove to wholly ignore each other during these mute periods. And a great wonder sprang up in the breast of each, as to how God had ever come to create the other.' Finally they killed each other.

London did much better; he moved into a nearby cabin, where he was welcomed by some friends who had not yet begun to irritate him so much. These were 'Doc' B. F. Harvey, a surgeon who had come north to escape drink; Judge E. H. Sullivan, a jurist turned argonaut; and W. B. ('Bert') Hargrave, who was to become a socialist largely through London's influence. Bert Hargrave tells of his meeting with Jack:

It was in October of 1897 that I first met him . . . . No other man has left so indelible an impression upon my memory as Jack London. . . . His cabin was on the bank of the Yukon, near the mouth of the Stewart River. I remember well the first time I entered it. London was seated on the edge of a bunk, rolling a cigarette. He smoked incessantly and it would have taken no Sherlock Holmes to tell what the stains on his fingers meant. One of his partners, Goodman, was preparing a meal, and the other, Sloper, was doing some carpentry work. From the few words which I overheard as I entered, I surmised that Jack had challenged some of Goodman's orthodox views, and that the latter was doggedly defending himself in an unequal contest of wits. Many times afterward I myself felt the rapier thrust of London's, and knew how to sympathize with Goodman.

Jack interrupted the conversation to welcome me, and his hospitality was so cordial, his smile so genial, his goodfellow-ship so real, that it instantly dispelled all reserve. I was invited to participate in the discussion, which I did, much to my subsequent discomfiture.[6]

Little further is known about Hargrave or Sullivan in the Yukon (Hargrave went to Dawson about the time London moved in), but Doc Harvey's name crops up frequently in the London correspondence. He was so full of tall tales that he was nicknamed 'Old Thousand and One Nights' Harvey; he liked to argue with Jack but was somewhat annoyed at the latter's atheism; and he eventually was to be London's companion in floating down to Dawson on a home-made raft after the spring thaw.

The most interesting story connected with Doc Harvey was the one about his operating on a man's ankle, using Jack's whisky as a pain-killer for both himself and his patient. London referred to the incident in *John Barleycorn*: 'In my personal medicine chest [crossing the Chilkoot] was a quart of whisky. I never drew the cork till six months afterwards, in a lonely camp, where, without anesthetics, a doctor was compelled to operate on a man. The doctor and the patient emptied my bottle between them and then proceeded to the operation.' From Emil Jensen we learn that the man operated on by Doc Harvey was named Charlie Borg; he had broken his ankle while crossing the Chilkoot and had failed to get it set properly. After he became one of Jensen's cabin-mates on Split-up Island, the foot began giving very serious trouble, threatening to cost its owner his life, possibly on account of gangrene. London provided the whisky when no regular anesthetic could be found after a frantic search of the camps.

'Good whisky it was, Doc. Harvey said so, and he knew. One quarter of the bottle, or jug, went down his throat to steady his nerves, and the remainder of the whisky saved the life of his patient. . . . Thanks to the benumbing effect of that whisky, my partner survived the butchering, for butchering it was, as cruel as it was necessary, and our skilful old "Thousand and One Nights" sickened as he completed his surgical job.' The result may have been one of the reasons that London later maintained that the Klondike fearfully mangled more than it killed.

Emil Jensen, fifteen years older than Jack London, so attracted the future novelist that he used him as a model for Malemute Kid, the near paragon who forms the central figure in the tales published as *The Son of the Wolf*. Jensen was also much drawn to London, and in 1926 typed out his glowing tribute and sent it to Charmian London. Though it is ineptly written and much too wordy for the information it includes, it manages to give a memorable portrait of the young adventurer. It tells of his popularity: '. . . the London cabin was always the centre of attraction'; of his love of discussion; of his hospitality; of his fruitless attempt to get Jensen to read Darwin and Huxley; of his going to great lengths to find a copy of Kipling's poetry for him; and of their meeting with an adventurer named Stevens and his sluttish female companion. The spirit of Jensen's sketch is best illustrated from the opening remarks:

'How do you do?' he greeted me, as I stood before him on the snow-covered river-bank. 'Where from, friend?'

'San Francisco,' I replied rather tersely as I tried to dislodge a heavy chunk of ice from my moustache, where it had grown beyond all comfortable proportions until it threatened a combination with the week-old stubbles on my lower lip.

'Bay man, I'll bet!' ventured the youth, nothing daunted, as he drew his right from his mit; 'and a sailor in the bargain,' he added as I shook the proffered hand. 'I can tell a boatman,' he continued, 'as far as I can see him, and I had my eyes on you as you "came to" out there on the ice. In spite of the current and the drift-ice you landed without a jar.'

The curly-haired, blue-eyed boy—he was little more than a lad—certainly pleased me by this remark, for I was rather proud of the way I had handled our boat on this turbulent and most trying of rivers. Besides, the smile on his lips was boyishly friendly and his eyes sparkled as they gazed straight into mine. His were the first words of welcome I had heard on the cold, inhospitable river front, and the feel of his hand sent a current of warmth through my numbed body.

'What a likeable youth,' I thought, as my eyes took in the lithe, strong young figure before me, and perhaps my face reflected the thoughts that flitted through my mind, as a responsive light came into his eyes and his smile broadened into a happy, comrade-like grin.

[141]

'My name is Jack London,' he volunteered in a soft, pleasing voice, and, with what I thought at the time, the suspicion of a lisp. 'I, too, come from San Francisco Bay; my home is in Oakland.'

Other acquaintances in the small island community can be identified by name or personality and sketched in without much detail. There was Louis Savard, a hospitable French-Canadian with a fireplace and a cabin big enough for bull sessions. Savard, who may have been sensitive about his accent, was very taciturn but very likeable; he probably suggested Louis Savoy of *The Son of the Wolf*. There was Elam Harnish, from eastern Oregon, who was successful enough as a miner to remain in the Klondike and who was to furnish London with a name for his leading character in *Burning Daylight*. There were Harnish's partners, a German by the name of Charley Meyers, who appears as a trader in London stories, a nameless French-Canadian, and an equally nameless Swede. There were others similarly vaguely defined: a young man named Mason, Will Harrington, the Stanford football star, Everett Barton, Clarence Buzzini, and 'Con' Gepfert, all of whom wrote to London many years later. Others even more shadowy were Wolf the 'Malignant'—who fought with his three partners every livelong day—John Dillon, Carthy (or Courthé), Prewitt, Keough—'the giant Irishman'—Peacock the Texan, Charley Meadow—'Arizona Charley'—Hank Putnam—the professional gambler—Sam Adams, and Del Bishop—a pocket-miner who appeared under his own name in *A Daughter of the Snows*. There were Taylor, a Kentuckian who had gone to Annapolis, and bighearted John Thorson—two companions who were to float to the mouth of the Yukon with Jack London. And above all there was Stevens, who was to appear by name as an adventurer and teller of tall tales in London's fiction.

Stevens and his mistress made lasting impressions on

London, but for different reasons. In writing to a friend still in the Yukon in 1901, London asked, 'Did you ever hear of the man Stevens in the Klondike, and if so, of what became of him? If you will remember when you first landed at Stewart, Stevens had a woman and a camp across on the opposite bank of the Yukon. He was a wild sort of chap, and either a man of marvellous adventures or marvellous imagination.'[7] And when Fred Lockley of Portland ran into Doc Harvey after he returned from the Klondike and settled in the Pacific North-west, the first thing Harvey did was to mention London's interest in the 'wild man' Stevens, and the red-haired, freckle-faced woman with whom he was living. Much the most detailed description of this pair of rogues lies in Emil Jensen's manuscript. Jensen states that Stevens' companion was the only white woman they saw that winter on Split-up Island and that Jack, who was 'much at ease before women', was decidedly interested. 'Breathing, as he did, health from every pore, a womanless-world did not appeal to his clean, strong nature.'

Jensen's account, written thirty nostalgic years after the event, makes one realize what an unnatural life these Klondikers were living.

With the exception of an occasional squaw [Charmian insists Jack never crossed the colour-line], we saw but one woman in our camp that winter. This one was a visitor from across the river. One blistering cold afternoon, I came upon her in Jack's cabin. She and 'her man' feeling lonesome and in need of diversion had crossed the river ice to pay our camp a visit. Jack's cabin being the nearest, and the most conspicuous, had been, of course, the one they chose. The man introduced himself as 'Stevens', and his companion he designated simply as 'the Missus'. 'Mrs Stevens', we addressed her but, as she volunteered later during the afternoon's conversation, she had no legal right to the name. She had come to the Yukon, she said, at the behest of a 'control' in the Spirit World, in the belief that an old man was to lead her to untold riches, and Stevens was old—twenty-five years her senior. All this given freely, and without the flicker of an eyelid.

It was stuffy and smokey in Jack's cabin that day, a fitful, vindictive gust of wind sending every now and then puffs of biting smoke to worry the nostril and the eye, and it might have been this blurred atmosphere that made me think her slovenly, even unclean. [This effort to present her in the best light makes Jack's statement to Charmian that Jensen was the 'noblest' man he ever knew more understandable.] Certainly her old, worn dress was not over neat. Yet, she was a woman, and a white woman, who—if not in the springtime of youth, at least had a goodly share of its magnetism. . . .

In spite of her smoke-tarnished complexion and the twenty-five or thirty years that had passed over her head, notwithstanding this and her bedraggled appearance generally, she was comparatively fair to look upon; besides, she was unreservedly frank and her voice was soft and caressing, like the south wind in the moonlight, and there was music in her laugh. Gradually she is fading from my memory, but I can still summon a vision of a buxom, houri-like form standing beside the stove as I enter, two plump hands raised to the brown, wavy hair in the act of straightening a stray, unruly lock that her fur cap had displaced. A pose? Well, perhaps; nevertheless she looked well that way, her head thrown back and a satisfied smile on the full, pouting lips. Despite the soiled, unkempt apparel, her small, well-rounded figure showed soft and yielding in the tight, delapitated dress. I remember well her dark blue eyes, the innocent, baby-like stare, and teeth small and white gleaming between red-blooded, rather sensuous lips. That she had brains was evident; enough, at least, to hold a real man, for Stevens, we found, was a man beyond a doubt. He liked to talk, and he talked well and interestingly, keeping us spellbound with a series of horrible, blood-curdling tales of killings and rape, and always there was gold at the headwater of the rivers.

Jensen says that Stevens told them of many of his adventures, particularly those in the jungles of the upper Amazon. Here was a red-blooded he-man surviving in the nature of tooth and claw.

He made it a rule to kill on sight, man or beast; and women he took where he found them. . . . Always in his wake there was blood, for he must kill if he would live. The tales as told had the stamp of truth, and yet I doubted. Many times I glanced at Jack, but the man Stevens had him hypnotized. All ears, he was blind to everything about him, even the woman, whose eyes seldom wandered from that young and handsome face. Until the man who was telling the thrilling tales had finished, she and all of us were as nothing in Jack's young life. It was almost dark when the two visitors rose and took their leave, the woman as she stepped through the cabin door inviting us all to their abode across the river. 'Come soon!' she said, her eyes on Jack as she spoke.

Naturally, much conversation followed the departure of the visitors. There was difference of opinion on the truth of Stevens' tales but no disagreement on the boldness of his female. Three days later Jack, in spite of Emil's warning that 'baby eyes in a woman of her age spells trouble', crossed the river to visit the 'old ferret-eyed man' and his buxom mistress. He was luckier at getting tales than making conquests. In their dirty cabin, Stevens outdid himself in piling horror upon horror while his 'Missus' played silent companion for hour on hour.

After a time, when Stevens apparently ran dry, the woman had her chance, and once more repeated her experience with the spiritualists and their golden prophecies to her, which rantings Stevens abruptly interrupted when, apropos of nothing, he suddenly asked, in the cold, even voice that seemed to be his regular mode of speech, 'Have you ever seen straight shooting, Mr London?' The small beady eyes looked straight and unwavering into Jack's, as, without waiting for an answer, he rose from the edge of the bed where he had been seated and took down a Winchester from its hook above the stove.

A reply being unnecessary, Jack too arose, buttoning up his mackinaw and drawing the fur on his cap about his ears as he stood up. Stevens without further words moved towards the door and the two men stepped out into the snow together.

'It surely was the quickest, straightest, surest shooting that I ever saw,' said Jack, near the end of his recital of the afternoon's experience, 'and it gave me an uncanny, shivery feeling. Nailing a piece of tin but little larger than his hand to a tree near the trail, without more ado he put ten bullets into it in what seemed only a second or two at the most. . . . That man,' ended Jack, 'has an eye as quick as thought and muscles as flexible as steel springs. He is afraid of nothing. Of nothing, I tell you, not even the truth as I have already remarked.'

With the possible exception of Stevens, the men London knew on Split-up Island were no more noble, adventurous, stimulating, or degraded than the average. Yet there was plenty of story material here for a future novelist with a good memory. As with all random groups, there were strong men and there were weaklings, there were novices right out of offices and experienced outdoorsmen who had followed gold before, there were homesick family men and there were restless wanderers who were happiest away from home. Most important, London was seeing a male society living under difficult conditions, exhibiting the heights of resourcefulness and companionship and the depths of weakness and hostility which emerge in such situations.

Not all the time that winter was spent swapping yarns around a hot stove. In so far as outdoor scenes outnumber indoor ones in London's Yukon fiction, one is inevitably faced with the question of how much Jack got away from the cabins and how much experience he had with the trail and dog-teams. There are hints but little more than hints in letters, autobiographical articles, and books. 'We [Harnish and London] travelled trail together a great deal that winter,' Jack affirmed in a letter.[8] 'I have travelled all day [at] . . . seventy-four degrees below zero,' he boasted in *The People of the Abyss*, his account of the London slums. 'I have . . . slept in the snow under two blankets when the spirit thermometer registered seventy-four degrees below zero,' he asserted in *The Road*. 'Never again can I run with the sled-dogs along the endless miles of Arctic trail,' he lamented in *John Barleycorn*. 'Sleeping out in cold weather

—the ice . . . —the utter fatigue [on trail]',[9] he jotted down in his notes for a lecture on the Klondike.

Fred Thompson said in 1937, when his memories of the Klondike were faulty in many ways, that he bought a sled and team of dogs and prospected up the creeks with London during the winter.[10] There is some evidence that Mason and London, conscious of the need for fresh meat to combat a companion's scurvy, made a trip into the woods for moose late in the winter, breaking trail for eighty miles in and back. Another version has Doc Harvey rather than Mason making the trip with London. (London's companion must have done the shooting, for London was no hunter and hated to kill animals or birds. For the rest of his life he was to be haunted by the memory of a beautiful bird, which he had shot for food, dying in the reddened snow.) And certainly London made short trips to nearby camps to borrow books and tobacco and to chat with anyone who wanted to talk. 'He stood ever ready,' writes Jensen, 'were it a foraging trip among the camps for reading matter, to give a helping hand on a woodsled or to undertake a two days' hike for a plug of tobacco. . . .'

How much experience he had with Northland dogs is a matter for conjecture. There were plenty of dogs around, and at least two of London's correspondents mention 'outside' dogs—Newfoundlands and St Bernards—who learned to hold their own with the Indian dogs on Split-up Island. One was 'Nig', Louis Savard's dog, who, according to Joan London, suggested one of Buck's companions in *The Call of the Wild*. Jensen noted: 'Then in our camp there was Nig, lovable Nig, the short-haired, outside dog. Some day, I shall write the story of Nig.' London also saw something of the highly efficient huskies, the Eskimo dogs, and he later wrote an undistinguished article about them for *Harper's Weekly*. The only hint of personal experience in it is the sentence: 'It is a very common sight to see these animals breaking the ice of a water-hole by rearing in the air and coming down upon it with their whole weight on their fore feet.'

London must have seen some of the best husky teams in the area, as the main trail from the outside world to the Klondike ran near the cabin where he lived. He may have thrilled when Andrew Flett, a Mackenzie River half-breed, brought the first small mail of the winter through in January with a four-dog outfit. It must have been a big day on the island when the Canadian Mounties with forty of 'the Queen's dogs' finally managed to bring in the first big batch of the tons of mail which had been so long stalled at the Little Salmon, up the Yukon. And perhaps he saw Pat Galvin taking the first government mail of the spring out to tidewater in March, making the trip from Dawson to Fort Selkirk, a distance of 175 miles, in the remarkable time of three and a half days. These are but a few of the dog outfits that passed the mouth of the Stewart that winter.

On trail, up the Yukon or Henderson or over the hills for moose, London gained impressions which he used later in his fiction. He knew the coming of snow when 'the sky drew still closer, sending down a crystal flight of frost—little geometric designs, perfect, evanescent as a breath, yet destined to exist till the returning sun had covered half its northern journey.'[11] Or, 'like another Crusoe', he came upon a track by the edge of the river, 'the faint tracery of a snowshoe rabbit on the delicate snow-crust.' Or he may have had his fire buried by a shower of snow from a spruce tree, like his protagonist in 'To Build a Fire'. Doubtless he had carried a lunch of biscuits and bacon warm against his chest, as he has a number of his characters do. And he surely helped (like Sitka Charley's companions in 'The Wisdom of the Trail') in pitching a fly at the end of a day's hike.

A light breath of air blew from the south, nipping the exposed portions of their bodies and driving the frost, in needles of fire,

[148]

through fur and flesh to the bones. So, when the fire had grown lusty and thawed a damp circle in the snow about it, Sitka Charley forced his reluctant comrades to lend a hand in pitching a fly. It was a primitive affair—merely a blanket, stretched parallel with the fire and to windward of it, at an angle of perhaps forty-five degrees. This shut out the chill wind, and threw the heat backward and down upon those who were to huddle in its shelter. Then a layer of green spruce boughs was spread, that their bodies might not come in contact with the snow.

Such a camp, primitive though it was, must have been welcome after a day of breaking trail with snowshoes, so poignantly described in 'The White Silence'. 'And of all heart-breaking labours, that of breaking trail is the worst. At every step the great webbed shoe sinks till the snow is level with the knee. Then up, straight up, the deviation of a fraction of an inch being a certain precursor of disaster, the snowshoe must be lifted till the surface is cleared; then forward, down, and the other foot is raised perpendicularly for the matter of half a yard. He who tries this for the first time, if haply he avoids bringing his shoes in dangerous propinquity and measures not his length on the treacherous footing, will give up exhausted at the end of a hundred yards.'

Most remembered of all was the feeling of isolation that came over one at the end of the day, with silence and whiteness making man small.

The afternoon wore on, and with the awe, born of the White Silence, the voiceless travellers bent to their work. Nature has many tricks wherewith she convinces man of his finity—the ceaseless flow of the tides, the fury of the storm, the shock of the earthquake, the long roll of heaven's artillery—but the most tremendous, the most stupefying of all, is the passive phase of the White Silence. All movement ceases, the sky clears, the heavens are as brass; the slightest whisper seems sacrilege, and man becomes timid, affrighted at the sound of his own voice. Sole speck of life journeying across the ghostly wastes of a dead world, he trembles at his audacity, realizes that his is a maggot's

[149]

life, nothing more. Strange thoughts arise unsummoned, and the mystery of all things strives for utterance.

A consideration of London's experience on the trail in the Split-up Island area cannot avoid the question as to whether he spent part of the winter in a cabin by his claim on the left fork of the Henderson. Yukon tradition today assumes this to be true; there is (in the little museum at White Horse) even a picture of the cabin in which he was supposed to have wintered. Moreover, an Alaskan weekly published an article about the cabin written by Katherine Patty, wife of Ernest N. Patty, president of the University of Alaska. Mr J. W. Hoggan, who was in charge of gold-dredging operations on the Henderson in 1954, told me in Dawson in that year that old-timers were sure London had used the cabin and later sent me pictures of the shelter, now in bad repair. Moreover, President Patty has written me that during the period he was in charge of gold dredging on the Henderson, before becoming president of the University of Alaska, he always assumed the cabin on the left fork was Jack London's. 'Mr Hoggan spent much of his youth in Dawson City and at Stewart City and environs, and it was he who pointed out the cabin on Henderson Creek which was supposed to have been occupied one winter by Jack London. Several of the other old timers around the Dawson area and also in the vicinity of Stewart City have mentioned that London spent at least part of a winter in this cabin on Henderson Creek. That is the basis for the story.'[12]

The question is a puzzling one, for there is nothing in the Jack London papers which supports the idea that London spent any time wintering on the Henderson. On the other hand, there is ample testimony that he spent all or most of the winter on Split-up Island, several miles up the Yukon from the mouth of the Henderson. As far as I can ascertain, London never spoke or wrote of staying in a cabin on the Henderson, a cabin which would be at least fifteen miles from the Stewart River camps. Yet the idea cannot wholly be dismissed on the basis of lack of evidence. The persistent tradition among old-timers on the matter carries considerable weight. There is no reason for associating London with the left fork of the Henderson unless he spent some time there, since the mere filing of a claim in the fall of 1897 would have made no lasting impression on inhabitants of the area, particularly as London was entirely unknown. Most telling of all is the curious fact that the action in one of London's best Yukon stories, 'To Build a Fire', concerns a man journeying alone in winter up the Henderson, planning to join his partners at a cabin or camp on the left fork of the Henderson. 'He was bound for the old claim on the left fork of Henderson Creek, where the boys were already. They had come over [from Dawson City] across the divide from the Indian Creek country, while he had come the roundabout way to take a look at the possibilities of getting out logs in the spring from the islands in the Yukon. He would be in to camp by six o'clock; a bit after dark, it was true, but the boys would be there, a fire would be going, and a hot supper would be ready.' President Patty points out that this man's winter journey up the Henderson was accurately described: 'London's description of the trail up Henderson Creek is so accurate and vivid that I found I could follow the story on the ground very vividly.' He also reports that tradition has it that some of the characters in *The Call of the Wild* were named after people who mined that winter on the Henderson. It certainly is not out of the question that London, alone or with a companion, trekked through the ice and snow to the site of his gold claim and may very well have camped in some deserted cabin in the area. That he spent any length of time there is highly unlikely, I believe.

The culmination of five months of unbalanced diet and insufficient exercise eventually brought to Jack London, as to a great many other Yukoners, an attack of the dreaded scurvy. Rarely proving fatal in the areas close to medical aid, it was at the same time the 'culminating misfortune' of the Klondike rush. Such a loathsome disorder that it was confused during the Middle Ages with leprosy and during modern times with gangrene, it was particularly disheartening because the much-desired remedies became more difficult to obtain even as the disease progressed. Its first symptom was lassitude, which, if not fought vigorously, automatically cut down on the exercise which was necessary to prevent the disorder from growing severe. Fresh meat, again, would help, and spruce tea and, best of all, raw potatoes (salad greens and lemons were, of course, not to be found). With the exception of spruce tea, these could be obtained only with considerable exertion and luck. London fortunately did not develop all of the concomitants of scurvy to an advanced degree; what could have happened is illustrated in Pierre Berton's description of the ravages of the disease: 'The legs go lame, the joints ache, the face becomes puffy, the flesh turns soft and pliable as dough, the skin becomes dry and harsh and mottled red, blue, and black. The gums swell and bleed, the teeth rattle in the head and eventually drop out. The breath becomes a stench, the face turns yellow or leaden, and the eyes sink into the skull until the victim, a living skeleton, expires.'

The several references to scurvy in London's Klondike fiction deal mostly with its early stages. In 'Argus' Tarwater fights off lassitude and stiffening joints, has the luck to get a moose, and survives, still perky in spite of his seventy years. A character in 'Finis' suffers first from lassitude and then, in spite of copious draughts of spruce tea, passes into the second stage of the disorder. 'At last the scurvy entered upon its next stage. The skin was unable longer to cast off the impurity of the blood, and the result was that the body began to swell. His ankles grew puffy, and the ache in them kept him awake long hours at night. Next, the swelling jumped to his knees, and the sum of his pain was more than doubled.' A more gruesome account is found in 'In a Far Country', in which two men, long isolated in the Porcupine cabin, suffer this disaster. 'In the absence of fresh vegetables and exercise, their blood became impoverished, and a loathsome, purplish rash crept over their bodies. Yet they refused to heed the warning. Next, their muscles and joints began to swell, the flesh turning black, while their mouths, gums, and lips took on the colour of rich cream.'

The evidence indicates that scurvy became a major problem with Jack London about the time of the spring thaw. It was then uncertain whether he would become seriously incapacitated before the river cleared of ice so that he could float down to Dawson. Already he could push dents into his skin that inelastically refused to go away; he was crippled so that he was bent almost double; his gums were swelling and separating from the teeth, threatening damage to the few good teeth he had remaining in his jaws.

The coming of spring was not an unmixed blessing. Scurvy was but one factor, albeit a very important one, in forcing a decision as to whether to remain in the Yukon and mine or to get out of the country and go home. All winter long that decision could be put off, and thousands of Klondikers had put it off; now the hour of decision was here, as the buds began to swell on the trees and the river groaned uneasily.

VI · THE BREAK-UP

'THE hard luck of other mining countries pales into insignificance before the hard luck of the North. And as for the hardship, it cannot be conveyed by printed page or word of mouth. No man may know who has not undergone.' When he made this comment in 'The Gold Hunters of the North', London was remembering the long pull over the Chilkoot, the windswept dash down the lakes and rapids, the cold cabins with the hot stoves, the bacon and beans and bread, the gold claim without the gold, the scurvy that puffed the flesh and ate at the bones, and the dark winter that seemed interminable. He was not speaking of the coming of spring, though even the coming of spring had its perilous side. Spring meant light, warmth, and a river to float on rather than a chaos of ice and snow to block men and discourage dogs. Spring came dramatically—late, and literally with a bang. By the end of the first week of May the Yukon was largely free of ice; the preceding fortnight saw an implacable winter vent its fury before it was spent. In the break-up, spring won but winter put up a good fight, using ice as its lethal weapon.

The hope for spring during the dead of the long winter is well-expressed in 'In a Far Country', that grim story of two misfits who spent the winter in an isolated cabin north of the Arctic Circle. 'The sun was coming back again. It would be with them tomorrow, and the next day, and the next. And it would stay longer every visit, and a time would come when it would ride their heaven day and night, never once dropping below the sky-line. There would be no night. The ice-locked winter would be broken; the winds would

[154]

blow and the forests answer; the land would bathe in the blessed sunshine, and life renew.'

An account of the coming of spring to Split-up Island is found in *A Daughter of the Snows*, London's first novel, which reflects extensively his still fresh memories of Yukon terrain and weather. In spite of the turgid rhetoric which so badly mars his early writing, particularly in this unsuccessful novel, something of the Yukon spring survives.

Spring, smiting with soft, warm hands, had come like a miracle, and now lingered for a dreamy spell before bursting into full-blown summer. The snow had left the bottoms and valleys and nestled only on the north slopes of the ice-scarred ridges. The glacial drip was already in evidence, and every creek in roaring spate. Each day the sun rose earlier and stayed later. It was now chill day by three o'clock and mellow twilight at nine. Soon a golden circle would be drawn around the sky, and deep midnight become as bright as high noon. The willows and aspens had long since budded, and were now decking themselves in liveries of fresh young green, and the sap was rising in the pines.

Mother nature had heaved her waking sigh and gone about her brief business. Crickets sang of nights in the stilly cabins, and in the sunshine mosquitoes crept from out hollow logs and snug crevices among the rocks—big, noisy, harmless fellows, that had procreated the year gone, lain frozen through the winter, and were now rejuvenated to buzz through swift senility to second death. All sorts of creeping, crawling, fluttering life came forth from the warming earth and hastened to mature, reproduce, and cease. Just a breath of balmy air, and then the long cold frost again—ah! they knew it well and lost no time. Sand martins were driving their ancient tunnels into the soft clay banks, and robins singing on the spruce-garbed islands. Overhead the woodpecker knocked insistently, and in the forest depths the partridge boom-boomed and strutted in virile glory.

But in all this nervous haste the Yukon took no part. For many a thousand miles it lay cold, unsmiling, dead. Wild fowl, driving up from the south in wind-jamming wedges, halted, looked vainly for open water, and quested dauntlessly on into the north. From bank to bank stretched the savage ice. Here and there the water burst through and flooded over, but in the chill nights froze solidly as ever. Tradition has it that of old time the Yukon lay unbroken through three long summers, and on the face of it there be traditions less easy of belief.

So summer waited for open water, and the tardy Yukon took to stretching of days and cracking its stiff joints. Now an air-hole ate into the ice, and ate and ate; or a fissure formed, and grew, and failed to freeze again. Then the ice ripped from the shore and uprose bodily a yard. But still the river was loth to loose its grip. It was a slow travail, and man, used to nursing nature with pigmy skill, able to burst waterspouts and harness waterfalls, could avail nothing against the billions of frigid tons which refused to run down the hill to Bering Sea. On Split-up Island all were ready for the break-up.

The suspense became almost unbearable. No longer was it possible to travel up or down the Yukon, up the Stewart, or even among the flat islands, for the river ice was now too treacherous to be trusted. At such a time whole parties could disappear through the ice, as did one described in *The Call of the Wild*, vanishing before the eyes of helpless onlookers. 'Mercedes's scream came to their ears. They saw Charles turn and make one step to run back, and then a whole section of ice give way and dogs and humans disappear. A yawning hole was all that was to be seen. The bottom had dropped out of the trail.'

As the men waited for the break-up, they prepared to depart for many destinations. Of course, no one planned to stay on Split-up Island, which might, in fact, be badly damaged by the ice jams. Those expecting to go upstream pitched their poling-boats and shod their poles with iron, and those bound down caulked their scows and barges and shaped spare sweeps with ax and drawknife. At long last, as described in *A Daughter of the Snows*, there was a hoarse rumble from upstream, a noise like a train crossing a trestle, followed by louder and closer rumbles during the day. The robins stopped their singing and the squirrels their chattering, while the human beings felt a tremor of fear at the terrific force of the powerful river.

Their concern was truly justified, for they lay just below the Stewart, whose ice had already broken and was slipping downstream under the Yukon ice, grinding, groaning, and then jamming. During the night the river rose eight feet, and the water began to run over the crust of old river ice. 'Much crackling and splitting were going on, and fissures leaping into life and multiplying in all directions.' All day long the noise increased, the river rose, and the islands trembled, for, caught in a jam, they would be scraped as if they were the bottom of a barrel.

The climax, reached the next day, was described through the eyes of the heroine; there is reason to believe that London saw it much as she did. 'The river was up. In the chill gray light she could see the ice rubbing softly against the very crest of the bank; it even topped it in places, and the huge cakes worked inshore many feet. A hundred yards out the white field merged into the dim dawn and the gray sky. Subdued splits and splutters whispered from out the obscureness, and a gentle grinding could be heard.' The water was, in fact, rising fast—at periods as fast as a foot an hour. The whole river was in movement now, with the surface ice moving slowly downstream. 'There was no commotion, no ear-splitting thunder, no splendid display of force; simply a silent flood of white, an orderly procession of tight-packed ice—packed so closely that not a drop of water was in evidence. It was there, somewhere, down underneath; but it had to be taken on faith.'

Gradually the ice picked up momentum, and a hum was heard which soon grew louder and more threatening. A jam began to develop in the mile-wide river at the bend just below Split-up Island where shallows and other islands lay in the path of the ice-torrent. 'A great cake had driven its nose into the bed of the river thirty feet below and was struggling to up-end. All the frigid flood behind crinkled and bent back like so much paper. Then the stalled cake

turned completely over and thrust its muddy nose skyward. But the squeeze caught it, while cake mounted cake
at its back, and its fifty feet of muck and gouge were
hurled into the air. It crashed upon the moving mass beneath, and flying fragments landed at the feet of those that
watched. Caught broadside in a chaos of pressures, it
crumbled into scattered pieces and disappeared.' As the
day grew brighter, the huge chunks pushed by the islands,
sometimes crashing against the shore, and once even reaching inshore like a huge hand, ripping three good-sized
trees out by the roots. Faster and faster the ice moved, and
down all its length the bank was being gashed and gouged,
while the island was 'jarring and shaking to its founda-
tions.' The action of the ice became fearful: 'Cake pressed
upon cake and shelved out of the water, out and up,
sliding and grinding and climbing, and still more cakes
from behind, till hillocks and mountains of ice upreared
and crashed among the trees.'

Then the jam downriver broke, and the water dropped
six feet in almost as many minutes, twenty feet in an hour.
This was followed by another jam, another flood. 'The ice
before them slowed down and came to rest. Then followed
the instant rise of the river. Up it came in a swift rush, as
though nothing short of the sky could stop it. As when
they were first awakened, the cakes rubbed and slid inshore over the crest of the bank, the muddy water creeping
in advance and marking the way.' The ice now stood
breast-high above the island like a wall. The islanders
climbed to the roofs of their cabins, fleeing the water but
fearing that the ice cakes would sweep away their perches
or even the island. Suddenly the jam broke again: 'The
whole river seemed to pick itself up and start down the
stream. With the increasing motion the ice-wall broke in
a hundred places, and from up and down the shore came
the rending and crashing of uprooted trees.' The river fell
rapidly again, down to its winter level, pounding its ice

glut steadily along. 'But in falling it had rimmed the shore with a twenty-foot wall of stranded floes. The great blocks were spilled inland among the thrown and standing trees and the slime-coated flowers and grasses like the titanic vomit of some Northland monster. The sun was not idle, and the steaming thaw washed the mud and foulness from the bergs till they blazed like heaped diamonds in the brightness, or shimmered opalescent-blue. Yet they were reared hazardously one on another, and ever and anon flashing towers and rainbow minarets crumbled thunderously into the flood.'

Three miles above the island, the first sizeable patch of clear water appeared, marvellous to behold after the granite winter. But the ice floes piled on the banks still offered a peril, as they broke and tottered and crashed into the river. The adventurers in *A Daughter of the Snows* finally succeeded in crossing the river in a Peterborough canoe in order to rescue a wounded man on the opposite bank. They did so by working upstream and then making their way diagonally across the current as they floated back towards the island. 'Stewart River was wide open, and they ascended it a quarter of a mile before they shot its mouth and continued up the Yukon. But when they were well abreast of the man on the opposite bank a new obstacle faced them. A mile above, a wreck of an island clung desperately to the river bed. Its tail dwindled to a sandspit which bisected the river as far down as the impassable bluffs. Further, a few hundred thousand tons of ice had grounded upon the spit and upreared a glittering ridge.' They landed at the foot of a jutting cake, climbed to its summit, and looked out over the dazzle. 'Floe was piled on floe in titanic confusion. Huge blocks topped and overtopped one another, only to serve as pedestals for great white masses, which blazed and scintillated in the sun like monstrous jewels. . . . Below, pastoral in its green quiet, lay Split-up Island.' One more great wall of ice came down

[159]

the river, crashed into trees and cabins, killed a couple of men, and then the river was open. Winter was over. The road to Dawson City and to the Bering Straits and to San Francisco was free and inviting.

Years later Jack London stated in an article in *The Reader* that he had intended to spend a second year in the vicinity of the Stewart River trying his luck at gold-hunting but that the spring thaw was so long delayed that his scurvy drove him out for medical help. It is probable that his scurvy did demand immediate attention, but it is also probable that his departure downstream for Dawson and the Outside was as certain as the break-up of the ice in the spring. He had 'seen the elephant' and there was little cause for him to linger.

It has also been asserted that the receipt in the spring mails of the news that John London had died in Oakland on the fourteenth of October, shortly after Jack reached the Klondike, played its part in making him decide to return home, and that he left the Yukon in order to help his mother, who would now need his aid more than ever. The evidence that he heard of the death while he was still in the North is, however, by no means conclusive, as testimony on the point is highly contradictory. For instance, he wrote in *John Barleycorn*, 'Back in California a year later, recovering from scurvy, I found that my father was dead. . . .' Moreover, mail service to Dawson was very undependable, and it is not certain that any letters were delivered during the winter to Split-up Island. Lack of luck with mining, the ravages of scurvy, and a need to get home may all have played their part. The central truth is that there was no good reason for staying on in the Klondike and the easiest way home was the best. In leaving, London was merely joining an exodus which was operating under a more reasonable force than the one which had brought him and his companions so far from home. Many gold-seekers were already eager to leave, and most of the rest would be out of the country within two years.

Getting down to Dawson was not so very difficult, in spite of scurvy. Doc Harvey and Jack London tore down their cabin, made a raft, and floated downstream with an additional raft of logs and driftwood in tow. Years later Doc Harvey was still telling how colourfully and explosively Jack cursed when he lost his sweep and nearly lost control of the rafts at one point on the journey. No doubt there were other profane moments as he worked with his crippled limbs, but the logs that had carried the two downstream were to bring them six hundred dollars in Dawson City, which was already beginning to bulge with newcomers looking for material to build cabins. And with his portion of the six hundred Jack London was able to get proper food and adequate medical attention for his scurvy.

As Jack London and Doc Harvey swung their cumbersome raft into the big eddy by the sawmill at Dawson, they found a community which was even less inviting than the shanty village Jack had known in the fall. After spending three and a half weeks in Dawson in May and early June, he was to bid it good-bye with no regrets, referring to it as 'dreary, desolate Dawson, built in a swamp, flooded to the second story, populated by dogs, mosquitoes, and goldseekers.'[1] The flood waters had mounted over the Yukon banks for several reasons. A sudden heat spell had melted the ice in upper tributaries like the White, the Pelican, and the Stewart, and in countless streams and pups like the Eldorado and the Henderson. The resulting high water could not rush to the ocean as the lower river was still clogged with ice floes, particularly near the mouth of the Porcupine at Fort Yukon. Moreover, the site of Dawson City was little more than a swamp; the Indians could remember paddling their canoes right up to the base of Moosehide hill during earlier floods. This year much of Dawson was awash. Even after the highest waters subsided, its main street was a sea of mud, with men and horses floundering together in the sticky ditch, like sinners in the slimy pockets of Dante's hell. Those who were lucky crossed the morass on boards thrown across the muck or stumbled along the high boardwalk that lined one side of the street.

And Dawson was crowded, for together with the flood of water had come a flood of cheechakos. Thousands of men who had camped during the winter beside the rivers and lakes between Dawson and Dyea floated into town, each determined to make his stake (or perhaps, like London, to get out as soon as possible downriver). A half-dozen canvas cities—Bennett, Lindeman, Sheep Camp, Dyea, Tagish, Teslin—had simply moved downstream to the mining centre. Tents were all over the place—in Dawson and Louse Town, across the Yukon in 'West Dawson', up the Klondike, even on the sides of the Moosehide Mountain. Though building was going on apace, the very circumstances which made it possible for London to turn a nice sum by floating a log raft down to Dawson made it impossible for him to rent a single room for less than a hundred dollars a month. He soon found Emil Jensen, however, and was immediately welcomed to his tent. There he remained for most of his stay. He may also have managed to get into St Mary's Hospital for a short period in order to obtain help for his scurvy.

St Mary's Hospital was run by the extraordinary Father William Judge, an ascetic Jesuit missionary with an El Greco face and a Henry Fielding heart, who had spent more than a dozen years in Alaska and was rapidly earning his title as 'The Saint of Dawson'. When Dawson was but a canvas and log village, he set about the tasks of building a church and a hospital. He was his own architect and his own workman. He did every job, including cooking for those who helped him. Naturally, the townspeople rallied round him, finding Father Judge an excellent conscience for them all. When his church burned, they passed the hat and collected enough for him to build a bigger one. Then they helped him raise $35,000 to complete the hospital, where he tried to cope with rheumatism, pneumonia, frostbite, and winter accidents. As might be expected, the hospital was jammed with scurvy cases before the winter of 1897–1898 was over.

Like everyone else who wrote about the Klondike, London mentioned the greathearted Jesuit in his fiction, telling of his story in *Burning Daylight* and having Smoke Bellew turn over to him a great percentage of his gambling profits. We know that London received help at the Catholic hospital in Dawson. Father Judge may have hospitalized him for a period. On the other hand, he may have done no more than give him curative foods. Charmian London testifies that Jack never ceased to enjoy telling how a raw potato and a lemon helped to straighten him out, and to reduce the puffiness of his skin and gums. He also based an entire episode of *Smoke Bellew* on the miraculous saving qualities of raw potatoes in a scurvy-ridden camp. He apparently recovered enough to earn miners' wages snagging logs floating down the Yukon and selling them to the lumber mill. He may also have collected firewood from the hills back of Dawson, a practice he described in a juvenile entitled 'Up the Slide'.

London's further activities and impressions during this short time in flooded Dawson can only be guessed at, with the emphases in his fiction furnishing some tenuous clues. For instance, in his stories he plays up the eagerness of the Klondikers to get news from the outside world, a world they had been almost completely shut off from for several months. Though the first boat from downriver bringing travellers and news from the Outside via the all-water route did not arrive until after London left Dawson, the overland invasion from Dyea and Skagway was, as we have seen, well under way. Ships were able to negotiate the comparatively warm inland passage long before the ice cleared in Bering Straits off St Michael, the point from which river boats started the long trip up the Yukon. To a land without telegraph or radio, the arrival of news was a very exciting event indeed. There is evidence that in May men were paying as much as fifteen dollars each for grease-streaked newspapers, long out of date, which had been hauled over the Chilkoot. London twice has characters in his writings make a bonanza by reading such a newspaper to crowds at the Opera House, charging so much a head for the privilege of listening. Such an action may or may not have happened when London was in Dawson; it is a recurring item in most books about the Klondike, and London may have been drawn to it as inevitably as he was to the howling of dogs at the aurora borealis.

More novel is his treatment of the behaviour of news-hungry Klondikers in 'At the Rainbow's End', a yarn about a mendacious gambler and confidence man named Montana Kid. Montana Kid, who had been plying his crooked trade in Dyea and Sheep Camp, managed to get through to Dawson on the last shaky ice before the break-up. Prevented by the Canadian Royal Mounties from capitalizing on his usual tricks, he decided in his resentment to fill law-abiding Dawson with lies in place of news. He manufactured tales of disaster concerning many a Yukon basin pioneer.

Dawson, always eager for news, beheld Montana Kid's sled heading down the Yukon, and went out on the ice to meet him. No, he hadn't any newspapers; didn't know whether Durrant was hanged yet, nor who had won the Thanksgiving game; hadn't heard whether the United States and Spain had gone to fighting; didn't know who Dreyfus was; but O'Brien? Hadn't they heard? O'Brien, why, he was drowned in the White Horse; Sitka Charley the only one of the party who escaped. Joe Ladue? Both legs frozen and amputated at the Five Fingers. And Jack Dalton? Blown up on the 'Sea Lion' with all hands. And Bettles? Wrecked on the 'Carthagina,' in Seymour Narrows—twenty survivors out of three hundred. And Swiftwater Bill? Gone through the rotten ice of Lake LeBarge with six Female members of the opera troupe he was convoying.

These and other whoppers told by Montana Kid were cleared up soon after he slipped out of town in the direction of Circle City, where he would be once more in American territory and be able to use his talents in a lucrative fashion. But the questions put to him throw some light on the topics discussed that May in Dawson. Word was beginning to come through of the sinking of the *Maine* and the war with Spain, but these far-reaching events were no more important to Dawson argonauts than the verdict on Durrant, the accused in the famous San Francisco murder case of 'the girl in the belfry'. Though the Dreyfus controversy was disturbing the civilized world, the result of the 'Thanksgiving game', the Big Game between Stanford and California, was probably more important to the cheechakos on the Yukon, the majority of whom hailed from the Pacific Coast. The reference to Swiftwater Bill (William Gates) reminds one that that flamboyant character was at this time making his way back from San Francisco with a group of dance girls for his dance hall and saloon called the Monte Carlo. There is some evidence that Jack London knew Gates, one of the most famous eccentrics of the Klondike rush, for Edward E. P. Morgan in *God's Loaded Dice* states that he often saw London and Swiftwater Bill together at the bars in Dawson City. If so, it was during the autumn, before Swiftwater made his famous trip out to the States to get more talent for his honky-tonk. The point is of some importance, for it is fairly certain that Swiftwater Bill is the original of Wild Water Charley, who plays a prominent role in *Smoke Bellew*.

The well-heeled Swiftwater Bill was inextricably mixed up with tales about the shortage of eggs and their consequent exorbitant prices. He is said to have cornered all the eggs in Dawson as a way of getting even with his current (but unfaithful) *inamorata*, Gussie Lamore, dance-hall queen. Ham and eggs was her favourite dish, a feast which almost repaid her for dancing all night. 'Now, we'll see if that damned tart will have any more fried eggs,'[2] he is reputed to have said. London alters and dresses up the yarn in telling it about Wild Water Charley in *Smoke Bellew*, and he also uses the shortage of eggs as his theme in 'The One Thousand Dozen'. It is true that the price of eggs in Dawson had risen to an outlandish figure during the winter; two hundred dozen brought in over the Chilkoot just before the break-up are said to have fetched $3,600. By the time London reached the gold town, however, there were little but wild stories left to indicate the egg shortage; once the river was open, so many consignments of eggs arrived in Dawson that the price dropped to a modest three dollars a dozen.

One of the few personal documents bearing on London's spring stay in Dawson is a letter he wrote to Charmian London five years later in which he mentions seeing a Klondike acquaintance on a trip down to Oakland from Glen Ellen. 'And who, of all people, do you suppose I ran into last evening, when Eliza and I was rummaging around the street-fair in Oakland?—Freda Moloof, fat and forty— doing the muscle dance in the Streets of Cairo! It was good to see her and talk over old times when I, all doubled up with scurvy, used to admire her dancing and her plucky spirit in Dawson. I've promised to send her a book I mentioned her in.'[3] London was certainly minimizing the situation when he spoke of mentioning her in a book. He had, in fact, given her a prominent part in 'The Wife of a King'; he had featured her in both the story and play versions of *Scorn of Women*, in which she was equipped with both a piano and a maid; and in time he was to pull her out of the river, an attempted suicide, in *Burning Daylight*. She was a most attractive, vibrant Greek dance girl in these stories, lovely to look at, witty to talk to, and motivated by a heart of gold. London must have cleaned her up a good deal for the part she had to play; the records show that she was too 'hot' even for a town where Dia-

Winter street scene, Dawson City

Up to the wheel hubs in mud on Front Street

Steamer leaving Dawson City for St. Michaels

mond-Tooth Gertie and Oregon Mare got away with murder. The Dawson police closed down her hootchie-kootchie act, though she tried to sound arty by billing herself as 'The Turkish Whirlwind Danseuse'.[4] They felt that her imitation of Little Egypt of the Columbian Exposition was too inflammatory for the citizenry. To London she must have had a notable *joie de vivre* which outweighed her coarser faults.

In a copy of *The God of His Fathers* (a book in which Freda is treated very kindly) in the London library, now owned by the Huntington Library, is pasted a letter from the dancer dated July 10, 1903, in which she says she has read London's story about her and admires it very much. She adds in her breezy fashion: 'I am here in Frisko now, I dont kno where I will go next, I have heard that Dawson is wide open igain, if so, I might go back.' It is signed 'Freada Moloof'. The letter still exudes a whiff from the Klondike world of 1898.

On the eighth of June, 1898, Jack London left Dawson and the Klondike on his long journey home. He was glad to get out of the jerry-built town where men sometimes went for their mail in canoes; where bartenders watered down bad whisky to a third of its strength and restaurant owners charged five dollars for a poor meal; where fleas and floozies vied with each other for the miners' attention; where there was no piped water and no sewer; and where dozens of new buildings were springing up in the mud to take care of the suckers moving down from the passes and lakes and up from Seattle and St Michael. He got out as soon as the river was navigable, in the cheapest and most reasonable way possible. There was no necessity for poling and paddling his way upstream to Bennett, crossing the Chilkoot, and getting a boat at Skagway or Dyea, nor was he interested in waiting another fortnight for a river steamer and paying $150 for deck passage to the Yukon mouth. Why else had he learned to sail a small boat?

Emigrant-built boats were being sold almost for the asking by those who needed them no longer, and negotiating the nearly two thousand miles of Yukon River down to its mouth on the Bering Straits was a snap for a seasoned sailor. Jack London let the river do his work and pay his passage while he took what he was later to call 'an Alaska vacation'. And he felt he had earned one.

VII · DOWNRIVER

IT WAS four o'clock in the afternoon when Jack London, 'big-bodied, big-hearted' John Thorson, and Charley Taylor, a Kentuckian who had studied at Annapolis, started down the Yukon in their small boat, 'home-made, weak-kneed, and leaky', heading for St Michael, the salt-water port near the mouth of the river. Their friends on the bank attempted a half-hearty cheer and 'filled the air with messages for those at home'. Most of them frankly expressed envy of those who were leaving.

The mood of the three companions was far from down-cast. As London put it, 'The three of us had sworn to make of this a pleasure trip, in which all labour was to be per-formed by gravitation, and all profit reaped by ourselves. And what a profit it was to us who had been accustomed to pack great loads on our backs or drag all day at the sleds for a paltry 25 or 30 miles. We now hunted, played cards, smoked, ate and slept, sure of our six miles an hour, of our 144 a day.' Though they seemed to be alone on the river, except for the passing steamboats headed toward the Klondike, they were in fact but one outfit in many making their way to the Outside by the easy method. Jeremiah Lynch, starting up the river from St Michael a month later, passed one hundred and eleven of these boats in one day. Most of the men who floated past Lynch were cheerful, but they advised almost uniformly against going to the Klon-dike. 'Bad news . . . cold winter, poor grub, no work, and hundreds starving. Go back,'[1] was the tenor of their warning.

The river which provided London and many another Klondiker such an effective escape route performs its function of reaching salt water in a most unusual way. It actually rises some fifteen miles from the Pacific Ocean and then wanders for some 2,500 miles across north-west Canada and Alaska before it finally reaches that same Pacific water. One of its headwaters is the trickle that runs out of Crater Lake, just across the Chilkoot from Dyea. From there it flows north-west through lakes and rapids, becoming a good-sized river before it reaches Dawson. After passing Dawson, it continues towards the Arctic regions for several hundred additional miles. As it approaches the Arctic Circle, it spreads out into countless channels across the dismal flats. Just after passing the Circle, where it is joined by one of its principal tributaries, the Porcupine, it makes a great bend and turns south-west, passing once more between hills and eventually losing itself in a great delta where its many mouths open upon the Bering Sea. When London floated down it, there were a few small settlements on its bank, some already well on the way to being ghost towns, others the beginnings of sizeable river villages. St Michael, the seaport which he eventually reached, eighty miles up the coast from the northernmost outlet of the Yukon delta, is now almost forgotten, but at that time it served as the navigational transfer point for all seaborne passengers and freight destined for the upper Yukon.

On the Tuesday that they left Dawson so late in the afternoon, London and his companions pulled up to shore in twilight at 10.00 p.m., planning to spend the rest of the night on land, where they could find adequate shelter from the light rain. They also needed to make final arrangements for their long downstream float. They had been so eager to get away from Dawson that they had not taken the time even to rig bunks in the boat. Now they proposed to turn their skiff into a living room-kitchen-bedroom combination in which they could travel in comparative comfort twenty-four hours a day.

By eleven the next morning they were ready to start

travelling in earnest. They had arranged to utilize the space in the small boat to its full capacity. The 'bed chamber', constructed of blankets laid on springy pine boughs, occupied the middle of the boat, just forward of the rower's bench. Jammed between the rower's bench and the seat for the steersman was the snug little kitchen, consisting principally of a Yukon stove, perhaps the most valued fixture of the Klondikers' outfits. These stoves were the miners' greatest friends. They consisted of one half of a sheet-iron barrel, together with a collapsible stovepipe, and were divided into two compartments, with the firebox in front and the oven in back. Almost every small boat on the Yukon from Lake Bennett to St Michael carried one of these stoves, and the sight of smoke puffing from its chimney meant that the travellers were cooking aboard. The woodpile in the bow of London's boat which fed the stove was frequently to require a river stop for replenishing.

Now that the boat was fit, it was time to come to an agreement about household and sailing tasks in the outfit. Taylor wanted to sleep at night and hated to get up early in the morning; it was accordingly decided that he would be cook, while Thorson, who seemed much more congenial and adaptable than the Kentuckian, shared the rotating watches with London. This was very much to London's liking, for he not only liked to sail a boat, he also enjoyed being awake during the long dusk of the twilight (it was never really dark in mid-June) when he could best observe, reflect, and plan undisturbed. He had now decided that the best way to salvage something from the Klondike experience was to use it as a subject for writing. For the first time during that long year he began to keep a diary, detailed and directed toward the articles and stories he wished to write. He was thinking of nature sketches for such journals as *Outing* and *Youth's Companion*, both of which he mentions in his notes. He seems also to have been contemplating fiction, particularly in connection with the Indians along the river. We know that he felt he was a good observer, with imagination; within the year he was to write to the San Francisco *Bulletin*, in support of an article he submitted: 'I have sailed and travelled quite extensively in other parts of the world and have learned to size [seize] upon that which is interesting, to grasp the true romance of things, and to understand the people I may be thrown amongst. I have just completed an article of 4,000 words, describing the trip from Dawson to St Michael in a row boat.'[2]

That article was to be turned down by the *Bulletin*, but a year later it was published by the Buffalo *Express*, under the title 'From Dawson to the Sea'. This article and the diary of the trip give us the most detailed record we have of any of London's Yukon experiences. The diary, particularly when weighed against the article, tells us much about his early writing tastes and techniques. Entries in the journal like, 'Small trees tender bark stripped, and stand stretching their bleached limbs heavenward, mute witnesses to the Ice God's wrath,' remind us that London was just beginning to write, while others like 'Sun rises like a ball of copper' give more promise. The finished article turned out to be crisp, vigorous, and thoroughly readable.

As the rough-hewn skiff, a boat so little cherished that it was apparently never named, floated rapidly between the hills and bluffs towards the Arctic Circle, it passed evidences of the changes brought on by the Klondike rush. These consisted principally of older camps which had been abandoned, knots of stranded Yukoners who had started for Dawson a year before and had been held up by winter ice, and riverboats making their way up the swollen, chocolate flood of the ice-freed river, straining to bring their cargoes into Dawson. The river still resembled in most of its length, however, the wilderness described by London in 'The Passing of Marcus O'Brien', in which, long before the discovery of gold in the Klondike, the settlers of Red Cow punished law-breakers by setting them adrift down the river in an open boat. 'The Yukon executed their decrees. Some two thousand miles below Red Cow the Yukon flowed into Bering Sea through a delta a hundred miles wide. Every mile of those two thousand miles was savage wilderness. It was true, where the Porcupine flowed into the Yukon inside the Arctic Circle there was a Hudson Bay Company trading post. But that was many hundreds of miles away. Also, it was rumoured that many hundreds of miles farther on there were missions. This last, however, was merely rumour; the men of Red Cow had never been there. They had entered the lone land by way of Chilcoot and the head-waters of the Yukon.'

The sight of abandoned towns reminded London and his companions that the wilderness could easily take over again. The second day out they passed Fortymile, once the thriving headquarters of the Alaska Commercial Company. It had been almost completely deserted since the day, two years before, when news of the discoveries of George Carmack, Skookum Jim, and Tagish Charley on the Klondike drained the town of its inhabitants, sourdoughs to a man. Equally deserted was nearby Fort Cudahy, started by the N.A.T. & T. in its attempt to cut in on the monopoly of the older Alaska Company. The next morning at 3.30 a.m., during London's watch, the boat crossed the line between Canadian and United States territory, and the wakened navigators went ashore at Eagle City, Alaska. With little gratitude toward a society which had given them safe shelter for the winter, they exulted at getting out from under British control. (Americans grumbled much about Canadian mining regulations and taxes.) 'What with the strange actions and heavy exactions of the North-west Territory officials, we gave vent to a most excessive enthusiasm on once more treading the soil of Uncle Sam.' They found the fifty inhabitants of Eagle City short of grub and waiting eagerly for upriver steamers to take them

[173]

to Dawson. In the meantime, even at four in the morning, they were bucking a faro layout. Much to London's amusement they halted the game in 'a vain attempt to sell us corner lots'.

For the same morning (Thursday, June 9, 1898), London's journal carries the entry: '9 a.m. Moose incident, excitement.'[3] This entry refers to the only attempt the voyagers made to get red meat on their way downriver. A good-sized moose had taken to the river in order to rid himself of mosquitoes. As London puts it dryly, he and his companions all sprang to arms; this did not amount to much, as their entire arsenal consisted of an axe and a rusty shotgun loaded with bird shot which usually misfired. When it did go off, one trigger persisted in firing both barrels. In proceeding to the attack Thorson rowed, Taylor manipulated the gun, and London flourished the axe and gave advice. A blast from the blunderbus failed to carry as far as the moose, but the noise drove him into the woods on the bank, with the Kentuckian in wild pursuit. London and Thorson, plagued even more than the moose by mosquitoes, at once started a smudge. The unlucky Taylor returned in a few minutes without any moose but so heavily bitten by mosquitoes that it took him a day to recover from the swellings.

The Yukon mosquito was, in fact, operating under optimum conditions in June at this latitude and was no pest to be laughed off easily. The predatory insects attacked in swarms as the party drifted through the dread Yukon flats, and the travellers were not to be rid of the insects before they reached salt water. The journal is dotted with phrases like: 'mosquitoes thick', 'Put up netting and fooled mosquitoes', 'Evening burned smudges', and 'Bite me through overalls and heavy underwear'. Neither smudges nor mosquito rigs solved the problem; there was nothing to do but suffer and curse. London granted that the mosquitoes were worthy opponents: 'Mosquitoes—One night badly bitten under netting—couldn't vouch for it but John watched them and said they rushed the netting in a body, one gang holding up the edge while a second gang crawled under. Charley swore that he has seen several of the larger ones pull the mesh apart and let a small one squeeze through. I have seen them with their proboscis bent and twisted after an assault on sheet iron stove.'

Provisioning, however, was no great problem for London and his friends. Doubtless they had some staples along, and they had money to buy ashore when they could find food for sale, though sometimes they found that none was available. Thus, at Circle City they tried to get sugar, butter, and milk without any luck. Elsewhere they fared better, and they could always trade with the Indians for provender. Their cuisine problem was not nearly as bad as that of the judge in 'The Passing of Marcus O'Brien', who was set adrift on the Yukon as a practical joke. He survived by living twenty-four days on a diet of the eggs of wild geese and ducks, which he ate raw before he reached Fort Yukon, cooked after he was able to get matches.

London and his companions were in no mood for such a limited fare. Though there were plenty of eggs obtainable with a little work, especially in the Yukon Flats, which London described as 'one of the greatest nesting grounds in the world, abounding with all kinds of ducks, brant, geese and swans', they preferred to obtain those they *had* to eat by barter with the Indians. 'While we did much of our own hunting, we did not waste time in gathering eggs or fishing, preferring to trade for such staples. However, we were usually disappointed in the eggs, not relishing the embryonic diet of ducks and geese which the natives so delight in.' Two weeks out of Dawson, London noted with relief, 'Above Andreasky had our last experience with eggs—large goose eggs.' And he added, in a more appreciative mood, 'Beautiful king salmon, cool, firm flesh fresh from icy Yukon.' The salmon they bought from the

Indians, finding that a cup or two of flour could be exchanged for a feast fit for kings.

They were 'indifferent' hunters, in both senses of the word. The moose having got away, the only game they bagged on the trip downriver was wild fowl. London does not say how many of these were brought down, but he implies that they were easy to get. In his article he played up their shooting as an attractive element in an idyllic picture. 'The hunting we could not forego. . . . Very pleasant it was during midnight lookouts, listening to the comrades snoring beneath the mosquito tent, drifting along the low-flooded banks, watching the sun above the northern horizon and dropping the startled wild fowl as they rose from the river.' It is a different story in his diary: 'Drifting the boat along the low, flooded banks during midnight watches while comrades snore under the mosquito netting, gun in hand, and dropping the wild fowl as they rise or metaphorically blessing the crazy gun for snapping. I will always recommend such a gun for amateurs. Always a reliable object at hand to lay bad markmanship to.'

Still, the diet was too limited for London's condition. It was not until the voyagers reached Anvik, more than halfway down the river, that he found some help for his scurvy. 'Hearty welcome we received. Given some fresh potatoes and a can of tomatoes for my scurvy, which has now almost entirely crippled me from my waist down. Right leg drawing up, can no longer straighten it, even in walking must put my whole weight on toes. These few raw potatoes and tomatoes are worth more to me at the present stage of the game than an Eldorado claim—What wots it, though a man gain illimitable wealth and lose his own life? How they got the potatoes? Quite a sacrifice on their part. White through and through.'

Even though the voyagers passed through long stretches of wilderness, they were not infrequently reminded that the outside world was rapidly penetrating the Yukon basin

[176]

because of the Klondike rush. One of the major evidences of this influx was the number of steamers they passed on a river which before this year had carried a minimum of navigation. On their first night out, the little *May West* chugged by, reputedly with six tons of whisky aboard, and Jack noted wistfully, 'Hot time in Dawson as a consequence.' The next morning at 2.00 a.m. the Alaska Commercial Company's *Victoria* passed London's party, loaded with hardware and apparently without a passenger aboard. Seven hours later it was the *Portus B. Weare*, pride of the rival N.A.T. & T., and it was clear that the movement to Dawson was well under way. It is true that none of these boats, nor the boats London was to see on the following days, had left salt water that spring. All had been frozen up for the winter; those which could manage it were making their belated trip upstream. Not until London and his friends reached the delta were they aware of passing their first boat from St Michael and the Outside, the *John J. Healey*. This is not surprising, for London notes in his diary that the first ocean vessel to get through the Bering Sea ice to St Michael arrived there on the sixteenth of June, eight days after he left Dawson.

It is not clear whether any downriver steamer overtook them as they floated down the Yukon. Certainly London mentions none in his diary. A passage in 'Flush of Gold', however, suggests that one passed them before they reached St Michael. 'You know what a Yukon steamboat is, but you can't guess what the *Golden Rocket* was when it left Dawson that June of 1898. She was a hummer. Being the first steamer out, she carried all the scurvy patients and hospital wrecks. Then she must have carried a couple of millions of Klondike dust and nuggets, to say nothing of a packed and jammed passenger list, deck passengers galore, and bucks and squaws and dogs without end. And she was loaded down to the guards with freight and baggage.'

Not all the steamers London saw on the river that summer were regular company boats, old or new, like the *Victoria* and the *Portus B. Weare*. Others bore more dramatic evidence of the unusual means by which Klondikers had tried to reach Dawson in the preceding fall. For instance, the ungainly *W. K. Merwin* was a seventeen-year-old stern-wheeler which looked like Noah's ark; it had been towed from Seattle to St Michael by a tug and was one of five vessels in the ill-assorted and ill-fated Eliza Anderson expedition. The *Merwin* had hardly entered the delta when the ice caught her, and her miserable passengers spent the winter near an Eskimo village. The little *May West*, first to reach Dawson with her whisky aboard, was built in the fall near St Michael by stranded argonauts, as was the *Seattle No. 1*, sometimes scornfully referred to as 'The Mukluk', after the Eskimos' footwear, because of its un-gainly appearance. Of the latter ramshackle craft London notes: '6.30 a.m.—passed Seattle No. One—*Mayor Woods* high and dry on a bar with 170 passengers. How they started last summer—frozen in 100 miles below Minook— etc. etc. Some discouraged and starting for St Michaels by our method.' Well they might have been discouraged. They were the survivors of a group of stampeders who had been led north by W. D. Wood, the former mayor of Seat-tle, who had resigned his position as soon as he had heard of the Klondike strike. Bad faith and bad luck had marred almost every day of the expedition's life; once the passengers had nearly lynched Wood, and later in the winter, after they had built their riverboat and got stuck in the ice, he had abandoned them to make his way back by foot to St Michael. They would eventually get off the bar where London saw them and make Dawson, where most of them would turn around and strike out for home. They were typical of the men who had been stranded along the Yukon in the winter of 1897–1898; it is estimated that of the eighteen hundred stampeders who took the all-water route in the fall, less than fifty reached Dawson before the freeze-up. Most of the rest survived, though a few perished, holed up at one spot or another along the river.

The two aspects of his river trip that figure largest in London's diary and article are his experiences in the flats where the Yukon made its big bend and his observations of the Indians along the lower river. He and his companions reached the Yukon Flats shortly after stopping for supplies and tobacco at Circle City, a nearly abandoned American mining settlement three hundred miles below Dawson and a short distance south of the Arctic Circle.

The Yukon Flats was an area dreaded because of its monotony, the absence of a clear channel, and the overpowering effect of heat and mosquitoes in the summertime. There was little to do here except drift and suffer; London accordingly increased the number of notes in his journal, hoping at least to get material for an article for some sportsman magazine. In 'From Dawson to the Sea' the results appeared.

The 'Flats' are a vast area of low country, extending for hundreds of miles in every direction, into which the Yukon plunges and is practically lost. The river, hitherto flowing between mountains, rugged and sternly outlined, with few islands on its breast, now begins its heartbreaking dividing and subdividing. One finds himself in a gigantic puzzle, consisting of thousands of miles of territory, and cut up into countless myriads of islands and channels. Men have been known to lose their way and wander for weeks in this perplexing maze. Great 'blind' sloughs, on every hand, lie in wait for the unwary. And most exasperating it is to labour several score of miles into one of these, to find that it is 'blind' (has no outlet) and that you must retrace your steps. The islands are well wooded, but, having also been well flooded, are miserable to land upon. . . . The adventurer who faces this soggy wilderness of water, mud, dank vegetation and mosquitoes, does not care to linger by the way, but, with an intense longing and exceeding haste, keeps to the largest channels and swiftest currents.

Still, the region was not without its unusual interests. Through all this portion of the trip it was hard to realize our

[179]

far-northerly latitude. It was more like an enchanted land, teeming with paradoxes. For instance, gasping for breath in the noonday heat and sweltering in a tropic temperature under Arctic skies or panting on top of the blankets at midnight, the red-disked sun poised like a ball of blood above the northern horizon. And the strange beauty and charm of the noonday nights—drifting, always drifting with the stream. Now slipping down a narrow channel where the wooded shores seem to meet overhead; now flashing into the open, where a thousand streams converge and form a mighty river; and again the diverging courses, the tiny channel, the overhanging forest, the smell of the land and the damp warmth of the vegetation. And above all, the hum of life, bursting into sudden gushes of song, slowly swelling to a great, dull roar of satisfaction or dying away into sweetly cadenced silence. Not a sound as we round the tail of a bar, disturbing a solitary crane from his ghostly reveries. A partridge drums in the forest, a moose lunges noisily as it takes to the water, and again silence. Then an owl hoots from some gloomy recess or a raven croaks gutturally overhead. Suddenly, the wild cry of a loon sweeps across a glassy stretch of river, awakening myriad answers. The robins open their full, rich throats and the woods burst into music. The tree squirrels play half a dozen instruments at once, while the blackbirds sing shrill choruses to the sharp-marked time of the woodpecker. The pure treble of the songbirds is accompanied by the steady boom boom of the partridge, till all is lost in the general pandemonium. Then the wild fowl of the swamp join the quick crescendo, and the finale, swelled to bursting, slowly dies away. A kildee calls timidly to its mate, and silence falls.

In the heart of the Yukon Flats, at the point where the Porcupine, the favourite explorer's route into the Yukon from the Mackenzie country, joined the mighty river before it plunged south-westerly back toward the hills, lay the old Hudson's Bay trading post of Fort Yukon. Here both of the Klondike trading companies had their big caches, caches which had played a prominent part during the winter shortage of food at Dawson. In Fort Yukon food had piled up when transportation had become so difficult that it could not be carried farther upriver. Much misunderstanding about the caches had risen in Dawson and the upper river camps, as is indicated by London's journal entries; at least once they had been broken open and plundered by indignant Klondikers who felt they had been unfairly deprived of sustenance. London noted: 'Capt. Ray defence of caches incident. Nearly all engaged have sledged to Circle City or otherwise disappeared.' London noted with interest that one of the caches was being emptied by Indians to fill the long-delayed *Bella*. The feverish activity, unusual among the natives, interested him and furnished material for a memorable scene in his article.

The steamer Bella, a year late, was industriously loading up. It was a peculiar scene of animation and excitement. Four o'clock in the morning, under the Arctic Circle, yet the sun was high in the heavens and it was already uncomfortably warm. It seemed more like some festival day at 3 o'clock in the afternoon. All was gaiety, noise and laughter. The bucks were skylarking or flirting with the maidens; the older squaws were gossiping in bunches, while the young ones shrank and giggled in the corners. The children played or squabbled, and the babies rolled in the muck with the tawny wolf-dogs. Fantastic forms, dimly outlined, flitted to and fro, surged together, eddied, parted, in the smoke-laden atmosphere. Only by nosing and poking about could one see anything; for the reeking smoke rose from untold smudges, bringing grief to the mosquito, tears to the soft eyes of the white men and giving to the whole affair a mysterious air of unreality.

Two more days of these surrealistic flats and the voyagers reached Minook, a very different sort of place from Fort Yukon or Circle City. Here was a spot with a future, brimming with emigrants who hoped that gold strikes which would put the Klondike in the shade would be made near at hand. The five hundred settlers had renamed the settlement Rampart City, for the river here flowed under tall bluffs. They had even made the famous old sourdough, Al Mayo, a sort of honorary mayor to give a bona fide flavour to the place. London noted in his journal that he had a talk with Captain Mayo, who had crossed the Chilkoot in 1873: 'Thirty years in [the] country.

Getting stout—very pleasant to converse with.' Mayo probably was the most genuine Alaska pioneer whom London met; he may have gained some useful impressions from him, but a few years later he was to remember him so dimly that he would refer to him as 'McQuestion', confusing him with Jack McQuesten, another famous old-timer who had been Mayo's partner in the upper Yukon. In Minook as elsewhere on the river London found the people avid for news—'war—football, Sharkey, Jeffries, Corbett, Fitz—did Durrant really hang—what did he say, etc.' It was constantly paradoxical to him that he and his two companions, coming downriver from the heart of the frozen north, thanks to the Chilkoot Pass should have more recent news than these people closer to the shipping lanes.

Another man whom London met at Minook (Rampart City) was Chestnut, an old acquaintance and a university man. This friend had a doleful tale to tell of hardships in coming up the river on the makeshift craft, *The Governor Stoneman*. It is unfortunate that London did not meet still another emigrant who had been stranded in Minook for the winter, Rex Beach, who was to rival London in stories of the Northland. According to Pierre Berton, Beach had been dumped at Rampart in the fall with 'a fur-lined sleeping-bag, a rifle, a dogskin suit, and a mandolin'.

For the next nine days London and his companions floated between hills, passing tributaries like the Tanana and the Koyokuk, up which prospectors were already searching for goldfields which would rival the Klondike. Perhaps the most famous of these strikes was to give rise to the town of Fairbanks. The voyagers were also entering the part of the Yukon basin which had figured in the Russian occupation, as some of the place-names testify. The perverse geography of Alaska continued to cause havoc with the weather as they moved farther south and west; whereas they had sweltered under the midnight sun above the Arctic Circle, they now shivered as they passed through mountainous country still covered with last winter's snow. They also saw many evidences of the ice jams and high water of the spring of 1898. The nearer they came to the mouth of the river, the more in evidence were the signs of the tremendous struggle between river and land which London had seen at Split-up Island.

It has been a very early spring, and the breaking of the Yukon was accompanied by the greatest high-water known for years. From Dawson to Kutlik, every station and long-established village had been severely flooded, many being washed away. If signs are to be trusted, the ice-run for the last 500 miles of river must have been terrific. Many portions of the mainland and whole islands had been swept clear of the timber which always clusters thickly in the bottoms. The large trees are up-rooted or literally gnawed in two by the grinding ice, while the smaller ones bend before it and are rubbed clean of bark, reminding one of well-picked bones on some endless battlefield.

In this section of the river, Jack London had the best opportunity to observe Indians that he had had during his stay in the North. As he was to write a good many stories about the natives, it is of importance to estimate just how much he observed of their behaviour. On his way into the Klondike the previous fall he had ridden in canoes paddled by short, heavy-set Tlingits, with 'Mongolian eyes and stringy mustaches', and he had seen the Dyea Indians earn an exorbitant tariff packing goods over the Chilkoot. Going downriver towards Dawson he had stopped at the Little Salmon to trade with 'a tough looking set' of Stick Indians. They wore large rings in their noses and little else; they smelled bad and at every turn they cheated. Doubtless at this stage London would have agreed with Kathryn Winslow's generalization in *Big Pan-out*: 'All the Yukon Indians were a grimy, louse-stuck bunch, reeking with rancid salmon and animal-hide clothing.' At Fort Selkirk he saw a more orderly settlement of Yukon River Indians, and he must have noted many of their cabins as he moved farther into the North-west Territory. Louse Town, or

Klondike City, still housed some Indians; the native village of Moosehide was just north of Dawson; and there must have been some families in the neighbourhood of Split-up Island, though doubtless most of the bucks were away for the winter hunting moose. Some of the dog trains that passed along the river trail were driven by natives or half-breeds like the fictional Sitka Charley, and pack-carrying Indians were a familiar sight in the area.

London must also have heard a great deal about the mating of Indian and white in an area where the white men so greatly outnumbered the white women. Legend has it that squaws were a dime a dozen. Many Klondikers insisted that, if you could stand the smell and the vermin, you could be downright comfortable. What interested him more than casual contacts, one judges from his stories, was the practice among the old-timers of marrying Indian women and treating them as social equals. Thus, as he points out in his fiction, it was the custom of the members of 'The Yukon Order of Pioneers', limited to sourdoughs who had come in before 1895, to bring their native wives to their big New Year's Eve ball in Dawson. According to Tappan Adney, who attended their party in 1897, they made a charming picture, with the women in their newest 'store clothes' and the plump babies, who played among the dancers' feet, most endearing in their little parkas. Naturally, the growth of Anglo-Saxon society after the rush created a new social atmosphere for these Indian wives and their white husbands to cope with.

It was the mixture—usually illicit—of Indian and white that interested London most as he floated down the river below Minook. The sight of this miscegenation constantly led the race-conscious London to speculate about the relative merits of the white and Indian stocks and the results arising from mixing them. As it was the fishing and trading season, he passed fairly large gatherings of Indians at the mouth of the Tanana and again a hundred miles farther down the Yukon; he also saw something of the Christianized natives at the missions maintained by the Episcopalians at Anvik and the Roman Catholics at Nulato and Holy Cross. His journal entries are studded with comments such as these: 'Ubiquitous Anglo Saxon White man from Sacramento living with them. . . .' 'Traces of white blood among the papooses everywhere apparent.'

Squaw three quarter breed with a white baby (girl) (2 yrs.) such as would delight any American mother. Unusual love she lavished upon it. An erstwhile sad expression. Talked good English.
'I have no man.'
'Father of child had deserted her.' Good natured joking, 'I'll be your man—I go St Michaels, come back plenty flour, bacon, blankets, clothes and grub of all kinds. You marry me.'
'Maybe I be married when you come back.'
'You marry Charlie?'
'No, I marry Indian, white man always leave Indian girl.'

This Indian girl might have been the original of El Soo of 'The Wit of Porportuk' or Madelaine of 'The Wife of a King', both of whom were attractive mission girls from Holy Cross who had run away with white men. That London felt stirred by the attractiveness of the Indian girls and moved by their plight is vividly apparent in the series of vignettes he eventually created from his journal and his memories.

Running the rapids below Minook, where the Yukon at some early period cut its way through the Rampart Mountains, we made Tanana station. Here also was the Indian town of Nuklukyeto, while several miles below stood the old mission of St James. Great was the merrymaking as we arrived in the wee, sma' hours. The spring run of salmon was expected at any moment, and [at] the mission, Tanana and Tozikakats were all assembled, to say nothing of the general sprinkling contributed by the several hundred miles of Yukon on either side the station. We landed our heavy craft amid the litter of flimsy bark canoes which lined the bank, and found ourselves in the great fishing camp. Picking our steps among the tents

[185]

and wading through the sprawling babies and fighting dogs, we made our way to a large log structure where a dance was in progress. After much pushing and shoving, we forced an entrance through the swarming children. The long, low room was literally packed with dancers. There was no light, no ventilation, save through the crowded doorway, and, in the semi-darkness, strapping bucks and wild-eyed squaws sweated, howled and revelled in a dance which defies description. With the peculiar elation of the traveller who scales the virgin peak, we prepared to enjoy the novelty of the situation; but, imagine our disappointment on discovering that even here, 1,000 miles beyond the uttermost bounds of civilization, the adventurous white man already had penetrated. In the crowded room, dizzy with heat and the smell of bodies, we at last discerned the fair bronzed skin, the blue eyes, the blond mustache of the ubiquitous Anglo-Saxon. A glance demonstrated how thoroughly at home he was.

One hundred miles below Nuklukyeto, our midnight watch was beguiled by a wild chant, which rose and fell uncannily as it floated across the water. An hour later we rounded a bend and landed at a fishing village, so engrossed in its religious rites that our arrival was unnoted. Climbing the bank, we came full upon the weird scene. It brought us back to the orgies of the cavemen and more closely in touch with our common ancestor, probably arboreal, which Mr Darwin has so fittingly described. Several score of bucks were giving tongue to unwritten music, evidently born when the world was very young, and still apulse with the spirit of primeval man. Urged on by the chief medicine man, the women had abandoned themselves to the religious ecstasy, their raven hair unbound and falling to their hips, while their bodies were swaying and undulating to the swing of the song.

Nor was the ubiquitous Anglo-Saxon absent; for there, between the flaps of a tent, with a nursing child at the breast, we found him staring at us through the eyes of a half-caste woman. Slender-formed, with her Caucasian features and delicate oval face, she seemed as a pearl cast among swine. Lafcadio Hearn had dwelt with great pathos upon the Japanese half-caste; but how much harder the lot of the Yukon Indian half-breed. It is a life of severest toil, coupled with extreme privation and misery. . . .

In the course of trading with the natives, one soon learns much of the sickness and misery with which their lives are girt.

[186]

From one end of the land to the other, the piteous cry for medicine goes up. In the most cursory intercourse, one stumbles upon pathetic little keynotes that serve as inklings to the solemn chords of heartache with which their lives vibrate. At the mouth of the Koyokuk, I wandered into a summer camp in the hope of picking up some specimens of beadwork. At one of the neatest tents of the encampment, I opened negotiations with a young half-breed woman for some exceptionally fine work, and, when I went away, I was filled with wonder at the bargain she had got. Nor was I at loss, for, before me, on a bearskin mat, had played a most beautiful child—flaxen-haired, blue-eyed and rosy-complexioned, a typical Saxon lass. As often as I stiffened the lines of the barter in accordance with Indian trading, I softened as I rescued my sheath-knife or tobacco pouch from the baby fingers, or gazed into the blue eyes of the white father. And, when I hardened my heart for the articles of the final agreement, the mother said, 'O you big white man, why so hard? I do much work. Oh, so much work, I get fish and moose and flour for two, and no man to help me.'

I pointed to the child with a glance of interrogation, and she answered, 'He go way—one—two—three years now.'

And the bargain she made caused great envy among her dark sisters huddled in the doorway.

London's ultimate comment on the Indians, modified but not seriously impaired by his sympathy for their suffering, is found in a journal note. 'Indian seems unable to comprehend the fact that he can never get the better of the white man.' Even though he might note the degeneracy of some northern settlers, like the squaw man at Bill Moore's near Kutlik who had lost all ambition and had sunk to the squalor of the natives, he thrilled constantly in the manifest destiny of the Anglo-Saxon, the pervasive strength of the blond conqueror. With not a jot less enthusiasm for the supremacy of his race than had Kipling, he gave the Indian sympathy but little genuine understanding.

Opinionated also was his judgement of the missions on the river, as might be expected from one who had already proclaimed himself 'a materialistic monist'. He was amused when the Episcopalian missionary at Anvik pressed them to stop over to spend 'at least one Christian Sunday'; he noted, after bartering a pack of cards for a crucifix with some Malemutes near Icogmute, that the conversion of some of the Indians was only skin-deep ('Several of my souvenirs will testify to the readiness with which they will trade a crucifix for an old pack of cards,' he later wrote); and he concluded that the Roman Catholics were more successful in influencing the natives than the Protestants because the former, in their emphasis on ritual, offered the Indians something that was both mystical (a pejorative word with London) and irrational. Even this appeal had proved ephemeral with the Russian Catholics, however. At Icogmute on the lower river, where he saw the Russian mission which had once been the headquarters of Russian missionary activities in North America, he found only sleepiness, 'a very miserable place', with only one Russian left to carry on.

Yet at Nulato he was moved by the Catholic service: 'Shrill chanting of Indian women combining with the basses of the father and brother—weird effect', he jotted down. Later he remembered with approval a Nulato missionary named Father Monroe, 'a cultured, and as rumour puts it, a very wealthy Frenchman', whose delicate features had struck him at the time. The talented Monroe, who had decided to devote his life to caring for savages, had spent five years at Nulato without losing any of his zeal. And when London floated around the bend and caught sight of Holy Cross mission, the headquarters of Roman Catholic activity in Alaska, he felt pangs of homesickness. 'Grassy hills, etc., fences, farm, etc. . . . Indian girls play-ing in school yard. Homelike.' These Indians were indus-trious, as the ones at Fort Yukon had been; they were busily making bark ropes, nets, and other objects. London had to admit that 'The Indians are always more energetic, thrifty, and of better appearance at the missions than elsewhere.'

Now that they had entered on the last leg of their journey, the passage of the vast wastes of the Yukon delta where the entering of the wrong slough might mean hours or days lost and perhaps lives thrown away, they saw no more white men and only natives of a very inferior nature. These were Malemutes, 'a sort of mongrel cross of Thlinket [sic] and Esquimau', whose unprogressive nature he was to use as the theme of 'Nam-Bok the Unveracious'. In his article he was to describe them as miserable folk. 'Poverty-stricken, with little energy and no ambition, they have not furnished much inducement to the white traders; hence, they continue to exist on a straight fish and meat diet, washed down with incalculable quantities of vile-smelling seal oil. Their houses are merely holes in the ground, shored with driftwood timbers. In the centre of this they build an open fire, the smoke of which escapes through a venthole in the roof. In the winter time, the men, women and children crowd into these burrows like sardines. The sanitary, social and moral conditions may be conjectured.' London found that the one thing of interest about the Malemutes was their fantastically decorated graveyards, dotted with totem poles and 'rain sheds', on which designs had been painted with soot and seal oil.

After threading their way one hundred and twenty-six miles through the Apkon channel, northernmost outlet of the delta, passing several deserted fishing villages, the lonesome trading station at Hamilton, and the dismal hovels of Bill Moore, the squaw man, they at last felt the pulse of the tide. When they reached the open sea at Kutlik, they gave vent to 'much foolish enthusiasm', deeming themselves to be nearly home, but they discovered that they still had eighty miles to go, eighty miles of rowing and sailing up the coast past Point Romanoff and through the canal to St Michael. It took them most of five days, with dirty weather for the final hours of their shallow-water voyage. 'Our last taste of Bering Sea was a fitting close to the trip. Midnight found us wallowing in the sea, a rocky coast to leeward and a dirty sky to windward, with splutters of rain and wind squalls which soon developed into a gale. Removing the sprit and bagging the after-leech, we shortened to storm canvas and ran before it, reaching the harbor of St Michael just 21 days from the time we cast off the lines at Dawson.'

One final adventure took place before bleak St Michael was reached. Soon after leaving Kutlik, off Point Roman-off, they picked up a Jesuit priest who was having a rough time of it in a three-hatch kayak, or as the Russians called it, a bidarka. 'Take him aboard—how unlike a father on first sight. Sits alongside of me while steering—ask him if smoke objectionable—on contrary pipe in bidarka. So all light up and are content.' London soon found that the priest's name was Father Roubeau and that he was a really inspiring character. 'He was an illustration of the many strange types to be found in the Northland,' London wrote in 'From Dawson to the Sea'. 'An Italian by blood, a Frenchman by birth, a Spaniard by education, and an American by residence, he was a marvellous scholar and his whole life was one continuous romance; but sworn to the oaths of his order, he had sacrificed twelve prime years of his life in bleak Alaska, and in all things, even to reducing the Innuit language to a grammar, was happy.'

London's journal plays up his absorbing conversation and his abrupt departure. '5 p.m. Father bids good-bye and goes on. Never heard of again—lost in some back slough most likely.' Not lost in reality. His 'tanned skin, brilliant black eyes . . . vivid play of emotion so different from the sterner, colder Anglo-Saxon'; his fur cap, coarse blue shirt, and mukluk boots; his zest for action and his frontier resourcefulness were all to be re-created when he appeared under his own name as one of the principal characters in *The Son of the Wolf*.

St Michael, with its depressing mud flats, its grey ware-houses, its rusty Russian cannon, and its pervasive smell of dead fish, was hardly the spot to go on a spree. Jack and his friends seemed rather to emerge from a dream, discovering that even their record of days spent floating down the river was uncertain. Suddenly Thursday, June 30, became Wednesday, June 28, and life seemed better under control. The last entry in the journal reads: 'Leave St Michaels— unregrettable moment.' Ever quick to seize an opportunity, London had obtained a job passing coal on a steamer pushing south to warmer waters. Somewhere between St Michael and Victoria, he burned himself so badly that he had to give up the job. Perhaps his scurvy crippled or weakened him enough to cause the accident. Or perhaps the explanation is found in a passage in *John Barleycorn*. 'I remember passing coal on an ocean steamer through eight days of hell during which time we coal-passers were kept to the job by being fed whisky. We toiled half drunk all the time. And without the whisky we could not have passed the coal.' Such conditions might easily have led to a serious burn. He travelled steerage from British Columbia to San Francisco, arriving home early in August.

Many years later he was to write in *John Barleycorn*: 'I brought nothing back from the Klondike but my scurvy.' Even in a narrow sense, this was not true; on August 6 he sold to Treager's Loan Office in Oakland gold dust from the Klondike for the sum of $4.50. In a larger sense the statement was wholly misleading; he never was to make a better investment than his winter in the North. In less than two years his first book, *The Son of the Wolf*, was to be published, and from the date of its publication his success as a writer was to be assured. Just as Herman Melville was to find that a whaling ship was his Yale College, and his Harvard, Jack London was to discover that his adventure on the Yukon was his entrance to a wider world. At twenty-four years of age, when he normally would have been graduating from the University, he had got his foot on the ladder of fame. And it was the Klondike that put him there.

[191]

VIII · BONANZA

———————

THE story of how Jack London became a successful writer is one which features talent, perseverance, and good luck. It is as difficult to weigh all the ingredients today as it was for London to do so. He told that story in many ways, each time assuming his success was a sort of minor miracle. For instance, in *John Barleycorn* he wrote:

Critics have complained about the swift education one of my characters, Martin Eden, achieved. In three years, from a sailor with a common school education, I made a successful writer of him. The critics say this is impossible. Yet I was Martin Eden. At the end of three working years, two of which were spent in high school and the university and one spent at writing, and all three in studying immensely and intensely, I was publishing stories in magazines such as the *Atlantic Monthly*, was correcting proofs of my first book (issued by Houghton Mifflin Co.), was selling sociological articles to *Cosmopolitan* and *McClure's*, had declined an associate editorship proffered me by telegraph from New York City, and was getting ready to marry.

London was mistaken in assuming that his success was a miracle unless one is to assume that all writing successes are miracles; the annals of literature are full of examples of men and women who developed very rapidly as writers. But that London's progress was dramatic cannot be denied. Though his story holds much in common with that of many other writers, in some ways it is highly individual, almost unique. A careful examination of the five years which followed his return from the Klondike should throw light on his progress if it does not and cannot wholly explain it. These five years ended with the publication in the summer of 1903 of *The Call of the Wild*; its appearance marked both the climax and the end of a phase of London's writing career.

One attempts this record and appraisal with the knowledge that London's best account of his struggles, his failures, and his successes in *Martin Eden*, less fictionalized than one might suspect, cannot be improved on, though it can be corrected and amended. It certainly cannot be improved through paraphrase and summary. The story of a questing mind, eager to understand, eager to be creative, is so dramatic in the novel that its spirit almost inevitably captures the loyalties of young readers today, who think timidly of doing what London did boldly. His formula is particularly appealing, for he says time after time that it is not inspiration but determination and hard work that bring success in writing, and then goes on to illustrate his thesis.

His belief that determination and hard work lay at the base of his success was often expressed in letters to young people trying to be writers. 'A strong will can accomplish anything,' he wrote to an aspiring writer. 'I believe you to be possessed of the same—why not form the habit of studying? There is no such thing as inspiration, and very little of genius. Dig, blooming under opportunity, results in what appears to be the former, and certainly makes possible the development of what original modicum of the latter which one may possess.'[1] Again, in an article in *The Editor* entitled 'Getting into Print', London advised the beginner: 'Don't loaf and invite inspiration; light out after it with a club, and if you don't get it you will nonetheless get something that looks remarkably like it.'

To dig, to battle in a confident attempt to master even the most difficult tasks, was certainly one of London's salient character traits. His picture of himself as the self-made man, the jack-of-all-trades, the resourceful frontiersman furthered his belief that he could do anything if he tried hard enough. To his sweetheart he wrote: 'If I die I

N　　　　　　　[193]

shall die hard, fighting to the last, and hell shall receive no fitter inmate than myself . . . . if I were a woman I would prostitute myself to all men but that I would succeed—in short, I will.'[2] In a more characteristically buoyant mood he later wrote to a friend: 'I may sometimes appear impatient at nothing at all, and all that; but this everybody who has had a chance to know me well [sic] have noticed: things come my way even though they take years; no one sways me, save in little things of the moment; I am not stubborn but I swing to my purpose as steadily as the needle to the pole; delay, evade, oppose secretly or openly, it's all immaterial, the thing comes my way.'[3]

Hard work with a grim determination to succeed does not tell the whole story, however. London was not by any means poorly equipped to go into the field of writing as he prepared to capitalize on his Klondike experiences. Ever since he had placed his sailing article with the *Call* when he was seventeen, he had been trying to learn to write in his odd moments. He had even spent a considerable period doing little else, the spring before he went to the Klondike. Since early childhood he had been an avid reader and was not by any means ungifted in appreciating and analysing good writing. It is true that he had had but little schooling, though more than Mark Twain or Herman Melville or even William Dean Howells had had, but he had benefited by taking both his high school and college work late, after roughing it had taught him to look more intelligently for what he wanted.

As any professional writer could have told him, schooling would always be a weak substitute for settling down to writing, yet it would help in the long run, if for no other reason than to give confidence. Though later he sometimes deprecated his schooling, he by no means regretted it at the time he was first publishing. It is to be noted that in the passage from *John Barleycorn* quoted at the beginning of this chapter, London made it clear that he had attended both high school and college in order to prepare himself to write. By the Christmas after he returned from the Klondike, he felt that he really was getting somewhere and that the hard-earned exposure to secondary school and college was paying off: 'I have learned more in the past three months than in all my High School and College; yet, of course, they were necessary from a preparatory standpoint.'⁴ But perhaps his greatest asset in becoming a writer was his extensive experience with occupations that could furnish subject matter for interesting articles, stories, and novels.

Like Martin Eden, Jack London found that the first and perhaps the greatest difficulty in gambling for success in a writing career was to keep himself alive while he was writing and seeking a market for his output. Some way or other he had to find time and energy to write. One way was to take a full-time job, save up some money, and then quit the job and write frantically. That would be the Belmont laundry experience over again. The other was to get some sort of part-time work and supplement his wages with all the additional resources available to him, such as pawning his belongings, in the hope that he could keep going long enough to earn recognition. It appears that it was largely luck in the character of a national depression which prevented him from following the first course. Because he could not find a full-time job, he resorted to the second and better way.

In *John Barleycorn* he ascribes his difficulty in finding work to hard times. 'Work of any sort was difficult to get. And work of any sort was what I had to take, for I was still an unskilled labourer. . . . Unskilled labour is the first to feel the slackness of hard times, and I had no trades save those of sailor and laundryman. With my new responsibilities I didn't dare go to sea, and I failed to find a job at laundrying. I failed to find a job at anything. . . . Yet I was a bargain in the labour market. I was twenty-two

[195]

years old, weighed one hundred and sixty-five pounds stripped, every pound of which was excellent for toil; and the last traces of my scurvy were vanishing before a treatment of potatoes chewed raw.'

He advertised in three newspapers and registered with five employment agencies. He persuaded all his friends to look out for jobs for him. Many occupations were closed to him because he belonged to no union, but he went the rounds to search for work as 'wop, lumper, or roustabout'. He offered to model for art students but found the market glutted. He hoped in vain to be a companion to some elderly invalid and even contemplated becoming a sewing-machine agent. As he was waiting for something to turn up, he joined a short-lived gold rush to the Sierras, panning no more dust there than he had in the Klondike. Finally he took the Civil Service examinations for a position in the postal service which would pay sixty-five dollars a month. He was placed at the top of the list and was told to wait until a position opened up for him. By the time notice arrived that he indeed was to have a job with the postal service, he had shifted his bets to the alternative of part-time work and the squeezing of pennies. Having spent his period of unemployment writing, he turned down the offer in order to continue, sensing that he was on the right track.

Jack's mother was very much in favour of this decision, according to Joan London, and at this time did everything she could to help Jack make something of himself as a writer. It is true that John London had left some debts, and it is also true that Flora London had given another hostage to fortune by taking charge of one of John London's grandchildren, whose mother was not in a position to care for him. Thus, there were three mouths to feed. Still, she had a small pension as the widow of a Civil War veteran, and she was being more than usually successful in getting piano pupils. She could also do fine needlework. Joan London writes: 'It was Flora who persuaded him to abandon his frenzied job hunting until he heard the results of the examination some weeks hence. She was making enough to feed them, the pension paid the rent, and other matters could wait. Jack compromised by doing odd jobs at intervals with which to buy tobacco, stamps and manuscript paper, and to rent a typewriter, and sat down at the old kitchen table in his tiny bedroom to write.' Of course, there were many expenses Flora did not include in her optimistic budget. One was the dentist. In May, 1900, Jack London wrote an old Klondike friend that he had had three sets of teeth since returning home and had broken two. 'Makes quite a difference in a fellow, a set of teeth,'[5] he confessed.

The odd jobs included mowing lawns and trimming hedges; washing windows; taking up carpets, beating them, and re-laying them; and similar tasks. Sometimes things went well, with plenty to eat in the house; at other times the pickings were slim, the fare featuring such items as pea soup, potatoes, beans, rice, and an occasional piece of round steak. Credit at the three neighbourhood grocers was stretched to the limit (about five dollars each), but the rent was paid regularly and conscientiously, for the landlady was a poor widow. When things got bad, Jack made one of his recurring trips to the pawnshop; the cancelled tickets still remain to give some idea how often he visited his 'uncle'. 'The situation was desperate. I pawned my watch, my bicycle, and a mackintosh of which my father had been very proud and which he had left to me.'[6] Sometimes he held manuscripts because he did not have the stamps to mail them; sometimes he went no further than a rough draft, having no paper on which to type the finished tale. 'Am out of paper', he wrote to Ted Applegarth in far from a disconsolate mood, 'so have not typed it yet. Sent off 10 mss. and have 9 more ready to go as soon as I get stamps. Revised 3 more yesterday and today, and expect to revise another 5,000-word one tonight.'[7] Later he had

[197]

to return the typewriter to the shop where he rented it, not having enough money to meet the monthly payments. This deprivation really hurt him. Such was the situation he contemplated at Christmas, the loneliest Christmas he had ever lived through, he complained to Mabel Applegarth (the bicycle was in pawn so that he could not ride down to College Park to see her).

It is a tribute to London's perseverance, and to Flora's pluck, that he stuck it out. There was little enough encouragement at the beginning. During the fall, the article on the trip down the Yukon, which Jack felt certainly would earn at least ten dollars, was returned by the San Francisco *Bulletin* with the comment: 'Interest in Alaska has subsided in an amazing degree. Then again so much has been written that I do not think it would pay us to buy your story.'[8] He abandoned the Klondike for the moment and, drawing on some of his youthful escapades, wrote a 21,000-word serial for *Youth's Companion*. 'I turned it out and typed it in seven days. I fancy that was what was the matter with it, for it came back.'[9] He dug out the essays, poems, and stories he had written before going to the Klondike and once more started them on their rounds; as his fund for postage stamps decreased, the pile of rejection slips impaled on a stiff wire mounted higher and higher. (Tradition has it that it finally reached a height of five feet!) He once sold an item three thousand words long for a dollar and a half. He even entered a contest put on by the Fifth Ward Republican Club for campaign articles and poems to be used in the fall elections; he stated the Republican cause so effectively that he won first prize for prose and second prize for verse. The next spring he was still trying to collect the prize money by suing for it.

Three months after he started his intensive writing programme he sold his first story. This was 'To the Man on Trail', a Klondike tale which was to be included in his first book, *The Son of the Wolf*. Though the *Overland*

[198]

Monthly was very pleased with the yarn and asked for more like it, they were able to pay only five dollars, a figure far beneath the sum London had assumed he would get for a good story. Even the five dollars was but a promise, and he had to make a personal visit to the editorial offices in San Francisco in order to collect it. Fortunately, on almost the same day that the acceptance letter arrived from the *Overland Monthly*, a cheque for forty dollars suddenly appeared from the *Black Cat*, which had bought 'A Thousand Deaths', written by London two years before. He rightly considered the latter a piece of hackwork and was bowled over at having it accepted. Now the grocers could be paid and the bicycle taken out of hock. Most important of all, two acceptances were just enough to keep his hopes up.

Though the *Overland Monthly* bought seven more of London's Klondike tales in 1898, raising their price to $7.50 a story and featuring the series as the work of a very promising local writer, the income with which London had to work was by no means extensive. The correspondence and figures available indicate that, during the fifteen months between August, 1898, when he returned from the Klondike and late October, 1899, when he received his first sizeable cheque, $120 from the *Atlantic Monthly* for 'An Odyssey of the North', he could not have made more than $150 at the most from his writing. That was an average of ten dollars a month, a sum which certainly couldn't have covered much more than tobacco, paper, stamps, and typewriter rental.

Odd jobs, short rations, and pawning were not the only resources on which the beginning writer could draw. During these fifteen months and for several years to follow, Jack London attempted to meet 'the landlady and stamp problem' by turning out a certain amount of 'hack'. Under this heading he included everything which he did not feel was 'serious' writing. To his editor at Houghton

[199]

Mifflin he spoke of hack as ranging 'from a comic joke or triolet to pseudo-scientific disquisitions upon things about which I know nothing.'[10] In spite of his advice to beginners in *The Writer*, composed in 1900, to avoid above everything else becoming a hack writer, 'a gibbering spectre of a once robust manhood', he was willing to take his chances by writing sudsy villanelles, turgid science fiction, light-hearted juveniles, and even jokes: 'A good joke will sell quicker than a good poem, and, measured in sweat and blood, will bring better remuneration.'

In 1901 London agreed to write feature articles for the San Francisco *Examiner* on such subjects as the *Schuetzenfest*, 'Girl-Fighting Duel', and the Ruhling-Jeffries prize-fight. The following year, however, he was explaining to George Brett of the Macmillan Company that he wanted very much to gain sufficient financial security so that he would not have 'to dissipate my energy on all kinds of hack'.[11] In 'Getting into Print' he thanked *The Editor* for having shown him where he might sell his cheaper writing. 'It taught me the market for hackwork and the prices I might expect. So I was enabled to do a certain quantity of hackwork each month, enough to pay expenses, and to devote the rest of my time to serious efforts, which are always hazardous financial undertakings.' Under the circumstances, the amount of hack which can be identified as London's is remarkably small; perhaps much lies unidentified in newspapers and journals of the day.

In the end it was the serious work, not the hack, that paid financially, and of course it was the serious work which brought London pleasure and a growing reputation. The publication of 'An Odyssey of the North' in the *Atlantic Monthly* in January, 1900, augured well for the first year of the new century, and the $120 he received was much the largest payment he had known. Even better was the offer by the highly esteemed house of Houghton Mifflin to issue the nine Klondike tales which had appeared in the

Overland Monthly and the *Atlantic Monthly* as a volume. The resulting *The Son of the Wolf* appeared in April of 1900 and was very well received by the critics. Two months later, S.S. McClure, who was always on the lookout for promising young talent to write for his magazine and publishing house, made an arrangement to pay London $125 a month as advance royalties while he worked on his first novel. This arrangement continued for nearly two years, although McClure's did not care to publish the novel (*A Daughter of the Snows*) when it was finished, and peddled it to Lippincott. The advance royalties were eventually paid off by the earnings from London's second volume of short stories, *The God of His Fathers*, and various tales and articles published in *McClure's Magazine*.

In the meantime, London had earned additional money from stories and articles published elsewhere than with McClure's; and early in 1902, an English publisher, Isbister and Company, was prepared to bring out English editions of his first two volumes of short stories. Isbister's English editions were the first of many foreign printings of London books. In the spring of that same year, London was approached by George Brett, president of the Macmillan Company, to see if he were interested in finding a new publisher. After talking with Brett in New York, London, who had grown dissatisfied with McClure's, made an arrangement whereby he received $150 a month regularly in advance royalties from his new publishers. In addition Brett paid London two thousand dollars outright for *The Call of the Wild* the following year. The publisher proposed that, if London would agree to a fixed figure for the book, he would turn out a very fine volume and advertise and push it to the limit. The gamble paid off well for Macmillan and the immediate returns to London were good; in the long run, however, he lost much in failing to receive continuing royalties. (By 1953 Macmillan had sold nearly two million copies of the novel.) *The Call of the Wild*, followed shortly by *The Sea-Wolf* and *White Fang*, fully established London as a successful writer, and it is estimated that before he died, in his forty-first year, he earned nearly a million dollars from his writing. During this lucrative writing career, Macmillan remained London's publisher, except for a short period when the novelist, in a huff, went over to Century. The successful relationship was due largely to the astuteness and understanding of George Brett, whose correspondence with Jack London shows both men at their best. To date the Macmillan Company has published nearly six million copies of London's books.[12]

When London was negotiating with Brett at the time he went over to Macmillan, he displayed what today appears to be a very modest estimate of the amount of money he would need to live on, assuring the publisher that it cost him only about $150 a month to meet his running expenses. 'We live moderately,' he wrote. 'One hundred and fifty dollars per month run us, though we are seven, and ofttimes nine when my old nurse and her husband depend upon us.'[13]

The large number of dependants which London mentions in this letter written in November, 1902, shows dramatically how London had stepped up his responsibilities as his earning power grew. He was now a married man, the head of a household. It is beyond the scope of this study to present London's amatory and marital career in any detail; the matter has been treated extensively, if not always accurately, elsewhere, and London himself felt there was so much to be said on the subject that he planned to write an autobiography in those terms. A cursory summary of that career is to the point, however. Soon after returning from the Klondike he quarrelled with (or drifted away from) his first sweetheart, the English girl named Mabel Applegarth, with whom he had fallen in love even before he attended the University of California. Doubtless the year of separation while Jack was in the

Yukon helped to terminate the friendship. At any rate, Mabel Applegarth, who had helped him a good deal when he needed most to gain confidence, deserved a better fate than to be embalmed in the shallow and priggish character of Ruth Morse in *Martin Eden*. Another friend who might have become London's wife but did not was Anna Strunsky, a spirited and talented Jewish girl whom London met at a socialist meeting in San Francisco in the fall of 1899. Together they were to write *The Kempton-Wace Letters* (1903), in which they expressed contrasting points of view on the subjects of love and marriage, Jack's being what one might call the economic-biological approach and Anna's the romantic-spiritual one. Though their private letters indicate that they deeply appreciated each other's friendship, disparities in age, temperament, and racial background probably precluded any great likelihood of marriage.

The young lady who did become Mrs London was Bessie Maddern, a niece of Minnie Maddern Fiske. London met Bessie in 1896 when she was engaged to his close friend, Fred Jacobs. After the latter's death in the Spanish-American war, Jack and Bessie were thrown much together. Friendly, intelligent, earnest, and hardworking, Bessie was preparing herself for college by going to night school and saving up money by tutoring in mathematics and English during the day. When she and London were married in April, 1900, the match appeared to be a most sensible one. Perhaps it was too sensible. In the same letter to George Brett in which London spoke of the size of his family, his two daughters Joan and Bessie having been born by that time, he wrote in his customary manner of the *reasonableness* of his marriage. 'When I returned from the Klondike I began to write. But when I returned from the Klondike I found my father dead and my mother in debt. I was a young fellow who had never been rash enough to anchor myself by marrying. Nevertheless I found myself with a household on my shoulders. I buckled down and began to write to support that household and at the same time to educate myself. Finding myself anchored with a household, I resolved to have the compensations of a household, and so I married and increased my household or the weight of my anchor.'[14]

In the summer of 1903 London separated from his wife and children, moving from his Piedmont home in the hills back of Oakland to single lodgings on Telegraph Avenue near the heart of the city. In the following year, after returning from serving as newspaper correspondent in the Russo-Japanese War, he was divorced by Bessie London with considerable attendant publicity. A year later, as soon as the interlocutory decree became final, he married Charmian Kittredge, who had been an active member of the circle of friends who had gathered at the London house in Piedmont. London's separation from his first wife effectively put an end to his long residence in Oakland. For the rest of his life he was to live on his ranch at Glen Ellen, north of San Francisco, with sea voyages to the South Pacific (on the *Snark*), around the Horn, and to Hawaii as outlets for his restlessness and desire for adventure.

The only other aspect of London's personal life during the six years following his return from the Klondike which need concern us before turning to an analysis of the writing methods which brought him fame, is the matter of his friendships. He often complained, as he looked back on his life, that he knew no authors at the time he decided to become a writer and that he was notably handicapped because of this lack. It is true that until he published *The Call of the Wild* none of his acquaintances had had much experience with writing or publishing, but he was by no means without encouragement from friends who wanted to see him make good. Even before he entered high school, Fred Jacobs and Ted Applegarth, both of whom had aspirations to write, exchanged manuscripts with him and encouraged him fervidly, and, he felt, indiscriminately. Mabel Applegarth and Bessie Maddern both took a good deal of interest in his writing, and Anna Strunsky was generous with her time, discerning in her comments.

As his contacts with the socialists in the Bay Region became more frequent, London met several men who were in a position to give him intellectual companionship, one of whom was Frederick I. Bamford of the Oakland Public Library, noted for his enthusiasm for young writers. Another figure was the intense, otherworldly Strawn-Hamilton, from whom, Joan London believes, her father learned most of his Spencer and Nietzsche. Joan also feels that her father learned much of his Marx from the very able labour attorney Austin Lewis, who was well informed in economics and political theory and never failed to tell Jack London where he felt he was making his mistakes. These active socialists were not only vitally interested in ideas but much concerned with having them expressed effectively both in speech and in writing.

Of more immediate help with his fiction was London's friendship with Herman ('Jim') Whitaker, who was trying to use his experiences as a farmer in Canada as a basis for stories. For a while, London gave over a day a week from his busy schedule to help teach Whitaker to write. Undoubtedly the aid was mutual, as so often happens between teacher and pupil. Perhaps most valuable of all was London's correspondence with another young writer of his own age, Cloudesley Johns, who wrote him a fan letter shortly after his first Klondike story appeared. A very active correspondence developed in which the two pooled information on the problems of writing. London's letters to Johns, together with those to Elwyn Hoffman, another young writer, and to Anna Strunsky tell more about the development of his writing attitudes and methods than do any other sources. How a busy man like London could have found time to write so often and at such length as he did to these acquaintances is hard to explain; that he did so shows how eager he was to share experiences in writing and publishing. Finally, as time went on and early friendships dropped away, London met George Sterling, and these two exchanged ideas on life, love, and writing. Possibly the closest friendship which London was to experience, this relationship ripened during the period when he was living in Piedmont near Sterling's home, just before his separation from Bessie.

Though he was clearly not entirely without friends with a common interest in writing, it remains true that Jack London was to a considerable degree a self-made writer. Like Martin Eden, he felt that he had taught himself almost everything he knew about writing. He learned through trial and error, often making mistakes, never curing himself of grievous faults which badly mar much of his prodigious output (he was to complete forty-nine books in eighteen years). His writing methods, together with his attitudes towards the several phases of his craft, developed and became fixed during the five years he spent primarily on Klondike materials. These merit careful consideration.

London took great pleasure in developing an adequate writing routine. It was a game, a conflict, a challenge. His approach reflects his remark in a letter to George Sterling: 'No, I don't approve of Pegasus ploughing if he CAN fly. But I believe in his plugging like hell in order to fly.'[15] 'Plugging like hell' included gaining as many hours each day as possible, at the expense of sleep; writing morning, noon, and night, until he discovered that one had the energy to write for only part of the day; and always finding as much time as possible to read, for books brought great pleasure to him and often helpful instruction. How much he enjoyed this full-time effort is implicit in such remarks as the following, which are always cropping up in his letters. 'At last am at work; have completed my day's stint; am now clearing up my correspondence; and as

[206]

soon as I finish this shall be off and away for a scorch on my wheel. Then tonight comes my studying as usual.'[16]

London had already discovered that long hours of writing and an output of three thousand words a day inevitably resulted in reaction and an inability to write anything at all. Eventually he settled down to a pace of about a thousand words a day, making his word count after each day's writing with the knowledge that eventually, 'brick by brick', the product would be finished. This remained his pace for the rest of his life, and in time he came to be able to write his stint in two or possibly three hours in the morning and leave the rest of the day for other things. He prided himself on turning out his thousand words, rain or shine, at home or travelling, on Sundays and holidays as well as on weekdays. He boasted that he never wasted more than five hours on sleep each night.

To help him learn how to write, he consulted such rhetorics and guides to narrative writing as came to his hand ('at first I was completely lost—had no conception even of the relative values of the comma, colon, and semicolon.')[17] He also read such professional journals as *The Editor* and *The Writer*; raced through as many novels and stories as he could find time for, choosing particularly those which seemed to use the idiom popular at the moment; and added to his vocabulary systematically by trying to learn a few new words each day. Like Martin Eden he wrote these additions to his vocabulary on bits of paper and strung them across the room, where they resembled socks on a clothesline; thus he would note them in passing from bed to table and fix them in mind. His next task was to work them into his writing, which he did sometimes in an unfortunately forced way.

When he first started writing, he made a point of trying as many forms as possible, feeling that he would thus rapidly improve his powers of communication. He spent much time on poetry, which he wanted very much to write

[207]

well; but his poetry was not good, and in time he came to defend the writing of it much in the terms of Benjamin Franklin, insisting that composition in verse sharpened one's knowledge of words and made one's prose clearer and more succinct. Thus, as an explanation for spending time on a triolet, London wrote Johns: 'The only reason I ever venture such things is a desire to practice up thinking in meter. And the more rigid or more intricate structures are good training.'[18]

Most important of all, he systematically copied page after page of successful writing by others, feeling that he could learn to express himself better by thus intensifying his perception of their methods. For this routine, Kipling was his favourite, just as in many ways he was his favourite author for narrative method and ideas. Like many another young writer from Norris to Hemingway, London was in no way apologetic that he began to speak in a voice that sounded like Kipling's. He wrote to Hoffman the year *The Son of the Wolf* appeared: 'A man doesn't take a ship to sea without a compass. . . . Any piece of writing ever produced, more nearly resembles one thing than another. . . . As for myself, there is no end of Kipling in my work. I have even quoted him. I would never possibly [have] written anywhere near the way I did had Kipling never been. True, true, every bit of it. And if several other men had never existed, Kipling would never have written as he did.'[19]

His methodical approach, as it developed, required concentration but no frenzy. As he worked on his first draft, he distrusted 'inspiration'. 'Never write any story at white heat,' he wrote an inquirer. 'Hell is kept warm by unpublished manuscripts that were written at white heat.'[20] As to revision, once London got into his stride, he worked over his phrases in his head before he put words to paper in longhand, and then sometimes touched up his material in typing his copy. As he wrote to Brett: 'Mr. Gilder speaks

[208]

of rough drafts. I do not make any. I compose very slowly, in long hand, and each day type what I have written. My main revision is done each day in the course of typewriting the manuscript. This manuscript is the final one, and as much time is spent on it as is spent by many a man in making two or three rough drafts. My revisions in proof-sheets are very infrequent, chopping a word or a phrase out here, putting in one or the other there, and that is all. So that, for me, a rough draft is an impossible thing.'[21]

Perhaps a more customary practice was that described to Johns in November, 1899: 'Every day sees what I have composed, all typed and ready to be submitted. I never polish. I write anywhere from ten to two hundred words in long hand, glance over it, and slap it through the machine.'[22] Again: 'I doubt if I shall ever be able to polish. I permit too short a period—one to fifteen minutes—to elapse between the long-hand and the final MS.'[23] London's fairly frequent insistence that he never revised his work once it reached the typed form is fully borne out by the condition of his many manuscripts stored in the Huntington Library. They are almost wholly free of inter-linear changes. It is probable that London would have improved his style had he revised more, although his temperament did not seem to be particularly suited to revision. It is to be remembered that he wrote at a time when the emerging school of American naturalists were inclined to revolt against the finely-moulded style. 'Tell your yarn,' asserted Frank Norris, 'and let your style go to the devil.'[24] It was a period of which London could write: 'It tolerates Mr James, but it prefers Mr Kipling,'[25] without much chance of running into a dissenting voice.

His indifference to the niceties of style, however, raises doubts about his motivation as a writer. The questions have often been put in connection with London's career: 'Did he write because he liked to or only to make money?' 'Did he start writing because he wanted to express himself,

o [209]

to be an artist, or was he merely trying to find a profession with which he could support himself with his brains rather than his brawn?' The issue has been more than a little clouded by London's repeated insistence late in his career that he hated writing and wished that he had been able to support himself in some other way. Even when he was starting out, he made such statements as 'If cash comes with fame, come fame; if cash comes without fame, come cash';[26] and, 'I was moved towards literature by belly need.'[27]

To judge London's artistic integrity is not so simple as one might wish. Like all men, he worked with mixed motives. He undoubtedly felt that it was nearly miraculous that he could, without further schooling, prevent himself from slipping from the lower fringe of the middle class into which he had been born, down into the proletariat. For a few years he had seen the likelihood of becoming a 'work-beast', and he had been fearfully frightened by the prospect. Writing not only saved him from this; it made him a companion to artists and intellectuals and an idol of a generation of readers. The truth appears to be that when he started writing he was motivated both by the 'belly need' and the urge to create. In this he was by no means unique.

The pleasure in creativity was strongly there. When asked his formula for success as a writer, he replied: 'The three great things are: Good health; Work; and a Philosophy of Life. I may add, nay, must add, a fourth—Sincerity.'[28] To George Brett he wrote: 'I have always insisted that the cardinal literary virtue is sincerity, and I have striven to live up to this belief.'[29] With London, to write with sincerity meant to try to be as good a writer as possible. No one reading the letters that he wrote to Cloudesley Johns, to Elwyn Hoffman, to Anna Strunsky, to George Brett can fail to note the eagerness with which he tackled the age-old problems of his craft. Surely there

were many moments when he felt as did his fictional counterpart, Martin Eden: 'Other men had discovered the
trick of expression, of making words obedient servitors,
and of making combinations of words mean more than
the sum of their separate meanings. He was stirred pro-
foundly by the passing glimpse at the secret, and he was
again caught up in the vision of sunlit spaces and starry
voids. . . .' And again, 'The toil meant nothing to him. It
was not toil. He was finding speech, and all the beauty and
wonder that had been pent for years behind his inarticulate
lips was now pouring forth in a wild and virile flood.'

Unless the joys and agonies of the creative artist were
upon London, how account for the reason for his refusal
of an editorship with McClure's? 'I want to be free, to
write of what delights me, whensoever and wheresoever it
delights me.'[30] To Johns he wrote at one moment: 'You
see, I am groping, groping, groping for my own particular
style, for the style which should be mine but which I
have not yet found';[31] and at another, 'Better one thousand
words which are builded, than a whole book of mediocre,
spun-out, dashed-off stuff.'[32] He was most patient in his
advice to Johns—he discussed pace, point of view, diction,
suspense, plotting, and other aspects of fiction with an
engaging enthusiasm. 'Pour all yourself into your work
until your work becomes you, but no where let yourself
be apparent.'[33] Work hard to attain better phrases: 'Sit
down and grope after them, hammer them out in sweat
and blood, endure your share of the travail of birth.'[34]
That travail did not end with the typing of a story. He
found cutting out twelve thousand words ('every word
essential to atmosphere')[35] from 'An Odyssey of the
North', at the editor's request, as bad as giving his pound
of flesh. Yet when he read 'The White Silence', one of his
first (and best) stories, in the *Overland Monthly* he admitted:
'I was sick at heart, felt that it was a most miserable performance, and was heartily ashamed that it had escaped the

waste-paper basket.'[36] Shortly before his death, when London was disillusioned with writing and almost everything else, he said to his daughter Joan: 'That's the way it is. You look back and see how hard you worked, and how poor you were, and how desperately anxious you were to succeed, and all you can remember is how happy you were. You were young, and you were working at something you believed in with all your heart, and you knew you were going to succeed!'

Jack London's bonanza was not all convertible into dollars and cents. The cash was accompanied by gains less material but far more vitalizing than the substance needed for paying grocers' bills.

IX · THE FICTIONAL
COUNTERPART

IN EVALUATING London's literary output, one must remember that unquestionably he placed substance above form, as did most of his contemporaries. At the threshold of his career he asserted to Elwyn Hoffman: 'After all, it is the substance that counts. What is form? What intrinsic value resides in it? None, none, none—unless it clothe pregnant substance, great substance.'[1] The substance of London's first successful writing was man's experiences in the Far North, together with such comments on his behaviour as seemed appropriate. The Klondike rush was at the heart of the fiction which made him famous. In 1900 he wrote to Con Gepfert, a Stewart River friend who had returned to the Yukon: 'I never realized a cent from any properties I had interest in up there. Still, I have been managing to pan out a living ever since on the strength of the trip.'[2] Earlier he had written to Mabel Applegarth: 'Dig is the arcana of literature, as it is of all things save being born with a silver spoon and going to Klondike.'[3] Failing to inherit the former, he took full advantage of the latter. Through his royalties he was to continue to cash in on a bonanza from the Klondike as long as he lived, although his almost exclusive concentration on that field in his writing began to taper off five years after he started washing out his tailings.

The extent to which London's success as a writer, both in the quality of his fiction and the size of his audience, arose from his use of his Yukon experience is well indicated by the extent of his concentration on this field between

1898 and 1903 and his return to it at various times during his later career. In 1899 he published nine Yukon short stories, most of them in the *Overland Monthly*, which were to form the bulk of his first book. In the following year ten more Klondike stories appeared, these in Eastern journals which paid more and had wider circulation than the local *Overland Monthly*. He continued to concentrate on Klondike material in his short stories for the next three years. In 1901 he published seven, in 1902 nine, and in 1903 four; he also published four juveniles using the Yukon scene in *Youth's Companion* and seven articles about the Far North in magazines such as *Harper's Weekly* and the *Review of Reviews*. His fifteen remaining Klondike stories appeared later at scattered intervals except for a cluster of six in 1908, written while he was cruising in the South Seas. In all he published six volumes of Klondike tales. He also published a play, *Scorn of Women* (1906), based on his short story of the same name, and he attempted unsuccessfully to get it produced. Though his principal interest in Klondike material began to wear off in 1903, about the time he turned to his sealing voyage as a background for *The Sea-Wolf* (1904) and developed an increased interest in Marxism which was to culminate in *The Iron Heel* (1908), he wrote some of his best tales about the North, such as 'Love of Life', 'To Build a Fire', and 'The Passing of Marcus O'Brien', long after his first burst of Klondike fiction.

He also wrote five novels set entirely or in part in the Far North. Though his unsuccessful *A Daughter of the Snows* was almost stillborn when it was published in 1902, *The Call of the Wild* was serialized in the *Saturday Evening Post* and appeared in book form the following year. Its companion novel, *White Fang*, repeated the success of *The Call of the Wild* in 1906. In 1910 London once more turned to the Yukon for the first part of *Burning Daylight*, and the following year he produced the loosely connected episodes of *Smoke Bellew* for *Cosmopolitan*. The book appeared in 1912. Thus, in all, London produced eleven volumes of Yukon fiction, one play, and a number of articles. Before the publication of *The Call of the Wild* only one volume not laid in the Klondike had appeared—the juvenile *The Cruise of the Dazzler*, in which he drew on his boyhood experiences sailing on San Francisco Bay.

An examination of the genesis and development of London's first three volumes of short stories, chronologically arranged, followed by a similar consideration of his Yukon novels, throws valuable light on his use of his Klondike experiences and on his writing techniques. The stories in *The Son of the Wolf* merit particular attention, as they brought him, even in magazine form, a critical acclaim and popular reputation which was to play a vital part in moulding his later fiction. They are held together by their northern settings and by the appearance and reappearance of a group of characters of whom Malemute Kid is the most noteworthy. Reviewers at once labelled Malemute Kid an Argonaut Mulvaney, recognizing the Kipling influence as truly in the central character as in London's use of the paragraph of aphorisms, 'the vague and choppy abstract', as one critic put it, with which he opened many of his tales. They also recognized that the Kid was a descendant of some of Bret Harte's characters. Malemute Kid is a sourdough with a heart of gold. Though he has 'lived on rabbit-tracks and salmon-belly' and can both think straight and act quickly and, if necessary, roughly, he is sensitive to all finer emotions. Much more youthful than his prototype, Leatherstocking, he is a born raconteur as well as an excellent drinking companion. An Indian describes him as 'a mighty man, straight as a willow-shoot, and tall; strong as the bald-faced grizzly, with a heart like the full summer moon.' He has as companions a number of old-timers, of which the adventuresome priest, Roubeau, the plucky Indian dog driver, Sitka

Charley, and the huge taciturn French-Canadian, Louis Savoy, are the most notable.

Though Malemute Kid does not dominate any story with the exception of 'The Men of Forty-Mile', in which he stops a fight between two of his friends by threatening to hang them both, he plays an active part as agent in the plot or raconteur in seven of the nine tales; that he had imaginative vitality is indicated by a letter London wrote to Johns after the first four tales had appeared in the *Overland Monthly*. 'I realize the truth in your criticism of ringing the changes on Malemute Kid. . . . But you will notice in 'The Son of the Wolf' that he appears only cursorily. In the June tale ['In a Far Country'] he will not appear at all, or even be mentioned. You surprise me with the aptness of your warning, telling me I may learn to love him too well myself. I am afraid I am rather stuck on him—not on the one in print, but the one in my brain. I doubt if I ever shall get him in print.'4

The stories of this first volume are laid partly in Yukon settlements like Fortymile during the times antecedent to the Klondike discoveries; partly at Split-up Island, where Malemute Kid has a cabin; partly at Dawson; and frequently on the snowy trail, as in 'The White Silence'. These settings we have already seen in considerable detail. The supporting characters include sourdoughs, who are uniformly hardy and resourceful, and cheechakos, some of whom are brave, like the desperate hero of 'To the Man on Trail', and many of whom are cowardly—misfits and weaklings, clearly unable to adjust themselves to life in the Northland. The plots are not complicated; the tales are usually expanded incidents illustrating certain basic themes. London stated his method succinctly in one of his letters to Con Gepfert. 'I rarely handle plots, but nearly always do handle situations. Take the different ones of my stories which you may recollect, and you will see that they are usually built about some simple but striking human situation.'[5] Ever on the lookout for such situations, London asked Gepfert to send him photos, tell him incidents which he saw or heard about. (He also admitted that he was aching to return to the Klondike. 'I can hardly contain myself, so strongly do I desire to go back.')

Thus the resourceful Malemute Kid buries his partner in the branches of a fir tree and dashes on with his dogs to escape the threatening cold; he tells lies to the Canadian Mounties in order to allow a father to return to his wife and children in the States; he threatens his close friends in order to maintain peace in the camp. In these tales, as in the title story, 'The Son of the Wolf', the white man must be very resourceful to cope with his unusual environment. His methods and attitudes are transmitted even to the Indians, as the Indian dog driver, Sitka Charley, demonstrates when he shoots two native helpers who have broken their white leader's orders and eaten of provisions needed by the entire party. The Indian, hard-pressed to hold his own with the white, occasionally attempts revenge, as when Naas, in 'An Odyssey of the North', trails a man all over the North in order to avenge the stealing of his native bride. The plight of the Indian mated to a white is already interesting London; in 'The Wife of a King' he has an Indian girl win back her wandering sourdough mate largely by learning and displaying many of the tricks of her fairer sisters from the south. Finally, in 'In a Far Country', there is a vivid account of what happens to two misfits when they are isolated in a cabin together for a long, cold winter.

The stories are by no means 'formula' stories nor do they often conform to the editors' demand for a happy ending which London was to cavil at so frequently during his writing career. He advised beginners: 'Avoid the unhappy ending, the harsh, the brutal, the tragic, the horrible—if you care to see in print the things you write. (In this connection don't do as I do, but do as I say.'[6]) His writing notes show him constantly searching for situations to illustrate major conflicts faced by man—man against nature, the white man against the Indian, the weak against the strong. A notebook of jottings entitled 'Alaskan Short Story Stuff' contains many such items, with varying degrees of promise:

'In a Bear-trap.' [Accompanied by clipping telling of how a man was caught in a trap and finally rescued.] 'Story of Jim Joy': How he loved dance-hall girl, who took all his money and gave him nothing. He is an Indian, and she put it over him dead-easy. Told him to bring more money. He goes out and murders. A story, embodying the Indian point of view and exemplifying the whiteman's superiority. [This deals with the white man's ability to outpack the Indian.] 'The Joy of Life.' Running with tireless muscles on some adventure through the snow.—Companion to 'The Law of Life.' A story in which a woman, finely bred, leaps upon another and takes away a letter or trinket or token or something from another . . . the animal in her coming to the surface—the panther. . . . A Co-operative society in the Klondyke. The problem of the craze of Gold. The shirkers, and the natural inefficients, arguing that they should all share alike. Road to Dawson. Party of miners. Dude type. Servants with them . . . . In the White Horse rapids they lose almost all their grub . . . . Men show themselves and take control. Put dudes on allowance. Starvation:—finding game and fighting off the hungry men. Look up moose thoroughly. A white woman marries Indian buck— a dashing Indian buck, and her disillusionment. I must write a powerful tale of a man and a wolf-dog. Also a wolf-dog (sort of biographical, like a man), indomitable, fearless, ferocious, and unscrupulous. Build for a scene where he faces a score of antagonists, knowing that they shall tear him to shreds.[7]

In a letter to Con Gepfert, London explained the emphases he sought in his tales. 'You see, I have had to take liberties, and to idealize, etc. etc. for the sake of the artistic effect, and often from the inherent need of the tales themselves, and for their literary value.'[8] In another letter he complained to Gepfert that many Klondikers failed to see the romance in the country. 'Nay, though they live romances, they are not aware of it.'[9] These are vague enough terms; yet one finds on reading London's Klondike stories carefully that, like Martin Eden, he felt a strong turn towards realism, not only in his reliance on scenes and activities which he had experienced, but in his concept of the purpose of fiction. On the use of experience, Martin clearly reflects London's attitude: 'While his imagination was fanciful, even fantastic at times, he had a basic love of reality that compelled him to write about the things he knew.' As to his concept of realism, he felt that he was constantly achieving it by dealing with 'fundamental' conflicts and basically true psychology, nor did he consider that the turn of his plots violated these principles, even though the outcomes might be bizarre.

Never very skilful at articulating his writing attitudes, he fumbles somewhat more successfully in that direction than usual in a letter written to Anna Strunsky. Angered by drastic and partially merited attacks on the accuracy of his portrayal of Indian life, about which he knew very little, he criticized the reviewer, William H. Dall, a well-known authority on North-west Indians, on the grounds that Dall was not an artist and had thus failed to appreciate the reasons for London's selection of details.

When I have drawn a picture in few strokes, he would spoil it by putting in the multitude of details I have left out. . . . His trouble is that he does not see with a pictorial eye. He merely looks upon a scene and sees every bit of it; but he does not see the true picture in that scene, a picture which can be thrown upon the canvas by eliminating a great mass of things that spoil the composition, that obfuscate the true beautiful lines of it. There is no colour scheme in the scene he sees, no line scheme, no tone scheme, no distribution of light and shading, nothing that may be gained by elimination. He does not understand that mine is not *realism* but is *idealized realism*; that artistically I am an emotional materialist. . . . Further, he has no comprehension of things subjective. Take, for instance, 'In a Far Country.' There the description of the silence, and cold, and darkness, and loneliness, is subjective.[10]

Careful selectivity was an ideal with London, not always easy to achieve. 'The art of omission is the hardest of all to learn, and I am weak at it yet. I am too long-winded, and it is hard training to cut down.'[11] Yet even at the beginning he rarely succumbed to the tendency to pile detail on detail so characteristic of the naturalistic school. Nor did he in these early stories often treat the gruesome and brutal with photographic detail. Though the reviewers pointed out that his tales dealt with 'wild, elemental savagery' and were literature of 'bone and sinew', they found no particular episode or description to object to. The situation might involve the cutting off of a man's head or the eating of a dog; he merely suggested the unpleasant physical activity and did not gloat over it. Sex he treated with even more reticence than the other naturalists of his day. Rare indeed is such a bold remark found as, 'Then he took her in his great arms, and when she tore at his yellow hair laughed with a sound like that of the big bull seal in the rut.'[12] And when S.S. McClure asked him to cut out some swear words, he cheerfully did so, implying that such trivia were of small moment to him. 'Of course I agreed.'[13] In a number of other instances he softened elements in his stories to meet the demands of editors.

London found even while finishing the last of the stories in *The Son of the Wolf* that he was having great difficulty in maintaining his initial level of performance in his Klondike tales. By the time he came to 'The Priestly Prerogative', he was using material uncongenial to him, and he contrived the poor 'The Wife of a King' out of three 'retired manuscripts' which he had earlier given up as hopeless. These two stories deal with the sort of domestic intrigue that London handled very poorly. In the first, Father Roubeau keeps a woman from committing adultery by telling a lie; and in the second, Malemute Kid and his friends teach an Indian girl to dress and dance like a white so that she can hold her sourdough husband. Nor was

London to regain his starting level in his second collection of Northern tales, *The God of His Fathers*. There was much here about the grit of women, both red and white, and on their holding or losing their mates. There is also a nightmarish tale about a man with a horrible scar on his face, who accidentally kills himself while trying to protect his money, and a grotesque yarn about the unsuccessful attempt of two sailors to hang their companion without the help of a scaffold or handy tree. The title story of the volume made a poor impression at the very start with most of the reviewers; 'The God of His Fathers' tells of how an agnostic was brave enough to sacrifice his life for his faith whereas a missionary turned coward and denied his God. The story idea may have had some possibilities, but by the time it was embodied in persons and actions, it had become ridiculous and somewhat offensive.

With *The Children of the Frost* London did better. This volume, made up of ten stories, most of which were published during 1902, concerns itself with Indians or with Indians in contact with whites. The tales are presented from the Indian's point of view. Though they show, as Dall pointed out, very little professional knowledge of the aborigines of Alaska and the Canadian North-west, scarcely discriminating between Indians and Eskimos and differing from the picture of red men elsewhere principally through the emphasis on cold and blubber, they embody effectively two of the themes which London could handle well: the struggle for survival in a primitive environment, and the weakening of a native culture by contact with the predatory Anglo-Saxons. The tales are by no means uniform in quality; perhaps the poorest, paradoxically, was 'Li Wan, the Fair', which was the only one of the group to earn a place on the august pages of the *Atlantic Monthly*. The magazine turned down the excellent 'The Law of Life' as being too forbidding and distressing. This story tells of how a white girl, whose parents had been massacred by the Indians when she was a baby and who had been brought up as an Indian, tries to establish her identity as a Caucasian by comparing the fairness of her breasts with those of a visiting adventuress from the Southland. Naturally, her Indian husband drags her off after such an unseemly display!

The more promising stories in the volume, with one exception, concern the effect of the white on the Indian. 'Nam-bok the Unveracious' deals with the very primitive natives who live in the Yukon Delta and tells of how Nam-bok, who fled his culture to spend some time among the whites, failed on his return to convince his family and erstwhile friends of the marvellous things he has seen. They prefer not to believe him. When he is banished from the tribe as a liar, his mother refuses to go into exile with him because she is afraid to leave the mud wattles and raw fish of her ancestors. In 'Keesh, the Son of Keesh', London speculates on the softening effect of missionary activity on the Indian. Keesh, who has learned from the missionaries to believe in kindness, is challenged by his betrothed and her tribe to fight, to kill. Accordingly, he tells the missionary he has decided to go to hell and soon thereafter appears beside the campfire of his beloved with four bloody heads in a sack, the heads of her father, her two brothers, and his rival. He then calmly cuts her throat. 'The Death of Ligoun' presents an old drunken native boasting of his early killings as he drinks 'Three Star' with a white companion.

The best of the stories in *Children of the Frost* are 'The League of the Old Men' and 'The Law of Life'. The former tells of a plot entered into by some old men among the Indians of the upper Yukon to murder all the whites they meet in camp or on the trail, hoping thereby to discourage the Anglo-Saxons from coming into the region and thus to prevent the disintegration of their native culture. Of course they fail, but something of their dignity and tragedy is embodied in the last survivor, one Imber, who turns himself over to the law in Dawson City. He tells his story in dramatic terms to a shocked audience. After a number of killings he has reluctantly come to the conclusion that the newcomers are much too numerous to be picked off one by one, that they are much too resourceful to succumb to guerilla tactics, and that, because they live by the law, they are certain of victory in the end.

London always affirmed that this was the favourite among his stories. 'I incline to the opinion that "The League of the Old Men" is the best short story I have written,' he stated. 'It has no love-motif, but that is not my reason for thinking it is my best story. In ways, the motif of this story is greater than any love-motif; in fact, its wide sweep includes the conditions and situations for ten thousand love-motifs. The voices of millions are in the voice of old Imber, and the tears and sorrows of millions are in his throat as he tells his story; his story epitomizes the whole vast tragedy of the contact of the Indian and white man.'[14] It is not hard to understand why London favoured this story, for it combined his sympathy for the Indians, and underdogs generally, with his belief in the survival of the fittest through the operation of manifest destiny acting through the Anglo-Saxons. But the story has little action and less atmosphere; it is too talky to hold its own with London's best stories.

Much closer to his true forte is 'The Law of Life', which tells of the approach of death to Old Koskoosh, once an able warrior, now abandoned in the snow by his tribe to meet the fate of the decrepit. As the cold moves up and the wolves close in, he stoically dreams of the old days, particularly of his experience with a grand old moose who had eventually been forced to give up just as he was doing.

This story is told effectively by a writer who had learned a great deal about his craft in two years. In a letter to Cloudesley Johns, London used it to illustrate points he wished to make about universality, objectivity, and control of point of view in writing.

It is short, applies the particular to the universal, deals with a lonely death, of an old man, in which beasts consummate the tragedy. My man is an old Indian, abandoned in the snow by his tribe because he cannot keep up. He has a little fire, a few sticks of wood. The frost and silence about him. He is blind. How do I approach the event? What point of view do I take? Why, the old Indian's, of course. It opens up with him sitting by his little fire, listening to the tribesmen breaking camp, harnessing dogs, and departing. The reader listens with him to every familiar sound; hears the last draw away; feels the silence settle down. The old man wanders back into his past; the reader wanders with him—thus is the whole theme exploited through the soul of the Indian. Down to the consummation, when the wolves draw in upon him in a circle. Don't you see, nothing, even the moralizing and generalizing, is done, save through him, in expressions of his experience.[15]

In 'The Law of Life' the Indian was forced to accept the principle that: 'Nature was not kindly to the flesh. She had no concern for that concrete thing called the individual. Her interest lay in the species, the race.' In this way London continued to dramatize his interpretation of Darwin, feeling that here the biological theory of survival of the fittest applied to the extinction of the moose and the old man just as in 'The League of the Old Men' it applied to the success of the virile, imaginative races like the Anglo-Saxons, 'the salt of the earth', as he liked to call them. He wedded Darwin and Kipling in this fashion—not as difficult a union to manage as the union of Darwin and Marx, effected in his later fiction by assuming that the survival of the fittest applied to classes as well as to individuals and that the proletariat was the class most fit to survive.

In these early stories as in almost all his fiction, London embodied his ideas in his action. He was particularly impressed with social and economic theories and felt that their exposition was an important function of the novelist. As he stated in 'The Material Side', a writer can present his ideas, and still make a living, by cloaking them in fiction which appeals mainly through its story line. Of messages, 'we will weave them about with our fictions, and make them beautiful, and sell them for goodly sums.'[16] In another article he urged every writer to develop a significant 'Philosophy of Life', a condition to be achieved by reading intelligently. He made no attempt to hide the enthusiasms he developed from what he called his 'collateral reading'. To Anna Strunsky he remarked, quite appropriately, 'The influences at work in me, from Zangwill to Marx, are obvious.'[17] There is much Darwin, Huxley, and Spencer in his Klondike fiction but surprisingly little Marx, considering the fact that he had for several years been an enthusiast for Marx. Nor was Nietzsche to leave any strong mark on his Yukon books; the latter was to play no prominent part in his writing until *The Sea-Wolf* in 1904. In the Klondike books, he was as good an imperialist as the rest; he praised predatory business methods in *A Daughter of the Snows* and elsewhere seemed unconcerned about the plight of the poor. The element in his nature which in the final analysis brought together all these seemingly incompatible elements from his reading and experience—the genuine sympathy with the dispossessed native, the pride in the predatory Anglo-Saxon, the enthusiasm for the revolt of the masses—was his joy in conflict, his feeling that the persecuted must fight, his admiration for the fighter that could win.

This glory in fighting to hold one's own came to its climax and most satisfactory expression in *The Call of the Wild*, London's second novel. Perhaps it was the lack of a strong, centralizing idea which had made his first novel, *A Daughter of the Snows*, such a patched-up piece of work. He once said of his virgin effort that he had squandered enough material in it for a dozen novels. He was not aware of this trouble when he started the book, for not long after he got under way at the suggestion of S.S. McClure, who had put him on a monthly salary cheque to write it, he confided to Johns: 'Since it is my first attempt, I have chosen a simple subject and shall simply endeavour to make it true, artistic, and interesting.'[18] He failed in all three aims. After five months of wrestling with his 'man's woman', Frona Welse, with her inconceivable friends (and enemies) and her unlikely experiences set against considerable detail of Klondike scenery and customs, London was ready to announce: 'Well, I am on the home stretch of the novel, and it is a failure.'[19] A month later he simply referred to it as 'N.G.' When McClure peddled it to Lippincott, London shrugged his shoulders. The trouble was that he had tried to write a romance with little knowledge of pace, sustained character development, or social comedy. It was not his kind of book. Eventually he reached the day when he was ready to put into practice the advice he had given to Johns early in 1899: 'So you have completed a novel? Lucky dog! How I envy you! I have only got from ten to twenty mapped out, but God knows when I'll ever get a chance to begin one, much less finish it. I have figured that it is easier to make one of [them] from thirty-five to sixty thousand words and well written, than one three or four times as long and poorly written. What do you think about it?'[20]

The Call of the Wild fortunately started out as a short story and ended up a novel. Not long before he began Buck's narrative, London had written a tale which he entitled 'Bâtard', but which the prudent *Cosmopolitan* had altered to 'Diable: a Dog', to spare their readers' sensibilities. It told of a bitter feud between a mongrel dog and his vicious master which ended in the dog killing the man. London confided to Anna Strunsky that his new dog story started out as a companion piece to this tale: 'I started it as a companion to my other dog-story, "Batard", which you may remember; but it got away from me, and instead of

[226]

4,000 words it ran 32,000 before I could call a halt.'[21] It was the story of a very different dog from Bâtard, a 'civilized' dog, a cross between a St Bernard and a sheep dog, which was stolen from his home in California and taken north to the Klondike, where he became a superior sled dog under the tutelage of a kind master, Thornton.

The two principal themes in the book were almost perfect reflections of London's thinking of this period. The animal's struggle to adjust to his new life as a sled dog brings out every element of adaptability, resourcefulness, and grit which Buck possesses. In coping with men and dogs, he learns to defend his rights and then thrusts on until he is a leader. With no more training to make him a good sled dog than London had had to be a writer, he uses brains and brawn to win his way. He is, of course, Jack London making his effort to be successful, to win in the fight, and to be loved, particularly in the episodes dealing with Thornton. The second theme, that of atavism, arose partly because of London's interest in evolution, partly through the pervasive wildness of the far northern lands. The idea of going backward in the evolutionary process appealed widely at this time. Note, for instance, Frank Norris' 'Lauth', in which he has a human being 'devolve' through various stages of animal life until he becomes nothing but a mass of protozoa. Buck dreams more and more of his wild dog ancestors and the primitive experiences of his kind. Eventually, after Thornton's death, he joins a wolf pack to live in the forest and howl under the stars for the rest of his life.

But the concept of 'the call of the wild' was not solely a reflection of the atavistic ideas arising from popular interest in the Darwinian theory. The part of Buck that was Jack London was escaping from the confining elements in society. For the contemporary reader, the 'call' represents the tug on all civilized men to get away from routine tasks, to simplify their lives in somewhat the same way Thoreau

[227]

wanted them simplified, to find adventure in nature far from cities and family responsibilities. It is because *The Call of the Wild* is one of the great victory and escape books in American literature that it has continued to be read by old and young. It is filled with soul-satisfying action in a setting which London handles vividly, carefully, and memorably.

It is a better book than *White Fang*, written a year later as 'a companion' to *The Call of the Wild*. Jack London defined the theme of *White Fang* in a letter to Charmian: 'Beginning at the very opposite end—evolution instead of devolution; civilization instead of decivilization.' He added, 'I shall not call it "Call of the Tame".'[22] He might have done so with reason, however; the conquering of the wolf by love is not nearly as appealing as the escape of Buck into the wild. White Fang is vital and interesting principally during the portions of the book in which the animal forages for its living as a wolf cub and, after its capture, fights for its life against vicious exploiters in the Yukon mining towns. Once the dog gets to California it is just one more dog, effective in attacking intruders on Judge Miller's estate, but sadly reduced in stature by the amenities of civilization.

In 1910, after reflecting other interests in such books as *Before Adam*, *The Road*, *The Iron Heel*, and *Martin Eden*, London once more turned to the Yukon for the setting of the first half of *Burning Daylight*. This latter novel was in part an attack on shoddy capitalistic behaviour, in part a reflection of London's enthusiasm for his Sonoma ranch, to which he had retired after his voyage on the *Snark*, and in part an attempt to testify that love conquers all. As his notes indicate, he would take a sourdough as his hero: 'Young man, *à la* Frank Densmore in Klondike, strikes it rich. Harsh. Has integrities. In the Battle of the Strong he has survived.' The resultant Elam Harnish, known in the Yukon as 'Burning Daylight', was inordinately successful

[228]

at Circle City and at Dawson, when gold was discovered on the Klondike. This portion of the novel moves vigorously and effectively. Harnish in civilization, however, is not so impressive. His writing notes show London's intent: 'Civilization. Wealthy, he plays the business game. No glamour about it. He knows it for what it is. Discovers that love is the thing.' He is to find the right girl and the right ranch and then be able to illustrate the theme: 'To stand on his own legs, to be beholden to nobody (the morality of the strong).'[23] Elam Harnish is both grotesque and sentimental in his adventures in California; it is unfortunate that London did not leave him in Dawson City.

Finally, London used the Yukon once more in *Smoke Bellew*. Smoke was created because the *Cosmopolitan* magazine wanted a series of stories centring around one adventurer and preferred to have him operate in the tried and true region of the Klondike. London had for some time been writing stories about the South Pacific, but he was willing to do what the magazine wanted. 'It was on THE COSMOPOLITAN's suggestion that I placed the scene in the Klondike. My own preference was for the South Seas. You see, I know the South Seas pretty thoroughly, and I felt that I could do better work on the South Seas.'[24] The resulting series of short stories, loosely tied together through chronology and the characters of Smoke Bellew, a San Francisco journalist, and some of his friends, is a poor book, full of outlandish and often stale material. It has some good touches, however, particularly the events of the first few episodes when Smoke, like another Humphrey Van Weyden of *The Sea-Wolf*, is making his way over Chilkoot to Dawson and is learning to be a man in the process. Still, he is by no means as interesting in his maturation as was Buck with his eager skill, or White Fang with his curiosity and bravery in the world of tooth and claw.

X · INTERPRETER OF THINGS
WHICH ARE

WRITERS of fiction have usually found that the sources
for stories fall roughly into two categories, those drawn
from the imaginative world and those recorded from the
actual world. Every novelist soon finds that he has just two
places to turn to for his plots—inside his head and outside
it. If he is a Hawthorne, he starts with a theme, a story idea,
and thinks up a plot to illustrate it; if he is a Dreiser, he
starts with an actual event which he has experienced or
read about and interprets it in his own way. Sometimes
there is a fortunate writer equally skilled in both approaches. Certainly every successful writer mixes both
methods to some degree to get his results; but usually the
craftsman in fiction finds one or the other creative process
more naturally his own. Jack London almost invariably
turned to the actual for his story plots and ideas.

At first London's inability to think up a story without a
stimulus from his experience bothered him a good deal.
He early confided his troubles to Cloudesley Johns: 'I
sometimes fear that, while I shall surely develop expression
some day, I lack in origination. Perhaps this feeling is due
to the fact that almost every field under the sun, and over
it too, has been so thoroughly exploited by others.'[1] To
Elwyn Hoffman he continued his lament: 'No, I'm damned
if my stories just come to me. I had to work like the devil
for the themes. Then, of course, it was easy to just write
them down. Expression, you see—with me—is far easier
than invention.'[2] He made a clearer analysis of his difficulties and abilities when he explained to Johns why he

[230]

was not entering a contest put on by the *Black Cat* for ingenious stories. 'I cannot even think of a suitable plot—my damnable lack of origination you see. I think I had better become an interpreter of the things which are, rather than a creator of the things which might be.'[3]

A Polish friend recently said to me that he always thought of Shakespeare as an 'essayist'. When I asked him why, he said that it was because Shakespeare was always telling stories he got from someone else and commenting on them as he interpreted them. Though the dictum is admittedly a limiting one, it has its validity in considering London's creative methods. He, too, was an essayist, finding his stories outside himself and commenting on them as he interpreted them for the reader.

As interpreter of 'things which are', he drew extensively on his own experiences in the Klondike rush, as has been amply illustrated in the central section of this book. After he returned to Oakland, he read avidly all the articles and books about the Far North that he could lay his hands on, keeping an extensive clipping file as well as building up a personal library. In attempting to discern the workings of London's creative mind, it is possible to compare both personal experiences and published sources with the fiction which emerged from them. Though the printed sources of such stories as 'Love of Life' and 'To Build a Fire' can be compared with their fictional offspring with considerable confidence that a true relationship has been established (but also with the knowledge that many elusive elements that entered the reaction have not been identified), attempts to relate London's experiences to his fiction cannot hope to be as satisfactory, with so many unknowns in the equation. In two or three instances, however, valuable light is thrown on London's writing methods by efforts in this direction.

Starting from what he saw and what he heard, London created stories which often came close to recording the

Klondike rush as he saw it; at other times, drawing largely from his imagination (when his 'origination' was not at its best), he floundered in the implausible, the contrived, the ridiculous. No better examples of these extremes can be cited than those found in 'Like Argus of the Ancient Times', in which London turned for the last time to the Yukon for story material, just a few months before he died. At the expense of repetition, it is worth while examining this story in some detail.

'Like Argus of the Ancient Times' is the story of the spunky spirit and remarkable fortitude of a seventy-year-old forty-niner who joined the Klondike rush, in spite of his children's opposition, and without funds or outfit succeeded in reaching the Far North and panning out half a million dollars in gold. The story was suggested by the behaviour of the oldster from Santa Rosa named Tarwater, who joined London and his partners a few days out of Dyea, went to work for them in exchange for food and transportation in their boat down the Yukon, and was last seen when he was picked up by the authorities in Dawson City and shipped down to Fort Yukon. London even retains Tarwater's real name, although he has his character come to be better known among the Klondikers as 'Father Christmas'. The old man was always welcomed because of his ebullient good-humour, his grit, and his song, with words set to the tune of the doxology:

> 'Like Argus of the ancient times,
>   We leave this modern Greece,
> Tum-tum, tum-tum, tum-tum, tum-tum,
>   To shear the Golden Fleece.'

In describing the trip from tidewater to Dawson, London introduces not only Tarwater but his three partners and himself under very thin disguises and with altered names. The half-pint Sloper becomes Anson; Goodman is called Big Bill Wilson; Thompson becomes, with possibly more modification in character than the others, Charles Crayton; and Jack London appears as the sailor Liverpool,[4] marked by hardiness, profanity, and generosity. In order to build up Tarwater and Liverpool, Charles Crayton is made into a penny pincher and poor sport, thus providing a conflict early in the story. But the real strength of the narrative lies in the vivid account of the five making their way over Chilkoot, and by boat beating their way 'into the teeth of the north'. Though the winter hovers slightly closer than it did in reality, and though the running of the Box Canyon and the White Horse Rapids is omitted, the account follows very closely the experiences of London and his companions as revealed in Thompson's diary. This part is excellent, compelling narrative.

The latter half of the story, in which Tarwater makes his pile after being sent down to Fort Yukon, is out of touch with reality, however, and as a result the yarn loses much of its effectiveness. Though he creaks in every joint, Tarwater is able to survive the most extreme conditions. Lost while searching for one of his traps which a bobcat had dragged away, the old man built a flimsy shelter, in which he survived for weeks on the meat from a wounded moose that conveniently wandered in and died almost at his feet. The red meat did not supply a sufficiently varied diet to check the scurvy which was already eating on his rheumatic limbs, and he lay in his bed for days on end, close to death and frequently delirious. In this situation, incidentally, London was able to introduce some of the ideas about racial memories he had picked up from Jung's *Psychology of the Unconscious*, which he had but recently discovered. 'And here, in the unforgetable [*sic*] crypts of man's unwritten history, unthinkable and unrealizable, like passages of nightmare or impossible adventures of lunacy, he encountered the monsters created of man's first morality that ever since have vexed him into the spinning of fantasies to elude them or do battle with them. In short, weighted by his seventy years, in the vast and silent loneliness of the North, Old Tarwater, as in the delirium of drug or anaesthetic, recovered, within himself, the infantile mind of the child-man of the early world'.

After twenty days of this caveman reverie, all taking place in a temperature which never rose above fifty below, Tarwater was wakened out of his stupor by another wounded moose, which obligingly blundered into the sights of his rifle. Roused, and determined to find the men who had wounded the moose, Tarwater staggered north and east on his scurvy-ravaged legs until, after God knows how many days, he struggled into a good camp on the Porcupine, where the old-timers not only cured him with moss, herbs, and kindness but gave him part of their diggings so that he might recoup his fortunes (lost through speculation long before in California). Noticing some moss on a bench-formation near at hand, he ripped it up by the roots. 'The sun smouldered on dully glistening yellow. He shook the handful of moss, and coarse nuggets, like gravel, fell to the ground. It was the Golden Fleece ready for the shearing.' Not long thereafter he returned to California with half a million, and the story ends with his thrashing his disrespectful forty-five-year-old son, who had tried to prevent his becoming a Klondiker by putting him in an asylum. Thus a good yarn, given dramatic cogency through the use of 'actuality', goes to pieces in its latter part, when it departs from London's experiences.

A more effective story based on an incident London learned about in the Yukon is 'The One Thousand Dozen', the source of which he acknowledged in a letter to a fellow Klondiker. When Georges Dupuy wrote to him asserting that 'The Relic of the Pliocene' was based on a yarn which the latter had heard in Dawson City in 1898, London replied: 'This is one of the few stories I have not based on actual events. You may be thinking of my story "The One Thousand Dozen", which was based upon the actual

[234]

experience of a man in Klondike, that occurred at the time you were there.'[5] 'The One Thousand Dozen' tells of how a Californian, hearing of the high prices eggs were bringing in the Far North, transports a thousand dozen eggs from San Francisco to Dawson City only to find on arrival that they had rotted in transit. As has been pointed out, there was a severe shortage of eggs during the winter that Jack London was in the Yukon, and several men rushed eggs to the region hoping to make a handsome profit. The first entrepreneur to reach Dawson with cargoes brought in by dog train did, in fact, dispose of his eggs for eighteen dollars a dozen.

London makes a good story of this activity by having his protagonist an amateur rather than a dealer, who was suddenly taken with the idea of turning a thousand dollars into five thousand by carting eggs north before anyone else could manage it. After mortgaging his property to buy the eggs and pay his travel expenses, he sets out confident of victory. The excitement and grim humour in the tale arise from the efforts of Rasmunsen to deliver his eggs in spite of cold weather and constant disaster. Once more London's knowledge of the drama of the trail from Dyea to Dawson is drawn on to make vivid the little egg dealer's experiences. Before he finally reaches 'golden, omeletless Dawson', he has left two toes with the surgeon at Sheep Camp, frosted his lungs and frozen one foot, lost two or three helpers through drownings, and has made a rush trip from Lake Marsh to California and back in order to raise more funds by means of a second mortgage to hire more Indians and dogs. He earns the justified reputation of being mad.

When he arrived at Stewart River, seventy miles from Dawson, five of his dogs were gone, and the remainder were falling in the traces. He, also, was in the traces, hauling with what little strength was left in him. Even then he was barely crawling along ten miles a day. His cheek-bones and nose, frostbitten again and again, were turned bloody-black and hideous. The thumb,

which was separated from the fingers by the gee-pole, had likewise been nipped and gave him great pain. The monstrous
moccasin still incased his foot, and strange pains were beginning to rack the leg. At Sixty Mile, the last beans, which he had
been rationing for some time, were finished; yet he steadfastly
refused to touch the eggs. He could not reconcile his mind to
the legitimacy of it, and staggered and fell along the way to
Indian River.

Small wonder he hanged himself when, after reaching
Dawson, his frozen eggs proved all to be rotten when they
thawed out!

Among other stories which London based on events
about which he may have heard in Dawson or on Split-up
Island are the exciting 'Too Much Colour', included in
The Faith of Men, and 'The Race for Number Three', one
of the best tales in *Smoke Bellew*. The two events which he
used in these stories both took place the fall before his
arrival, and had already become a part of the saga of the
country. He could hardly have helped hearing about them
in the Yukon, but he may have supplemented oral tradition with printed sources by the time he got around to
writing his stories.

In 'Too Much Colour' he gives his interpretation of the
incident in which Charley Anderson, known thereafter as
the 'Lucky Swede', bought a supposedly worthless claim
(Eldorado Twentynine) while drunk and took a fortune
from it after he sobered up. London's version presents the
story from the viewpoint of the two sourdoughs who could
not tell a good claim when they saw one, and became victims of their own slickness when they decided to trick the
gullible 'Ams Handerson', whom they considered necessarily stupid because he was both a Swede and a cheechako.
Skilfully handling the well-tried biter-bit formula, London
adds a dimension to his story by demonstrating that even
for experienced prospectors the grass on the other side of
the fence always looks greener.

In 'The Race for Number Three' he based his narrative

on a curious incident which arose when the mining recorder discovered that Sixty Above on Bonanza, smack in
the heart of the richest Klondike diggings, had been staked
but not recorded. When, at midnight sixty days after the
first staking, it was opened for reassignment, sourdoughs
from all over the region were gathered to stake and dash
for Dawson, where the first man to reach the Recorder's
office would win the rich prize. The contestants were
eventually reduced to a Scotsman and a Swede, who, after
driving their dogs through the rest of the night and half a
day, staggered across the office threshold in a dead heat.
The claim (which ironically proved worthless) was divided
between them. In adapting the incident to fiction, London
made a very exciting matter of the race, once more giving
a detailed, graphic picture of the winter trail; and, by having Smoke Bellew one of the two winners, he pits cheechako
against sourdough, with a moral victory for the newcomer.

London's use of his experiences in the Klondike as the
subject for stories sometimes led him in the wrong direction.
The plausible incident which could be given universal
overtones elicited his best work, but the fantastic and improbable elements of Northern life often led him astray.
One such idea which he worked with for some time was that
of using Stevens, the 'wild-man' whom he had met at
Split-up Island, as the raconteur and central figure in a
series of tall yarns. He intended these tales to deal with the
improbable in a plausible manner, as a Coleridge or Poe
might handle them. London's notes indicate that his plans
for the series took him far afield. In addition to two such
stories which he wrote and published, 'A Relic of the
Pliocene' and 'A Hyperborean Brew', there were to be
several others, the wild nature of which is indicated by his
jottings: 'III. Mirage City. IV. Massacre of Indians. V. A
Dream of Gold. VI. Descendants of the Sir John Franklin
Expedition. VII. Lake draining—Gets all the tribe a working, and when it breaks, drowns them all.'[6]

A number of other similarly fantastic ideas are scattered throughout London's 'Alaska Notes'. It is evident from these notes that London planned to add to Stevens' improbable tales some of the yarns spun by a sourdough named Peter de Ville, whom he interviewed in San Francisco in 1901 when he was doing feature articles for the San Francisco *Examiner*. Though de Ville or 'French Pete' was at the time selling vegetables on Pacific Street, he maintained that he had wandered for thirty years in the Far North. In the 'Moon Country' he had not only seen three suns at a time and suffered from a fluttering compass but he had run into mastodons, fifty-foot-tall bats, and white men who were probably descendants of the members of the lost Franklin Expedition. London reported in the local press that French Pete had brought home to support his wild statements an animal which had the body of a bear, the forepaws of a wolf, and the head of a Malemute, and the *Examiner* ran a picture of the two-hundred-pound monstrosity. Many of the bizarre incidents which London was to use years later in the latter part of the *Smoke Bellew* series, in which the tales grow more preposterous with each episode, apparently also derived from contacts with Stevens and de Ville.

Though Stevens proves to be an interesting character as a Yukon Münchhausen in the framework of the two stories London published, the yarns which he spins do not amount to much. 'A Relic of the Pliocene', telling how Stevens captured a mastodon by closing the entrance of a canyon and running him to death, has the flavour but not the naïve plausibility of a good folktale. 'A Hyperborean Brew' proves to be too much of a mishmash of London, Stevens, de Ville, and Kipling. This latter story is principally of interest in illustrating London's method when he imitated the story concept of another fiction writer, a practice which he found unrewarding and used very sparingly. Both the framing and the action of London's tale are reminiscent of Kipling's 'The Man Who Would Be King', but where Kipling succeeded in riding the perilous line between romance and reality in his tale of the calamitous adventures of two rogues who took over a native kingdom in the wilds north of Afghanistan, London produced nothing but a tedious grotesquerie in his yarn concerning two adventurers who took over a tribe in the wilds north of the Yukon by building a still which brewed fearfully powerful firewater. Clearly London could learn much from Kipling's structure, stylistic devices, and general attitudes towards Anglo-Saxon adventure, but he could not use his plots satisfactorily.

A more effective use of a story situation developed by another writer and adapted by London is found in 'In a Far Country', which, as Sam Baskett has pointed out, bears a strong resemblance to Joseph Conrad's 'An Outpost of Progress'. 'In a Far Country', London's fifth published story, which appeared in the *Overland Monthly* in June, 1899, clearly owes a good deal to Conrad's story which had appeared the year before in his *Tales of Unrest*. There are many evidences that London was very fond of Conrad, and a letter he wrote to the senior novelist years later includes the statement: 'I had just begun to write when I read your first early work.' In developing 'In a Far Country' London for the first time abandoned his Kid Malemute technique, and, as he pointed out to a friend, tried what was for him a new formula.

The parallels between the Conrad and London stories are extensive and fundamental; both deal with the degeneration of two 'incapables' exposed to a wild and lonely environment—Conrad's to an isolated post on the Congo and London's to an isolated cabin between the Mackenzie and the Yukon. In both stories the men at first get on famously with an emphasis on loafing but eventually come to blows, in both cases over the short sugar supply. In both tales, one man kills the other and then succumbs himself, in Conrad as a suicide, in London as a victim of his wounds and the cold.[7]

There are also many ways, however, in which London made 'In a Far Country' very much his own. This story gave him an opportunity both to expose the plight of weaklings in the struggle for survival and to air his prejudices against types he did not like. One man was a clerk, obviously a victim of the petty commercial world and clearly not very imaginative, or he would never have been a clerk. The other was a rich playboy, who had been inevitably spoiled by his parents and friends. The awful lonesomeness of the snow-covered cabin in the silent Arctic was made fearfully real; the occupations of the men as they struggled to keep going were those which inexperienced men in northern regions would resort to. There is little sense of the gradual encroachment of evil from without and corrosion from within that one finds in the Conrad story; for that matter, there are no natives in the Northern story as there were, so prominently, in the Congo one. London's tale, rather, gives a good dramatic impression of two men without resources rubbing each other the wrong way until they finally have it out.

More helpful in throwing light on London's creative powers at work, however, than the study of his interpretation of story concepts borrowed from other writers, or even the examination of his utilization of his own experiences as bases for his narratives, is a comparison of identifiable printed sources, factual books and newspaper records with the stories or parts of stories he evolved from them. As one would expect, he used these sources in varying ways. Two such variant methods are illustrated by his use of details from Egerton R. Young's *My Dogs in the Northland* while writing *The Call of the Wild*, and the 'fictionalizing' of a news item in the Sunday section of the San Francisco *Examiner* in creating 'The Unexpected'.

Young's *My Dogs in the Northland* appeared late in 1902,

just a few months before London started *The Call of the Wild*. In his genial book, Young, a missionary in the Lake Winnepeg area, tells about the many dogs he used in his travels among the Indian villages. London, who was eager to write a book about a sled dog, seized upon this account as an important source of information to supplement his rather limited knowledge of the behaviour of draught dogs in the Arctic regions. Here he read about how one experienced dog could be trusted to whip a whole team into shape: about how dogs would burrow in the snow to find a good sleeping spot, some showing great discretion in choosing a spot to leeward of the wind, others, the white ones, using their slumber-holes as hideouts, still others stealing warm spots while the original occupants were foraging for food. Here, too, he learned how a dog would aid his master in removing the ice from his paws and coat after he had fallen in the freezing water; how dogs with tender feet were provided with moccasins and soon learned to hold their sore feet in the air to be shod with hide or leather. Young's dogs customarily howled at nine, twelve, and three o'clock during the nights, thus furnishing a dramatic sequence which London used in his novel. Several of Young's dogs even suggested character traits which appeared in the dogs in *The Call of the Wild*. Young's Jack, a St Bernard, has some of Buck's feeling of responsibility; Cuffy, a Newfoundland, is not unlike the feminine Curly; the one-eyed husky lead dog Voyageur may have contributed to the portrayal of unsociable, one-eyed Solleks; the behaviour of Young's Rover, who constantly licks the wounds of the other dogs in the team, may have suggested the role of doctor dog assumed by Skeet in London's novel. All these touches gave a feeling of authenticity to London's masterpiece and added richness and variety to the narrative. They were helpful but not basic. Available data in a technical field, they were worked skilfully into the narrative so that they fitted London's pur-

Q [241]

pose. They had little effect on plot, less on theme, and none at all on overtones and allegory.

'The Unexpected', one of the stories in *Love of Life*, is a tale that takes its plot almost unchanged from a newspaper account of a real event. The details of its development have been provided by London as interpreter of things as they are. When 'The Unexpected' originally appeared in *McClure's Magazine* in August, 1906, the story carried a footnote: 'Mr London's story is a real human document, based upon actual incidents. Michael Dennin was hanged at Latuya Bay by Mrs Nelson in 1900.' When a controversy developed over whether such happenings as London described had ever taken place, he wrote to the editor of the Seattle *Post-Intelligencer*, pointing out that his information had come from a news story which appeared in the Sunday section of the San Francisco *Examiner* on October 14, 1900. The anonymous author of the article in the *Examiner* stated that Mrs Edith Nelson and her husband, Hans, had taken justice into their own hands in an isolated spot in Alaska by hanging one of their mining companions named Michael Dennin. They had executed Dennin in order to avenge the deaths of two other members of the party of five which had set out to search for gold in the lonely Latuya Bay region a few months before. Dennin had arrived late to breakfast one morning with a shotgun in his hands, had fatally shot his two bunkmates at the table before anyone realized what was happening, and might have succeeded in reloading and murdering the Nelsons had not Mrs Nelson sprung at his throat just in the nick of time. After the Nelsons had disarmed Dennin and tied him up in his bunk, the murderer confessed that he had decided to kill the others in order to get all the gold, which by agreement was to have been shared five ways. According to the *Examiner*, his confession was written down and witnessed by local Siwash Indians, the only other human beings in the area. After waiting for ten days in the hope

[242]

that some passing boat would put into shore in response to their distress signal, the Nelsons decided that they could no longer stand the strain and danger of guarding the criminal night and day. Accordingly, they hanged him, with a circle of Siwashes as witnesses. Months later, after they had returned to Skagway, they were said to have laid the matter before a United States court, and were not only exonerated from any blame, but Mrs Nelson in particular was commended for her bravery. The article was entitled 'Woman Hangs a Man and the Law Upholds Her' and was illustrated with drawings.

This news story apparently struck London as an excellent example of reality that could be used as a basis for strong fiction. In creating his tale he even retained the original names, the general location, and almost all the details of action as reported in the newspaper. But he developed each of the characters in such a way as to make the action more plausible and fitting; he changed the season to midwinter so that he could accentuate the loneliness and strangeness of the environment and the helplessness of the Nelsons in getting outside aid, and he supplied the story with a generalizing theme. Though civilization tended to make most people less and less able to cope with the unexpected, there were rare exceptions on the frontier, individuals whose fitness in adjusting to totally unexpected circumstances made for their survival. Such a person was Edith Nelson, who proved to be the strong character in the plot. Little in her background as a girl in England or a maidservant in early life could account for this later alertness. But after marrying Hans Nelson, who had within him 'that Teutonic unrest that drives the race ever westward in its great adventure', she discovered that she was more adaptable than she realized and that she had imagination as well as persistence. As the Nelsons drifted westward and northward in the search for gold, she not only learned how to make pan-fried sourdough bread, to serve up a succulent boiled moccasin in lean times, and to 'build a fire of wet wood in a downpour of rain and not lose her temper'; she also stored up the resourcefulness and faith in law, including vigilante law, which were to make her come through in the time of crisis.

London furthered his purpose of drawing a convincing figure in Edith Nelson by having her husband well-intentioned but slow-moving, a naturalistic figure with a berserk streak which was aroused by Dennin's action. Thus Mrs Nelson had not only to act quickly to save both their lives, she also had to fight her husband, in whom the animal was barely beneath the skin, to keep him from shooting Dennin in his blind fury. Eventually, helped by the frequently cheerful and co-operative behaviour of the criminal, who confessed that his motive for the crime was to get enough money to make his mother back in Ireland comfortable for the rest of her life, she managed to get not only a semblance of a trial, but a hanging with decent protocol. All the way along, however, her nerves were wearing thin, and her control was maintained barely long enough to see justice done. After the hanging she went to pieces.

She turned her back, thrusting her fingers into her ears. Then she began to laugh, harshly, sharply, metallically; and Hans was shocked as he had not been shocked through the whole tragedy. Edith Nelson's breakdown had come. Even in her hysteria she knew it, and she was glad that she had been able to hold up under the strain until everything had been accomplished. She reeled toward Hans.

'Take me to the cabin, Hans,' she managed to articulate.

'And let me rest,' she added. 'Just let me rest, and rest, and rest.'

With Hans's arm around her, supporting her weight and directing her helpless steps, she went off across the snow. But the Indians remained solemnly to watch the working of the white man's law that compelled a man to dance upon the air.

'The Unexpected' is a competent fictional metamorphosis of a real event. The trouble with the story, however, is that it once more illustrates the adage that truth is stranger, and less plausible, than fiction. The actual event remains quite incredible, even if it really took place, and the story based on it suffers in consequence.

The opportunity to study London's imagination operating on identifiable material can hardly be bettered than in the composition of 'Love of Life', one of his most famous short stories and the one Lenin praised in such glowing terms. It tells of the struggle for survival of an injured prospector who lived without food for many days on the Barren Lands between the Great Bear Lake and the Coppermine River. It ends happily when the unnamed hero, kept alive by the blood of a sick wolf he has strangled, crawls to the shore of Coronation Gulf on the Arctic Ocean, where he is rescued by members of a scientific expedition sailing far-northern waters. London's story was suggested by the experiences of Charles Bunn, a member of a small Canadian exploration party which had looked for mineral deposits in the Barren Lands of northern Canada during the summer of 1900. Left with a companion to make his way back to the base camp, Bunn was abandoned by that companion, lost his way, and wandered for eight days with an injured ankle and no food before he stumbled into an Indian camp, where his needs were cared for.

London learned of Bunn's ordeal from an eight-page article about him entitled 'Lost in the Land of the Midnight Sun', which appeared in *McClure's Magazine* in 1901.[8] It was written by two journalists, Augustus Bridle and J. A. MacDonald, who had interviewed Bunn. London probably clipped the article at the time and used it as the basis for his story several years later. 'Love of Life' appared in *McClure's* in December, 1905. It was an excellent product of the process which London called in a letter to *The Editor* 'turning journalism into literature'.

As he developed his story, many of the changes London made were of a routine nature, to be anticipated in any well-written piece of fiction. For instance, he greatly reduced the exposition dealing with Bunn's activities before he sprained his ankle, confining the story of his protagonist to those few details necessary to explain his presence in the bleak Barren Lands. He also withheld these details until he had fully established the plight of the hero and a feel for the country, and when he did supply some exposition it was presented through the protagonist's reverie. The point of view became strictly controlled, although the narrative is in the third person. We are seeing everything from the hero's view throughout the story (except for the rather weak epilogue), and the perspective alters as the emotional states of the hero shift from confidence through panic and delirium, to a final almost animal-like persistence, based largely on instinctual responses. The geography of the story was changed so that London's hero would emerge on the Coronation Gulf on the Arctic Ocean rather than return, as Bunn did, to the Great Bear Lake area. The decision to have his hero wander north rather than west and south was probably dictated by a desire to have him rescued by the members of a scientific expedition rather than by a group of Indians, as Bunn had been, and to accentuate the bleakness of the environment and the lonesomeness of the ordeal. Early in the story we are told that the hero is north of the Arctic Circle, and by the time he has reached help it is far behind him. He is wandering towards the North Pole.

In other ways London made his story remarkably graphic and memorable. Although Bunn lost his way for a while (it must have been but a short while, as he emerged from his delirium at almost the exact point where he wished to go), London's prospector loses his way through circumstances carefully arranged to make his wanderings plausible. The weather is clear as he confidently sets his course by the position of the sun when he was first abandoned. Dense overcast, snow, and fog follow each other during the days when emotional changes make for loss of orientation. Thus the weather echoes or symbolizes the wanderer's mental state. The weather clears up at about the time the hero's mind clears. His body is now weak to the point where he can merely crawl, but he can see the Coppermine, the bay, and the ship clearly below and in front of him and can tell what they are.

Similarly, time has been handled much more skilfully than it was in the journalists' account of Bunn's wanderings. There the eight days were described with a monotonous regularity, with a statement at the very beginning giving the length of Bunn's ordeal. London establishes an awareness of time at the moment his hero's companion abandons him without a word of farewell, by having his hero refer frequently to his watch and wind it every night before going to sleep. In spite of this care, however, he loses track of time, and as his ordeal grows more intense he can hardly tell day from night, much less one day from another. As the outcome is not known until the end of the story, the suspense is maintained and built up by many different devices. Such suspense was denied the readers of the article, for they knew the end before they had hardly begun reading.

The action was made more dramatic by careful selection of details for effect, by proper timing, and by expansion when necessary. Whereas Bunn's companion had abandoned him after Bunn had sprained his ankle in crossing a stream, he left him with the words (and possibly the intent) that he would go on ahead to build a fire so that Bunn might recuperate on catching up. The authors suggest that there had been bad blood between the two men but never make it clear whether this was the reason that the two became separated. London uses the companion's silence and inexorable movement as a means of establishing

[247]

the hostility between the two and of accentuating the plight of his hero.

'I say, Bill, I've sprained my ankle.'

Bill staggered on through the milky water. He did not look around. The man watched him go, and though his face was expressionless as ever, his eyes were like the eyes of a wounded deer.

The other man limped up the farther bank and continued straight on without looking back. The man in the stream watched him. His lips trembled a little, so that the rough thatch of brown hair which covered them was visibly agitated. His tongue even strayed out to moisten them.

'Bill,' he cried out.

It was the pleading cry of a strong man in distress, but Bill's head did not turn. The man watched him go, limping grotesquely and lurching forward with stammering gait up the slow slope toward the soft sky-line of the low-lying hill. He watched him go till he passed over the crest and disappeared. Then he turned his gaze and slowly took in the circle of the world that remained to him now that Bill was gone.

Similar dramatizations took place with London's treatment of his hero's search for food. Both men started out by eating muskeg berries. The article reads: 'From ledge to muskeg and from muskeg to ledge he went, and at every muskeg he stooped under his pack, and pulled the pale, water-flavoured berries from the ankle-high scrubs. There is as much food for a man's body in muskeg berries as in drops of dew.' London wrote: 'He had not eaten for two days; for a far longer time he had not had all he wanted to eat. Often he stooped and picked pale muskeg berries, put them into his mouth, and chewed and swallowed them. A muskeg berry is a bit of seed enclosed in a bit of water. In the mouth the water melts away and the seed chews sharp and bitter. The man knew there was no nourishment in the berries, but he chewed them patiently with a hope greater than knowledge and defying experience.'

So it was, not only with the vain attempt to shoot a caribou with an empty rifle—much better than Bunn's

[248]

similar attempt with his last cartridge, which persiste
failed to fire—but also in the agonizing pursuit of the
ptarmigan, the grouse of the Arctic Regions. From tne
mere mention of a try on Bunn's part to catch some ptarmigan with his hands, London built up an elaborate stalk-
ing operation which at first resembled that of a cat
approaching a sparrow. Eventually his hero's cautious
approach brought some results, for he not only clutched
three tail feathers of one bird but sometime later stumbled
full upon a ptarmigan nest, where he found four day-old
chicks, which he crunched 'like egg-shells between his
teeth' while the mother beat him frantically with her wings.
His appetite merely whetted, he went after the mother
with a stick, then succeeded in breaking her wing with a
rock thrown with more precision than he had thought
himself capable of; but in the culminating duel with the
injured bird, he could not summon up enough energy to
carry through. 'He exhausted the mother ptarmigan; but
he exhausted himself. She lay panting on her side. He lay
panting on his side, a dozen feet away, unable to crawl to
her. And as he recovered she recovered, fluttering out of
reach as his hungry hand went out to her. The chase was
resumed. Night settled down and she escaped.'

The adventure with the ptarmigan and her chicks illustrates two elements which London introduced into his
story to make it more effective than the factual account.
One was the development of a variety of successful ways of
getting food, which not only made his protagonist seem
more resourceful than had Bunn, but added to the suspense
in the story, as it gave the hero some chance of survival on
the basis of his ingenuity. He may have failed with the
caribou and got no more ptarmigan than chick feathers
and barely-clothed bones, but he was quite successful in
catching minnows in the small pools on the barrens,
botching his first attempt, but eventually catching enough
so that he could save one for breakfast. He also got some

nutriment from succulent grasses, and he came upon the bones of a caribou calf killed by wolves 'clean-picked and polished, pink with the cell-life in them which had not yet died.' For a moment he thought of how his fate might be like that of the caribou, but he did not speculate for long. 'He was squatting in the moss, a bone in his mouth, sucking at the shreds of life that still dyed it faintly pink. The sweet, meaty taste, thin and elusive almost as a memory, maddened him. He closed his jaws on the bones and crunched. Sometimes it was the bone that broke, sometimes his teeth. Then he crushed the bones between rocks, pounded them to a pulp, and swallowed them.'

The nameless wanderer's experiences with the ptarmigan, the minnows, and the caribou bones not only spoke of his resourcefulness, they also testified to the increasing emergence of the animal in him, the naturalistic animal which not only worked almost blindly for survival but also was cruel and ugly and lacking in the softer human qualities which were uppermost during less fearful moments. Even eating grass was pictured in animal terms: 'He threw off his pack and went into the rush-grass on hands and knees, crunching and munching, like some bovine creature.' At first he approached his fishing in a rational manner, carefully thinking out a technique for catching the elusive minnows. This was hardly the method he resorted to, however, when he tried to outcrawl the ptarmigan or when he sucked and chewed the caribou bones. His kinship with the animal life around him was becoming more and more pronounced. Nothing demonstrated this more than the noises he made, for London's hero, unlike Bunn, broke the silence of the Barrens with more and more outlandish cries. At first he sobbed and shouted, but as his desolation increased he began to scream loudly (though intermittently) as he hobbled along on his injured ankle, now swollen to the size of his knee. The ptarmigan rising, whirring, before him annoyed him with their 'ker-ker-ker', and he cursed them and cried aloud at them with their own cry. The climax of this vocal activity came when he met and outgrowled a bear.

His desperate courage was evicted by a great surge of fear. In his weakness, what if the animal attacked him? He drew himself up to his most imposing stature, gripping the knife and staring hard at the bear. The bear advanced clumsily a couple of steps, reared up, and gave vent to a tentative growl. If the man ran, he would run after him; but the man did not run. He was animated now with the courage of fear. He, too, growled, savagely, terribly, voicing the fear that is to life germane and that lies twisted about life's deepest roots. The bear edged away to one side, growling menacingly, himself appalled by this mysterious creature that appeared upright and unafraid.

The instinct for survival which had caused him as a civilized man to wind his watch each night, to boil his kettle of water before going to sleep; to count his matches, and divide them into three packets and distribute them in different spots on his body so that he would not lose all at once—the human warmth of brotherhood which kept him from picking the bones of Bill, his former companion, when he found them where the wolves had left them, or even pre-empting Bill's nuggets, abandoned on the muskeg—these traits gradually disappeared, and about all that remained were the animal impulses which kept him going in the face of seemingly insuperable difficulties. 'He, as a man, no longer strove. It was the life in him, unwilling to die, that drove him on.'

The struggle to survive reaches its climax with the deadly duel between the protagonist and a sick wolf, and the hero's victory over the wolf marks the culmination of this onward thrust of the animal spirit. As in Bunn's narrative, the wolves, 'their howls weaving the very air into a fabric of menace', had pressed in closer and closer on London's wretched wanderer. They did not quite dare to attack. Though they had devoured Bill, they had chosen to attack caribou calves rather than to press in to the kill on this creature who might still be able to scratch and bite. The exception to this behaviour came from a sick wolf, which followed the man at what seemed a safe distance because it did not have enough strength to hunt with the pack.

The man became aware of the wolf just after a clearing consciousness had made him realize that what he took to be a mirage was actually a bay with a ship in it. It was near enough to bring fierce hope but so far away that he knew he did not have strength to reach it, for by now all he could do was barely to crawl along. The discovery of the wolf helped, in fact, to clear up his mind and bring him once more back into contact with reality.

He heard a snuffle behind him—a half-choking gasp or cough. Very slowly, because of his exceeding weakness and stiffness, he rolled over on his other side. He could see nothing near at hand, but he waited patiently. Again came the snuffle and cough, and outlined between two jagged rocks not a score of feet away he made out the grey head of a wolf. The sharp ears were not pricked so sharply as he had seen them on other wolves; the eyes were bleared and bloodshot, the head seemed to droop limply and forlornly. The animal blinked continually in the sunshine. It seemed sick. As he looked it snuffled and coughed again. This, at least, was real, he thought . . . .

At first he did not look upon the wolf as a possible source of food. It was merely a representative of the life that was around him on these Barren Grounds—life with which he would have to compete were he to survive.

Throughout the night he heard the cough of the sick wolf, and now and then the squawking of the caribou calves. There was life all around him, but it was strong life, very much alive and well, and he knew the sick wolf clung to the sick man's trail in the hope that the man would die first. In the morning, on opening his eyes, he beheld it regarding him with a wistful and hungry stare. It stood crouched, with tail between its legs, like a miserable and woe-begone dog. It shivered in the chill morning wind, and grinned dispiritedly when the man spoke to it in a voice that achieved no more than a hoarse whisper.

As the wolf waited for the kill, the man's strength ebbed so that he was crawling less and less distance each day. The fifth day after sighting the ship he was still seven miles away and unable to make even a mile a day. His knees were now as raw as his feet, and the wolf was hungrily licking his bleeding trail. 'He saw sharply what his own end might be—unless—unless he could get the wolf. Then began as grim a tragedy of existence as was ever played—a sick man that crawled, a sick wolf that limped, two creatures dragging their dying carcasses across the desolation and hunting each other's lives.'

Once, after one of his numerous fainting spells, he was awakened by a wheeze close to his ear. He knew that the wolf was closing in, and he also knew that he did not have enough strength to crawl the remaining distance to the ship. The good weather of the lingering Indian summer only made his plight more fearful. Unlike the wolf, however, he could plan ahead, could draw on resourcefulness which the wolf lacked, could use hands which had done so much in helping man to cope with his environment. He decided to feign death, hoping that the wolf, the terribly patient wolf, would come close enough so that he could grasp him. For half a day he lay on his back, fighting the spells of unconsciousness which came more and more frequently and could mean his end. More than once the wolf eluded him, but he stayed with his plan. At last he succeeded.

He did not hear the breath, and he slipped slowly from some dream to the feel of the tongue along his hand. He waited. The fangs pressed softly; the pressure increased; the wolf was exerting its last strength in an effort to sink teeth in the food for which it had waited so long. But the man had waited long, and the lacerated hand closed on the jaw. Slowly, while the wolf struggled feebly and the hand clutched feebly, the other hand crept across to a grip. Five minutes later the whole weight of the man's body was on top of the wolf. The hands had not sufficient strength to choke the wolf, but the face of the man was pressed

[253]

close to the throat of the wolf and the mouth of the man was full of hair. At the end of half an hour the man was aware of a warm trickle in his throat. It was not pleasant. It was like molten lead being forced into his stomach, and it was forced by his will alone. Later the man rolled over on his back and slept.

In this stark narrative, with its symbolic overtones, the man had survived because he had combined the will, imagination, and skill of his human side with the animal cunning and instinctive drive which complemented them. His love of life was a fearful thing, but at the end it brought him through to the 'scientific' expedition, capable even of recovery, though for some time he would be ridden by a compulsive tendency to hoard food. Both the man's persistence and his ruthlessness are essential to the story. It is a grim apotheosis of the struggle to survive.

A companion story to 'Love of Life', but one which deals with failure resulting from human ineptitude rather than survival in the face of almost insurmountable odds, is 'To Build a Fire', one of the most memorable of London's Yukon tales. Because of the unusual history of this story, there is available perhaps the most complete data extant to trace in detail the genesis and development of a narrative idea in London's fiction. An examination of the various stages through which it passed throws a good deal of light on the relationship of his 'invention and expression', as London put it. It started as what London considered an inconsequential juvenile entitled 'To Build a Fire', part of his hackwork, which appeared in *Youth's Companion* on May 29, 1902. In this sketch he told of a miner nearly freezing to death on a tributary of the Yukon because he failed to follow a major rule in the sourdough's unwritten law—always travel with a companion. He had slipped through the crust of snow into a pool of water caused by one of the soda springs which abounded in the neighbourhood; with his feet freezing almost at once, only a fire could save his life. After a good deal of difficulty he succeeded in

[254]

Newcomers selling out to go home

Bound for home on the Yukon River

First page, manuscript of short story "To Build a Fire"

building the fire, but all his life he bore scars which re-minded him of his fearful ordeal. This sketch was doubtless based on London's knowledge of the Henderson Creek area and tales he had heard during his winter on the Yukon. As he later wrote to one editor: 'Man after man in the Klon-dike has died alone after getting his feet wet, through fail-ure to build a fire.'[9]

In 1904 an English company published Jeremiah Lynch's *Three Years in the Klondike*. This book contained a dramatic description of the discovery of the body of a man who had frozen under conditions similar to those London had described in his sketch. London, following his practice of obtaining all the books on the Klondike as they appeared, ordered a copy from a book-dealer in England. It was pro-bably shortly after its arrival that he made the following note, filed under 'Future work'. 'Story—a study of a strong man wetting his feet, freezing to death and struggling to make a fire—See Lynch's "Three Years in Klondike," pp. 64–66.'[10] Presumably he had this story in mind when he set out from San Francisco on the *Snark*, as the hand-written manuscript of the completed tale carries the note: 'Finished Pearl Harbor, May 29, 1907,' a week after the *Snark* reached Hawaii. On June 21, 1907, the story was refused by *Success Magazine* on the grounds that it was too gruesome. It was eventually sold late in November by London's agent, who had had further trouble placing it because it was depressing and had finally accepted what he considered a low figure (four hundred dollars) from *Century* magazine. There it appeared in August, 1908, two years later, and it was included in a volume of short stories entitled *Lost Face*.[11]

It is noteworthy that when London turned his juvenile into an adult story, he changed the theme from one of adventure to one of tragedy. He did this in spite of the fact that he had found time after time that he had trouble selling stories with unhappy endings. The shift in his theme

[255]

doubtless received impetus from Lynch's true story, for now London could apply art and imagination to fact with an even greater conviction that the grim ending was more appropriate. Lynch's account reads as follows:

The day after (November 18) there came to us at Dawson the news of a dreadful death. No one seemed surprised, no one made many comments; it appeared so possible, so natural, so easy to believe, that we simply drew closer to the fire, and wondered where we should be next winter. A miner was walking up the Klondike ten miles from here going to his claim. The Klondike is fed by numerous soda springs rushing down the banks during the long, hot summer days. These are so potent that even the winter's cold fails to close them entirely. Apparently the soda or alkali in these springs resists the action of frost better than simple water; so, therefore, it often happens that, walking on the edge of the ice near the shore, the footsteps suddenly sink through the weakened ice and into the bubbling alkaline waters that have stealthily worked their way beneath to the deep-flowing stream at the bottom. It was only 6 inches of water that the miner stepped into, and in a moment he was out, and, hastening to the brush hard by, started to light a fire: for the clothes freeze, the feet freeze, and in five minutes one may find that part of his body and garments which has been immersed in the water, though only a few inches deep, as rigid as solid steel. Rapidly he cut a few fragments of wood with his heavy pocket-knife. But the unlighted match dropped from his already chilled fingers, for he had rashly removed his mitts in order to use the knife with more freedom. Then he lighted a second and a third, and finally several at one time; but either his haste, or perhaps a sigh of the air, caused them to fall on the ever-ready snow. And all this time the frost was seizing his limbs, his body, his heart, his mind. He turned to the fatal mitts, which he never should have taken off; but his already frozen fingers could only lift them from the ice where they had fallen, and after a vain attempt he hurled them from him, and strove once again to light a last match. But it was too late. Though only five minutes could have gone by, the terror of death was upon him. The Ice King slew him with appalling rapidity, and when his companion arrived, scarce fifteen minutes later, he found the body already cold and rigid, kneeling on the snow and ice, while the hands, partially closed together and uplifted as if in adoration or prayer to God, held yet within their palms the unlighted match. They said that particles of the ice-laden air, minute and invisible, floated down to his lungs and killed him as would prussic acid. It was found impossible to remove his arms and hands from the attitude of entreaty in which they were placed, and the body was brought so to Dawson, and later buried without attempting to change their position.

From these ingredients—Lynch's graphic report, London's own sketch for *Youth's Companion*, his knowledge of the Far North, and his imagination—he created a story about man's struggle with nature in which a particular, representative man shows great ingenuity, with the odds against him, but loses out in the end. The margin is close; if the man had had more experience, he probably would have won out; and, if he had had more imagination, he probably would have won out. But as the man had neither the experience nor the imagination to meet his problem, he lost the battle.

As in 'Love of Life' London leaves his protagonist nameless, feeling, perhaps, that his anonymity will make him more typical of all human beings and will increase the starkness of the struggle with nature. Though he uses the third person, he is inside the man's mind throughout the story except at the very end, when the man's mind ceases to function. During the action the man's attitude shifts from confidence because of bodily well-being to apprehension, fear, panic, and eventually, when all is clearly lost, to resignation—an unhealthy resignation which leads to drowsiness, coma, and death. The passage of time furnishes the punctuation. Even though the day is but dimly lit, its beginning and end parallel the man's rise and fall. He is pleased with his progress in the morning, and feels that he is easily able to cope with any danger; he is successful in lighting a fire for lunch and smacks his lips over his biscuits: 'For the moment the cold of space was outwitted.' He feels triumphant later in the day when, after wetting his feet, he succeeds again in lighting a fire. Then he is horrified when he sees the loosened snow from a spruce tree fall on his fire and put it out. He uses every resource at his disposal to meet the emergency, but his hands are too nearly frozen to start another fire. His spirit ebbs with the dark. In the morning he has taken joy in the long amber crystal beard that he has built up with tobacco juice; in midafternoon, after he managed to scratch his entire supply of sulphur matches—seventy of them—in one big flare, he realizes his hands are burning, not through feeling them but smelling them. It is not surprising that he panics and runs blindly up the trail.

London sees to it that as his protagonist grows more helpless, nature becomes more formidable. It is indifferent rather than hostile. It is there in terms of darkness, silence, and cold.

The man flung a look back along the way he had come. The Yukon lay a mile wide and hidden under three feet of ice. On top of this ice were as many feet of snow. It was all pure white, rolling in gentle, undulations where the ice-jams of the freeze-up had formed. North and south, as far as his eye could see, it was unbroken white, save for a dark hair-line that curved and twisted from around the spruce-covered island to the south, and that curved and twisted away into the north, where it disappeared behind another spruce-covered island. This dark hair-line was the trail—the main trail—that led south five hundred miles to the Chilcoot Pass, Dyea, and salt water; and that led north seventy miles to Dawson, and still on to the north a thousand miles to Nulato, and finally to St Michael on Bering Sea, a thousand miles and half a thousand more.

Not only his isolation but the cold and its perils were elements with which the man was poorly prepared to deal. He was not only a cheechako, he was simply not of the resourceful type to become a sourdough.

The trouble with him was that he was without imagination. He was quick and alert in the things of life, but only in the things, and not in the significances. Fifty degrees below zero meant eighty-odd degrees of frost. Such fact impressed him as being cold and uncomfortable, and that was all. It did not lead him to meditate upon his frailty as a creature of temperature, and upon man's frailty in general, able only to live within certain narrow limits of heat and cold; and from there on it did not lead him to the conjectural field of immortality and man's place in the universe.

He was in a spot where the sun, the source of life, never came up to cheer him: 'The bulge of the earth intervened between it and Henderson Creek, where the man walked under a clear sky at noon and cast no shadow.' London made him represent man at his loneliest and weakest. 'The cold of space smote the unprotected tip of the planet, and he, being on that unprotected tip, received the full force of the blow.'

Thus London gave Lynch's man a personality and emotions, he motivated his actions, he built up the details into a prolonged and exciting conflict rather than a short one, he made the antagonist tangible. And, most interesting of all, London gave his man a companion—a dog. The dog is there every moment of the time from dawn to dusk. It is a companion who eventually ceases to be a companion because of the man's folly. It represents warmth, which is partly illusory and is drawn away as surely as the sun. It is a symbol of the instinctive, sensing always the peril of its situation, knowing instinctively what to do; and yet it is quite unable to help the man. It is bothered by the cold; it goes ahead to feel out the snow; it yearns after the noon fire; it is a wistful watcher as the man desperately tries to get the flames going when they are most needed; it becomes, as the afternoon wears on and the end comes nearer, an object of envy, a tempting source of warmth (the man tries to kill the dog to warm his hands in its body but cannot do so because his hands are frozen), and at the end it is a puzzled observer of destruction and death. London makes no attempt to use Lynch's account of a corpse with hands frozen in the position of prayer; his ending, rather, stresses loss of light, loss of consciousness, and capitulation to the natural world.

Then the man drowsed off into what seemed to him the most comfortable and satisfying sleep he had ever known. The dog sat facing him and waiting. The brief day drew to a close in a long, slow twilight. There were no signs of a fire to be made, and, besides, never in the dog's experience had it known a man to sit like that in the snow and make no fire. As the twilight drew on, its eager yearning for the fire mastered it, and with a great lifting and shifting of forefeet, it whined softly, then flattened its ears down in anticipation of being chidden by the man. But the man remained silent. Later, the dog whined loudly. And still later it crept close to the man and caught the scent of death. This made the animal bristle and back away. A little longer it delayed, howling under the stars that leaped and danced and shone brightly in the cold sky. Then it turned and trotted up the trail in the direction of the camp it knew, where were the other food-providers and fire-providers.

*　　*　　*

Almost seven decades after London spent his winter in the Yukon, the writings which emerged from his experience retain much of their vitality and popularity. Of the fifty volumes from his pen, most of the dozen Alaskan books have survived remarkably well. The play has long since been out of print, but the best of the short stories are reprinted constantly in new editions of London's tales and occasionally in anthologies. Macmillan has kept the hardcover editions of *The Call of the Wild* and *White Fang* in print and there are also available several paperback editions of these two favourites, as well as occasional reprintings of *Smoke Bellew, Burning Daylight,* and *A Daughter of the Snows.*

Serious competition with the Alaskan fiction is provided by only *Martin Eden* and *The Sea-Wolf.* Of course, there is a considerable market in London secondhand copies, as anyone attempting to make a collection of first editions will have discovered. It is difficult to estimate which titles are most popular with the secondhand book browsers. This is the picture in the United States. The weighting towards the Yukon fiction is likely to increase rather than diminish with Alaska gaining statehood and the Yukon Territory booming. Abroad, particularly in Europe, Jack London has apparently a more constant public than in America. This fact has been extensively publicized particularly in connection with Russia, where his following is truly prodigious. Translations of his novels began appearing there during his lifetime, as they did in most European countries; by 1911, five years before the Revolution, the first 'collected' edition was announced. Since then there have been at least five more or less complete editions; one, in 1928–29, ran to twenty-four volumes. An eight-volume edition of London's novels, short stories, and articles, published by subscription in 600,000 copies, was sold out in five hours in 1956. In 1948, *A Guide to Soviet Russian Translations of American Literature* recorded that seven and a half million copies of London's books had appeared in Russia between 1917 and 1947; this was three times as many books as those of his closest American competitor, Mark Twain. Vil Bykov, of the University of Moscow, estimated recently that nearly seventeen million copies of London's books have been sold in Russia, and stated flatly: 'Jack London's fiction is more popular in the U.S.S.R. than that of any other foreign author.'[12]

Mr Bykov maintains that London's socialism plays a very minor part in his popularity in Russia. This view is borne out, as a whole, in Deming Brown's *Soviet Attitudes toward American Writing* (1962). The UNESCO records also show that London's most widely read works in the Soviet Union are not *The Iron Heel* or 'The Mexican' but the Yukon stories together with *Martin Eden* and *The Sea-Wolf*, none of which has any extensive commerce with socialism. Mr Bykov believes that the Russians like London because of his creation of an 'atmosphere of heroism and struggle' in his books. Even against the greatest odds the London hero persists with resourcefulness and bravery. The Russian critic makes his case in these terms:

Russia in the last fifty-five years has undergone three revolutions. In this short time the people have turned their fatherland from a country of paupers and illiterates into a power with advanced science and technology. This required gigantic efforts and the people's belief in their own strength. The people had both, therefore, the activity and life-sustaining spirit of the books of the eminent son of California, which are close to them. The process of building, the attacks on nature, the struggles for a better present are continuing and expanding; thus the stature of Jack London does not diminish. I risk the accusation of propagandizing, but these are historical facts which cannot be avoided and without which it is impossible to understand the reasons for the wide reputation of Jack London in Russia.[13]

The *Index Translationum*, compiled and published by the League of Nations from 1932 to 1940 and by UNESCO from 1948 to date, throws additional light on London's popularity abroad. This annual record of translations which have appeared in member nations, though admittedly incomplete and at times overlapping, is very valuable as a gauge of reading interests in most countries where books are published in any number. When it is remembered that London was extensively translated and published in many of these countries before the tabulations were begun, it is truly astonishing to find him at or near the top of American writers translated and printed in new foreign editions year after year. To be so he must keep ahead not only of Cooper, Mark Twain, and O. Henry, but of Lewis, Faulkner, and Hemingway. In making a rough tabulation of the reports which have appeared in the *Index Translationum* since its inception, I have been surprised to find that not the Soviet Union but Italy reported the greatest number of translations, 96; Germany was second, with 86, while Yugoslavia had 82, the U.S.S.R. 73, Poland 67, Norway 58, France 41, Czechoslovakia 38, Sweden 26, and Denmark 20.

In all, thirty-one nations reported London translations.

Though I have been unable to identify a few of the titles in the *Index Translationum*, largely because of lack of opportunity to examine the books, the following rating of the various London books according to popularity is approximately accurate. Apparently Europeans (for these reports are preponderantly from European countries) prefer the taming of a wolf cub to the turn to savagery of a civilized dog, for *White Fang* leads with seventy-eight translations and *The Call of the Wild* comes second at sixty-eight. The next eight are *Martin Eden* (44), *The Sea-Wolf* (32), *Smoke Bellew* (31), *Burning Daylight* (29), *A Daughter of the Snows* (28), *John Barleycorn* (21), *Adventure* (21), *The Iron Heel* (20). Thus the five Yukon novels are included in the first seven listed. In addition, there have been some sixty collections of short stories published in foreign languages during the period of reporting, almost all of which have presumably featured some of the Klondike tales. Of the six volumes in which London originally collected his Alaskan short stories, *The Son of the Wolf* appears most often, with ten translations. The data in the *Index Translationum* thus show that there is little doubt of the continued attraction of London's Northland fiction throughout Europe and parts of Asia and South America. I have compiled no figures on London's popularity in English-speaking countries other than the United States nor on the number of his books read in English by non-English-speaking peoples.[14]

It is always hazardous to assert the causes of a writer's popularity or to guess why one book appeals more than another. With books like *White Fang* and *The Call of the Wild* there is undoubtedly a large body of juvenile readers; for that matter, most literate Westerners read them in their childhood as automatically as they read *Robinson Crusoe* or *Huckleberry Finn*. With London's Yukon fiction generally, it can be asserted that he frequently tells a story well. He may not be subtle and he is as a whole unpolished, but he tells a yarn with excitement and graphic vividness. Who, once he has read, will forget climbing the Chilkoot with Frona Welse, or accompanying Burning Daylight on his mad dash over the winter trail to tidewater, or watching the race to record Number Three, or surviving starvation in the Barren Grounds, or learning with Buck to be a good sled dog (and thus going through another initiation) or with White Fang a good fighter? London's stories have the compelling quality of truly exciting fiction.

There are many other elements which make his tales vital. Their settings almost invariably have a romantic appeal. Often with simple directness they lay bare the horror and loneliness of a strange life. They are imbued with the zest for battle, whether it be with a man or an animal, with ravaging hunger or with bone-biting cold. The principal characters, such as Malemute Kid and Burning Daylight, act with bravery and with a disinterested friendship for their fellows. The publisher's reader who approved *The Son of the Wolf* summed up many of London's virtues in easy, straightforward terms. 'He draws a vivid picture of the terrors of cold, darkness, and starvation, the pleasures of human companionship in adverse circumstances, and the sterling qualities which the rough battle with nature brings out. The reader is convinced that the author has lived the life himself.'[15]

On the other hand, the extolling of physical strength, the emphasis on the 'blond beast', the toying with atavism have frequently turned readers against London. His enthusiastic social Darwinism seems dated, his naturalism reflects a school which has played itself out, his jingoism is an offence now that we know his ethnology was inaccurate, and his historical determinism was far off the mark. Yet there is a very important place in our sophisticated and often tired world for London's hero who fights even while he is falling, and he by no means always falls. T. K.

Whipple in *Study Out the Land*[16] pointed out two decades ago what seems even more important today; in discussing London's heroes he stated: 'Physical stamina, physical courage and endurance and hardihood—the "wild and free" strength which has so little place in our business civilization—surely these things are good in themselves, and there is no telling when we may need them again and need them badly.'

Finally, there is courage to be obtained from reading London, for in spite of his often confused social thinking and in spite of the bitterness which creeps into much of his later writing, he was at heart one who believed strongly in his fellow man. He was, in the purest sense of the term, a humanist. He was passionately of the conviction that man could be a reasonable creature, that he had the elements of greatness in the face of adversity, that he could survive in the wilderness and build a better society in his cities. Because he based his hope on the natural rather than the supernatural, but also because he has his transitory doubts of man's capabilities as well as a recurring confidence in his future, he seems today most human and most timely. His attitude towards man and his future is nowhere better expressed than in a curious prose poem found among London's papers. This had never before appeared in print in any language until it was translated into Russian and published by Vil Bykov in an issue of Moscow's *Komsomol Pravda*.

'Of man of the future! Who is able to describe him?
Perhaps he breaks our globe into fragments
In a time of warlike games.
Perhaps he hurls death through the firmament.
Man of the future! He is able to aim at the stars,
To harness the comets,
And to travel in space among the planets.'[17]

[265]

NOTES ON SOURCES

The idea for this study developed when, after doing
extensive research on Jack London's life and writings, I
made a trip in 1954 up the Alcan Highway with George R.
Stewart, who was collecting material for his *N.A.1: The
North-South Continental Highway*. Side trips from White
Horse to Skagway and Dawson not only turned me into an
enthusiast for the Yukon country but convinced me that a
detailed presentation of London's experiences in the
Klondike and his use of them in his fiction would throw
important light on his writing methods and his literary
fame. Not only did I gain a vivid sense of topography
from this trip, but also I had an opportunity to interview a
number of sourdoughs in Dawson and to check such local
records as remained after nearly sixty years of the mining
centre's decline into ghost-town status. My disappointment at finding nothing of significance at the Barracks of
the Royal Canadian Mounted Police (the North-west
Mounted Police) or the local Catholic hospital was more
than compensated for when I discovered the records of
gold claims filed by Jack London and his friends at the
Office of the Mining Recorder at Dawson. And I went on
my way to Fairbanks and Circle City with the feeling that
I was a true student of ecology. Thus my examination of
topographic maps put out by the Canadian Department
of Mines and Resources determined, among other things,
the spelling of Yukon place names, so variable in accounts
of the gold rush.

Since returning, I have received photos of the supposed

Jack London cabin on the Henderson from Mr J. W. Hoggan, dredging superintendent on the Henderson; and from Kathryn Winslow pictures of what is left of the settlement on Split-up Island at the mouth of the Stewart. I had met both of these very helpful people when I was in Dawson. Later President Ernest N. Patty of the University of Alaska sent further information on the stories about the cabin on the Henderson. In Dawson I had no difficulty obtaining copies of E. A. Hegg's contemporary photographs to use as illustrations in this study. To one long gone I give my thanks and admiration as well as recommend to those interested that they look up Hegg's entire pictorial record of the Klondike rush published in Ethel Becker's *Klondike '98* (Portland, Oregon, 1949). I have also consulted with profit the unpublished account of Louis and Marshall Bond's Klondike experiences written by Marshall Bond, Jr., of Santa Barbara, California.

Among the many books dealing with the Klondike rush I have relied most heavily on Tappan Adney's *The Klondike Stampede* (New York, 1900), the record of a *Harper's Weekly* correspondent whose letters to that journal have also proved helpful; and the more recent *Big Pan-Out* (New York, 1951) by Kathryn Winslow; and the very comprehensive *The Klondike Fever* (New York, 1958) by Pierre Berton. I have relied on Harold A. Innis' *Settlement and the Mining Frontier* in Vol. IX of *Canadian Frontiers of Settlement* (Toronto, 1936) for details on mining methods in the Yukon. I have found Robert B. Medill's *Klondike Diary* (Portland, Oregon, 1949) helpful because its compiler duplicated London's journey over the Chilkoot and down the river to Dawson just a month after London; and I have trusted Edward E. P. Morgan's account of meeting Jack in Dawson as well as his quiet, sober picture of Dawson life in *God's Loaded Dice* (Caldwell, Idaho, 1948). The following books have furnished help on special points: the flamboyant *The Many Mizners* (New York, 1932) by Addison Mizner;

the very readable *Three Years in the Klondike* (London, 1904) by Jeremiah Lynch; and Hamlin Garland's account of his attempt to reach the Yukon overland through Canada in *The Trail of the Gold-Seekers* (New York, 1899).

For primary materials on Jack London I have worked most extensively in the indispensable London collection at the Henry E. Huntington Library, San Marino, California. This consists of a basic collection of holographs, manuscripts, and scrapbooks acquired in 1925 from Charmian London (Jack London's second wife), and similar materials obtained from the same source a quarter of a century later. These two acquisitions included most of the London estate papers, many of which had been used by Charmian London in writing *The Book of Jack London* (New York, 1921). Since 1950 the London holdings at the Huntington Library have gradually been augmented, most notably by Anna Strunsky's gift of her letters from London, by the acquisition of the Cloudesley Johns correspondence (quoted only in part by Charmian London), and by the purchase of the books from Jack London's library. The Huntington Library holdings have further been enriched through the acquisition of the correspondence between London and Elwyn Hoffman, another writer, like Johns, of London's own age; and the papers of Fred Lockley, editor of the *Pacific Monthly*. I have gone through all the London materials at the Huntington Library, but I have drawn principally on London's correspondence with friends of his early life such as Mabel Applegarth, Anna Strunsky, Cloudesley Johns, Elwyn Hoffman, and George Sterling; with agents and editors, notably George P. Brett of the Macmillan Company; and with Klondike acquaintances of London such as Clarence Buzzini, Del Bishop, Everett Barton, and W. B. Hargrave. Among diaries I have found London's notes on his trip downriver from Dawson to the sea most helpful, but even more important to this study is Fred Thompson's diary of his trip with London and his companions from San Francisco to Dawson City. I have also quoted extensively from Emil Jensen's unpublished account of his memories of London entitled 'Jack London at Stewart River'. Finally, I have found London's rough writing notes valuable, particularly the sheaf entitled 'Alaskan Short Story Stuff'.

Though not as extensive as the Huntington Library materials, several other collections of London items have proved valuable. The Cresmer Collection at the University of Southern California, Los Angeles, contains much miscellaneous material, apparently collected by Harvey Taylor. It includes several manuscripts of early unpublished London stories and articles, the writing notes for London's projected autobiographical work which was to be entitled 'Jack Liverpool', and an extensively annotated bibliography, possibly prepared in collaboration with Charmian London. In the Special Collections department of the University of California at Los Angeles, Irving Stone has deposited his notes of interviews, etc., which he used in writing *Sailor on Horseback*. The Bancroft Library at the University of California at Berkeley contains, among many London items, an excellent collection of London's early printed stories and articles, his correspondence with Blanche Partington, and photostats of his interesting exchange of letters with a Klondike acquaintance, Cornelius ('Con') Morgan Gepfert, the originals of which are owned by his son, C. L. Gepfert. Mr Gepfert, as well as the Bancroft Library, has graciously allowed me to quote from the Gepfert letters, and the Bancroft Library has also allowed me to quote from the holograph of James Hopper's memoir of Jack London at the University of California. Stanford University Library, Stanford, California, owns a file of London's correspondence with his British agent, James B. Pinker; and Mills College, Oakland, California, has a convenient set of copies

[269]

of the Cloudesley Johns correspondence in its Bender Collection.

Among papers in private files, I have found those of Joan London, Jack's eldest daughter, very helpful. Also a rich find was the collection of Mrs W. R. Holman of Pacific Grove, California, who purchased the material collected for years by Richard Francis, as well as his pioneer bibliography. In this material may be found even London's pawn tickets and the receipt for the sale of his gold dust. Mr Denison Ayer of Oakland has the only complete file of London's Oakland High School *Aegis* items that I know. I am most grateful to Joan London, Mrs Holman, and Mr Ayer for generously allowing me to freely consult their London holdings.

In collecting biographical information on London, I have had helpful interviews with several of the friends of his youth, including Frank Atherton and Ted Applegarth as well as Anna Strunsky (Mrs William English Walling), whose acquaintance I have found a genuine delight. Before his death James Hopper reminisced with me about London's Oakland and Carmel days, and William McDevitt provided memories of some first-hand contact with London's socialist experiences. Among biographies of London I have drawn slightly on Charmian London's *The Book of Jack London*, although I have made a practice of quoting only from the originals of letters and manuscripts which she used except for W. B. Hargrave's memories of London in the Klondike, the original of which I have been unable to locate. Joan London's excellent *Jack London and His Times* (New York, 1939) has been of great help to me, as has been our long friendship and her cordial aid at every turn. Finally, I have used the newspaper files of the Bancroft Library and the University of California General Library rather extensively in obtaining background material for this study.

Quotations of London's treatment of the Klondike in

fiction and article are taken invariably from the first editions, and the source is usually identified in my text. For ease of reading, some obvious spelling and punctuation errors have been altered in quotations from manuscript sources. In addition, London's spelling has been uniformly anglicized in quotations from both printed and manuscript materials. A list of London's Klondike writings, arranged chronologically, within categories, is here offered for the reader's convenience. This list is followed by a chapter-by-chapter indication of sources not mentioned in the text, including identification of all quoted holograph and manuscript materials. Finally, I am depositing my own London collection, including my notes, correspondence, photostats of fugitive London items, and copies of Jack and Charmian London's letters to Frederick I. Bamford, in the Huntington Library for the use of such scholars as may wish to consult them.

II

Novels and plays

A Daughter of the Snows. J. B. Lippincott Co., Philadelphia,
1902.
The Call of the Wild. The Macmillan Co., New York, 1903.
Scorn of Women. The Macmillan Co., New York, 1906.
(Play)
White Fang. The Macmillan Co., New York, 1906.
Burning Daylight. The Macmillan Co., New York, 1910.
Smoke Bellew. Century, New York, 1912.

Collections of short stories

The Son of the Wolf. Houghton Mifflin Co., Boston, 1900.
'The White Silence'
'The Son of the Wolf'
'The Men of Forty-Mile'
'In a Far Country'
'To the Man on Trail'
'The Priestly Prerogative'
'The Wisdom of the Trail'
'The Wife of a King'
'An Odyssey of the North'
The God of His Fathers. McClure, Phillips and Co., New
York, 1901.
'The God of His Fathers'
'The Great Interrogation'
'Which Make Men Remember'
'Siwash'

'The Man with the Gash'
'Jan, the Unrepentant'
'Grit of Women'
'Where the Trail Forks'
'A Daughter of the Aurora'
'At the Rainbow's End'
'The Scorn of Women'
Children of the Frost. The Macmillan Co., New York, 1902.
'In the Forests of the North'
'The Law of Life'
'Nam-Bok the Unveracious'
'The Master of Mystery'
'The Sunlanders'
'The Sickness of Lone Chief'
'Keesh, the Son of Keesh'
'The Death of Ligoun'
'Li Wan, the Fair'
'The League of the Old Men'
The Faith of Men. The Macmillan Co., New York, 1904.
'A Relic of the Pliocene'
'A Hyperborean Brew'
'The Faith of Men'
'Too Much Gold'
'The One Thousand Dozen'
'The Marriage of Lit-Lit'
'Bâtard'
'The Story of Jees Uck'
Love of Life. The Macmillan Co., New York, 1907.
'Love of Life'
'A Day's Lodging'
'The White Man's Way'
'The Story of Keesh'
'The Unexpected'
'Brown Wolf'
'The Sun Dog's Trail'
'Negore, the Coward'

Lost Face. The Macmillan Co., New York, 1910.
'Lost Face'
'Trust'
'To Build a Fire'
'That Spot'
'Flush of Gold'
'The Passing of Marcus O'Brien'
'The Wit of Porportuk'

London volumes containing one or two Klondike items

Revolution. The Macmillan Co., New York, 1910.
'The Shrinkage of the Planet' (Article)
'The Gold Hunters of the North' (Article)
The Night Born. Century, New York, 1913.
'The Night Born' (Story)
The Turtles of Tasman. The Macmillan Co., New York, 1916.
'Finis' (Story)
'The End of the Story' (Story)
The Red One. The Macmillan Co., New York, 1918.
'Like Argus of the Ancient Times' (Story)

Items which London left uncollected

'Through the Rapids on the way to Klondike.' *The Home Magazine*, June, 1899. (Article)
Reprinted in *Jack London's Tales of Adventure*, 1956.
'From Dawson to the Sea.' *Buffalo Express*, June 4, 1899. (Article)
Reprinted in *Jack London's Tales of Adventure*, Garden City, New York, 1956.
'The King of Mazy May.' *Youth's Companion*, Nov. 30, 1899. (Juvenile)
'Economics in the Klondike.' *The Review of Reviews*, Jan., 1900. (Article)

'Pluck and Pertinacity.' *Youth's Companion*, Jan., 1900.
(Juvenile)
'The Husky.' *Harper's Weekly*, June 30, 1900. (Article)
'Housekeeping in the Klondike.' *Harper's Bazar*, Sept. 15,
1900. (Article)
'Thanksgiving on Slav Creek.' *Harper's Bazar*, Nov. 24,
1900. (Story)
'Bald Face.' *The News*, Dec., 1900. (Juvenile)
Reprinted in *Dutch Courage*, 1922.
'To Build a Fire.' *Youth's Companion*, May, 1902. (Juvenile)
'The Fuzziness of Hookla Heen.' *Youth's Companion*, July,
1902. (Juvenile)
'My Best Short Story.' *The Grand Magazine* (London),
Aug., 1906. (Comment on 'The League of the Old
Men')
'Up the Slide.' *Youth's Companion*, Oct. 25, 1906. (Juvenile)
'Chased by the Trail.' *Youth's Companion*, Sept. 26, 1907.
(Juvenile)

III

The following identifications refer to Jack London (JL)
books or manuscripts unless otherwise stated. The symbol
HEH is used to indicate that the manuscript source is in
the Huntington Library.

Chapter I: Background to Adventure (pp. 11–48)

When not identified in the text or listed below, the
London quotations are taken from *John Barleycorn* or, in
matters dealing with bumming on the railroads and the
experiences with Kelly's Army and in the penitentiary,
from *The Road*. Josiah Flynt's *Tramping with Tramps* (New
York, 1899) has been used to supplement London's account
of tramping. The locations of Jack London's boyhood residences have been worked out from local directories, with
additional aid from Rev. C. Jones Tyler, who has special-
ized in this field. The secondary-school and college records
were obtained from Oakland High School and the University of California. Further information on the *Sophia
Sutherland* voyage and the composition of *Martin Eden* can
be found in my Afterword to the Signet Classic edition of
The Sea-Wolf (New York, 1964) and in my chapter on
Martin Eden in *The American Novel* (ed. Wallace Stegner)
issued by Basic Books (New York) in the fall of 1965.

1. JL to Houghton Mifflin Co., Jan. 31, 1900. Joan
   London Collection.
2. *Revolution*, pp. 153–4.
3. *The God of His Fathers*, pp. 230–1.
4. Notes for autobiography: 'Sharks'. HEH.
5. Clipping of A.P. interview, Aug. 26, 1905. London
   Scrapbook, Vol. V. HEH.

6. *War of the Classes*, p. 268.
7. JL to Mabel Applegarth, Nov. 30, 1898. HEH.
8. *The Road*, p. 160.
9. JL to Cloudesley Johns, March 30, 1899. HEH.
10. Quoted in letter to the author from Erie County Penitentiary, Nov. 13, 1952.
11. *War of the Classes*, pp. 274–5.
12. JL to Houghton Mifflin Co., Jan. 31, 1900. Joan London Collection.
13. Ibid.
14. Passim. James Hopper MS on JL at University of California, Bancroft Library.
15. Letter from Anna Strunsky to the author, March 16, 1953.
16. JL to Houghton Mifflin Co., Jan. 31, 1900. Joan London Collection.
17. Clippings from Oakland *Times* and *Item* in London Scrapbooks, Vol. I, pp. 66–8. HEH.
18. JL fragment to Mabel Applegarth, n.d. (probably Jan., 1899). HEH.

Chapter II: Over Chilkoot (pp. 49–73)

Data on the arrival of news about the Klondike strike and the sailing of the *Umatilla* are found in the San Francisco and Oakland newspapers from July 14 to July 26, with much of the detail of the sailing taken from the San Francisco *Examiner*, July 26, 1897. Jack London is listed as 'J. Goudon' in the published passenger list. All the manuscript quotations in this chapter are taken from the diary of Fred Thompson, London's companion on the journey: 'Party:—Jack London, Mr Shepard, Merritt Sloper, Jim Goodman and myself'; the diary runs from Thompson's departure from Santa Rosa on July 23, 1897, to his arrival with Jack London and two others at Dawson on October 18, 1897. Dates from the diary are sufficiently identified in the text. All quotations from London's books are identified in the text except two from 'Like Argus of the Ancient Times' (*The Red One*). These are:

1. *The Red One*, p. 109.
2. Ibid., pp. 106–7.

Chapter III:
'Into the Teeth of the North' (pp. 74–100)

The eight manuscript entries in this chapter are all from Fred Thompson's diary, sufficiently dated in the text. All quotations from London books are identified except, on p. 74, 'perilous traverse of . . . ,' which is from 'Like Argus of the Ancient Times' (*The Red One*), p. 115.

Chapter IV:
Gold Creek and Gold Town (pp. 101–124)

The three Thompson diary quotations used in this chapter are easily identified as to date. Jack London quotes not identified in the text are listed below.

1. Files of Mining Recorder, Dawson, Y.T. Grant No. 2080.
2. JL to Con Gepfert, May 5, 1900. Bancroft Library.
3. Quoted in Pierre Berton, *The Klondike Fever*, p. 172.
4. Ibid., p. 178.
5. *Scorn of Women*, p. 180.
6. Letter dated Dec. 17, 1897, quoted in Harr Wagner's *Joaquin Miller and His Other Self* (1929), p. 178.
7. Addison Mizner, *The Many Mizners*, p. 120.

Chapter V: Split-up Island (pp. 125–153)

Though the area was not uniformly known as Split-up Island, this was a common name for the locality in which Jack spent his winter in the Klondike, and it was the name he used in his fiction. An excellent description of dog-sledding upriver in the winter is found in the account of Burning Daylight's dash from Circle City to Dyea and back to win a bet (*Burning Daylight*, pp. 35–57). It is too long to quote in this study. Sources not identified in the text of this chapter are as follows:

1. *Smoke Bellew*, p. 83.
2. *The God of His Fathers*, pp. 157–8.
3. W. B. Hargrave quoted by Charmian London in *The Book of Jack London*, I, 237–9.
4. *Jack London, by Himself.* Pamphlet issued by the Macmillan Co. HEH.
5. Emil Jensen MS entitled 'With Jack London at Stewart River.' HEH.
6. Hargrave in Charmian London, *The Book of Jack London*, I, 234–5.
7. JL to Con Gepfert, Sept. 20, 1901. Bancroft Library.
8. JL to Clarence Buzzini, Jan. 13, 1915. HEH.
9. Notes for lecture on Klondike. HEH.
10. Notes of interview with Irving Stone at University of California, Los Angeles.
11. *The Son of the Wolf*, p. 65.
12. Letter of Ernest N. Patty to the author, June 24, 1959.

Chapter VI: The Break-up (pp. 154–168)

There are additional vivid descriptions of the break-up of the ice on the Yukon in *Burning Daylight*, pp. 75–8, and *The Call of the Wild*, pp. 148–9.

1. 'From Dawson to the Sea', in *Jack London's Tales of Adventure*, p. 42.
2. Quoted in Edward E. P. Morgan, *God's Loaded Dice*, p. 128.
3. Quoted in Charmian London, *The Book of Jack London*, I, 244.
4. See Berton, *The Klondike Fever*, p. 321. Berton spells her name 'Maloof.'

Chapter VII: Downriver (pp. 169–191)

Most of the material in this chapter is based on London's holograph 'Yukon River diary' (covering June 8 to June 30, 1898; HEH) and printed almost verbatim in Charmian London's *The Book of Jack London*, I, 248–57; and the article based on the diary, 'From Dawson to the Sea,' Buffalo *Express*, Buffalo, New York, June 4, 1899. Quotations from the articles are distinguished from those from the diary by comment in the text or by the marked difference in style between the two.

1. Jeremiah Lynch, *Three Years in the Klondike*, p. 17.
2. JL to the San Francisco *Bulletin*, Sept. 17, 1898, exhibited at Jack London State Park, Glen Ellen, and reprinted in *Jack London's Tales of Adventure*, p. 49.
3. The incident of the hunting of the moose, here summarized, is described in 'From Dawson to the Sea'.

Chapter VIII: Bonanza (pp. 192–212)

Most of the material for this chapter is taken from correspondence.

1. JL to Cloudesley Johns, March 30, 1899. HEH.
2. JL to Mabel Applegarth, Nov. 30, 1898. HEH.
3. JL to Johns, July 29, 1899. HEH.
4. JL to Mabel Applegarth, Christmas, 1898. HEH.
5. JL to Con Gepfert, May 5, 1900. Bancroft Library.
6. *John Barleycorn*, p. 235.
7. JL to Ted Applegarth, quoted in Joan London, *Jack London and His Times*, p. 194.
8. Endorsement on *Bulletin* letter cited in Chap. VII.
9. *John Barleycorn*, p. 238.
10. JL to Houghton Mifflin, Jan. 31, 1900. Joan London Collection.
11. JL to George Brett, Nov. 21, 1902. HEH.
12. Sale of London books. George Brett wrote the present author on April 6, 1953, that the Macmillan

Company had sold 5,677,000 copies of London books; 1,700,000 of *The Call of the Wild* alone.

13. JL to Brett, Nov. 21, 1902. HEH.
14. Ibid.
15. JL to George Sterling, July 11, 1903. HEH.
16. JL to Johns, Sept. 26, 1899. HEH.
17. JL to Johns, March 7, 1899. HEH.
18. JL to Johns, April 22, 1899. HEH.
19. JL to Elwyn Hoffman, Oct. 27, 1900. HEH.
20. JL to Ethel Jennings, Feb. 5, 1915. HEH.
21. JL to Brett, n.d. (apparently Aug., 1903). HEH.
22. JL to Johns, Nov. 21, 1899. HEH.
23. Ibid., June 12, 1899. HEH.
24. Frank Norris to Isaac Marcosson, *The Letters of Frank Norris*, p. 31.
25. JL in 'The Phenomena of Literary Evolution,' *Bookman*, Oct., 1900.
26. JL to Johns, Nov. 21, 1899.
27. 'The Material Side', *Junior Munsey Magazine*, Dec., 1900.
28. 'Getting into Print', *The Editor*, March, 1905.
29. JL to Brett, March 7, 1907. HEH.
30. JL to Johns, Dec. 22, 1900. HEH.
31. Ibid., June 12, 1899. HEH.
32. Ibid., June 16, 1900. HEH.
33. Ibid.
34. Ibid., Dec. 22, 1900. HEH.
35. Ibid., July 29, 1899. HEH.
36. Ibid., Feb. 27, 1899. HEH.

Chapter IX:
The Fictional Counterpart (pp. 213–229)
1. JL to Elwyn Hoffman, Jan. 6, 1900. HEH.
2. JL to Con Gepfert, Nov. 5, 1900. Bancroft Library.
3. JL fragment to Mabel Applegarth, n.d. (probably Jan., 1899). HEH.

4. JL to Johns, April 17, 1899. HEH.
5. JL to Gepfert, Nov. 5, 1900. Bancroft Library.
6. 'Getting into Print', *The Editor*, March, 1903.
7. 'Alaskan Short Story Stuff.' HEH.
8. JL to Gepfert, May 5, 1900. Bancroft Library.
9. Ibid., Nov. 5, 1900. Bancroft Library.
10. JL to Anna Strunsky, Dec. 20, 1902. HEH. The Dall review was in the *New York Times*, Dec. 6, 1902.
11. JL fragment to Mabel Applegarth (probably Jan., 1899). HEH.
12. *The Son of the Wolf*, p. 225.
13. JL to Johns, Feb. 10, 1900. HEH.
14. 'My Best Short Story,' *The Grand Magazine* (London), Aug., 1906. MS in HEH.
15. JL to Johns, Dec. 22, 1900. HEH.
16. 'The Material Side,' *Junior Munsey Magazine*, Dec., 1900.
17. JL to Anna Strunsky, Jan. 21, 1900. HEH.
18. JL to Johns, Sept. 9, 1900. HEH.
19. Ibid., Feb. 13, 1901. HEH.
20. Ibid., March 15, 1899. HEH.
21. JL to Anna Strunsky, March 13, 1903. HEH.
22. JL to Charmian Kittredge, Dec. 6, 1904, quoted in Charmian London, *The Book of Jack London*, II, 12.
23. Writing notes. HEH.
24. JL to Karl E. Harriman, editor, *The Red Book*, Dec. 23, 1910. HEH.

Chapter X:

Interpreter of Things Which Are (pp. 230–265)

For further information on London's difficulty of thinking up plots see the author's article: 'Jack London's Use of Sinclair Lewis Plots,' *Huntington Library Quarterly*, XVII (Nov., 1953), 59–74. Considerable groundwork on this chapter was done by Joan Landis in preparing an M.A.

thesis under the author's direction. The thesis is entitled 'Narrative Techniques in Jack London's Alaskan Short Stories', Mills College, Oakland, Calif., 1956.

1. JL to Cloudesley Johns, April 22, 1899.
2. JL to Elwyn Hoffman, June 17, 1900. HEH.
3. JL to Johns, Sept. 6, 1899. HEH.
4. London apparently planned to write an autobiography dealing with the 'seamy' side of his life, in which he intended to refer to himself as Jack Liverpool.
5. JL to Georges Dupuy, Dec. 1, 1910. HEH.
6. 'Alaskan Short Story Stuff.' HEH.
7. On Conrad and London, see Sam Baskett's 'Jack London's Heart of Darkness,' *American Quarterly*, X (Spring, 1958), 66–77.
8. *McClure's Magazine*, XVIII (Dec., 1901), 152–160.
9. JL to R. W. Gilder, editor of *Century* magazine, Dec. 22, 1908. HEH.
10. 'Notes for Future Work.' HEH. The episode which London used was actually found in Lynch, *Three Years in the Klondike*, pp. 66–7.
11. The holograph of 'To Build a Fire' is in HEH.
12. Vil Bykov: 'Jack London in the Soviet Union', *Quarterly News Letter*, The Book Club of California, San Francisco, XXIV (Summer, 1959), 52.
13. Ibid., p. 55.
14. The *Index Translationum* figures have been examined through 1959.
15. Quoted in Irving Stone, *Sailor on Horseback*, p. 123.
16. Published by University of California Press (Berkeley, 1943).
17. Translated back into English by the author's colleague Robert L. Johnston, from Vil Bykov's 'In the Footsteps of Jack London', *Komsomol Pravda*, Sept. 20 and 23, 1959.

Index

John J. Healey (ship), 177
Johns, Cloudesley, 205, 208, 209, 210, 211, 216, 223, 226, 230, 268, 270
Judge, Father William, 109, 162–3
Juneau, 45, 50, 52
Jung, Carl, 233

'Keesh, the Son of Keesh', 222
Kelly's Army, 28, 33
Kempton-Wace Letters, 203
Kipling, Rudyard, 33, 35, 135, 238, 239
Klondike City, 184. *See also* Louse Town
Klondike River, 109
Korbo, John, 112
Koyokuk River, 182
Kutlik, 189, 190

Lake Bennett, 55, 75, 80, 81, 82
Lake Laberge, 75, 91, 92, 95, 98
Lake Lindeman (Linderman), 45, 57, 73, 74–5, 76, 77, 79, 80, 100
Lake Marsh, 75, 83
Lake Tagish, 51, 75, 83
Lamore, Gussie, 165
'Law of Life, The', 221, 222, 223, 224
'League of the Old Men, The', 116, 222, 223
Lenin, Nikolay, 245
Lewis, Austin, 205
Lewis River, 83
'Like Argus of the Ancient Times', 61, 65, 77, 80, 93, 137, 152, 232–3; quoted, 73, 81, 93–4, 96–7, 232
Lindeman (Linderman), Lake. *See* Lake Lindeman
Lindeman (town), 162
Little Salmon River, 95, 96, 183
Livermore, Calif., 17, 18
'Li Wan, the Fair', 221
Lockley, Fred, 143, 268
London, Bessie (daughter), 203
London, Bessie Maddern, 35, 203, 204, 205, 206
London, Charmian Kittredge, 82, 91, 125, 137, 138, 141, 143, 144, 163, 166, 204, 228, 268, 269, 270, 271
London, Flora Wellman, 11, 16, 18, 196, 197

London, Joan, 91, 147, 196, 203, 205, 212, 270
London, John (father), 11, 12, 16, 17, 18, 19, 160, 196
Long Lake, 80
Lost Face, 255
Louse Town, 106, 116, 162, 183, 184
Love of Life, 242
'Love of Life' (story), 214, 231, 245–54; quoted, 248, 251, 252, 253–4
Lynch, Jeremiah, 135, 169, 255, 256, 257, 268
Lynn Canal, 52

McClure, S. S., 201, 220, 226
McDevitt, William, 270
MacDonald, J. A., 245
McQuesten, Jack, 182
Mammy Jennie. *See* Prentiss, Virginia
Martin Eden, 33, 43, 192, 193, 195, 203, 206, 207, 211, 219, 260, 261, 263; quoted, 34, 35
Marx, Karl, 33, 205, 225
'Material Side, The', 225
Mayo, Al, 181, 182
Mayor Woods (ship), 178
May West (ship), 177, 178
Meadow, Charley, 142
Medill, Robert B., 267
Melville, Herman, 191
'Men of Forty-Mile, The', 216; quoted, 96, 97
'Mexican, The', 261
Meyers, Charley, 142
Miles Canyon. *See* Box Canyon
Miller, Joaquin, 12, 47, 118
Milton, John, 135
Minook, 181, 182, 185
Mizner, Addison, 66, 115, 267
Mizner, William, 66
Mizner, Wilson, 66
Monroe, Father, 188
'Moon Country', 238
Moore, Bill, 187, 189
Moosehide Mountain, 108, 109, 161, 162
Morgan, Edward E. P., 111, 112, 165, 267